How the States Shaped the Nation

CHICAGO STUDIES IN AMERICAN POLITICS

A series edited by Benjamin I. Page, Susan Herbst, Lawrence R. Jacobs, and Adam J. Berinsky

Also in the series:

Additional series titles follow index

How the States Shaped the Nation

American Electoral Institutions and
Voter Turnout, 1920–2000

MELANIE JEAN SPRINGER

The University of Chicago Press
Chicago and London

Melanie Jean Springer is assistant professor of political science at the University of California, Santa Cruz.

The University of Chicago Press, Chicago 60637
The University of Chicago Press, Ltd., London

23 22 21 20 19 18 17 16 15 14   1 2 3 4 5

ISBN-13: 978-0-226-11418-7 (cloth)
ISBN-13: 978-0-226-11421-7 (paper)
ISBN-13: 978-0-226-11435-4 (e-book)
DOI: 10.7208/chicago/9780226114354.001.0001

Library of Congress Cataloging-in-Publication Data

Springer, Melanie J., author.
    How the states shaped the nation : American electoral institutions and voter turnout, 1920–2000 / Melanie Jean Springer.
        pages cm — (Chicago studies in American politics)
    ISBN 978-0-226-11418-7 (cloth : alk. paper) — ISBN 978-0-226-11421-7 (pbk. : alk. paper) — ISBN 978-0-226-11435-4 (e-book)   1. Elections—United States.   2. Voter turnout—United States.   I. Title.   II. Series: Chicago studies in American politics.
    JK1967.S775 2014
    324.973′09—dc23
                                                                        2013025705

♾ This paper meets the requirements of ANSI/NISO Z39.48–1992 (Permanence of Paper).

For Joey, my love

CONTENTS

ILLUSTRATIONS

ACKNOWLEDGMENTS

This book would never have been possible without the steadfast support and encouragement I received from my colleagues, family, and dear friends. I offer my most sincere thanks and appreciation to this tremendous group of people.

First, and foremost, this work benefited greatly from the input of several generous scholars at Columbia University. There is no doubt it was improved by their attention, suggestions, and criticism. I especially thank Bob Erikson, who fostered my interest in voting and elections during my first months in graduate school, and who encouraged this work from the very beginning. I also thank Ira Katznelson for championing and guiding my interest in political history and for his one of a kind insights that never fail to inspire. I also offer my heartfelt thanks to John Lapinski, Rob Lieberman, Bob Shapiro, and Greg Wawro for their guidance during many important moments along the way, and to Mat McCubbins, who urged me to pursue this path in the first place.

After I left graduate school, Saint Louis was my home. I offer my utmost gratitude to my colleagues at Washington University. It was a privilege to begin my career supported by such wonderful scholars and friends. I especially thank Randy Calvert, Bill Lowry, Andrew Martin, Sunita Parikh, John Patty, Steve Smith, and Jim Spriggs for their encouragement and sound advice over the past several years. I also acknowledge the stellar research assistance I received from Morgan Hazelton, and generous funding from the Murray Weidenbaum Center on the Economy, Government, and Public Policy.

This work has evolved greatly thanks to the input of scholars far and wide. Although the individuals who helped shape this book are too numerous to name them all here, I especially thank Chris Achen, Becky Morton,

Bob Stein, Caroline Tolbert, and Dan Wirls for their very helpful suggestions. I also thank my good friend and collaborator Elizabeth Rigby, who graciously offered her expertise and never wavered in her enthusiasm for this project.

I also offer my utmost appreciation to John Tryneski, Rodney Powell, the editors of the American Politics Series at the University of Chicago Press, and all the scholars who anonymously reviewed my manuscript. It was an absolute privilege to work with such a supportive team. There is no doubt that their commitment to this endeavor and their invaluable suggestions greatly improved this book. To Rick Valelly, whose sage advice sparked a new direction at a critical time, I am especially indebted. Last, I must convey my immeasurable gratitude to Jamie Druckman, who has been a true mentor since my days as an undergraduate and an unwavering champion of me and my work—thank you Jamie.

I also offer my deepest thanks to my incredible family and friends, whose consistent love and friendship has brightened my life infinitely. Specifically, I thank my parents, John and Kathy Beamer, and my sister, Tiffany Campbell, who were my first teachers and encouraged my love of books. I thank Debby Springer, and the rest of my dynamic family, for supporting this pursuit every step of the way. I also acknowledge my father-in-law, Bill Springer, whom I miss dearly. And I thank my amazing friends—Michelle Hall, Guinevere Jobson, Liz Mosco, Gabrielle Muse, and Jocelyn Pietsch—who have tirelessly cheered me along throughout this journey and many others. I am so lucky to be able to share my life with each of you.

Last—but far from least—there are not enough words to thank my incredible husband and best friend, Joey. You are a remarkable partner. You have supported me endlessly, offered reassurance at every fork in the road, and urged me to persevere when I doubted. You have helped me overcome what seemed insurmountable, and you fill my days with hope and laughter. I am immensely grateful for your constant love, friendship, and unmatched ability to convince and inspire me with your even-handed sensibilities. There is nobody I would rather have by my side. Although it is a small token compared to all that I owe, I dedicate this work to you, Joey. Thank you for always being you, and for always believing in me.

ONE

Introduction

The presidential election held on November 7, 2000, was historic on many counts. One of its lasting legacies was bringing the rules governing American voting to the forefront of political debate and public conversation. This was not the first time the American public had confronted the political ramifications of the country's variable electoral systems; yet in the aftermath of this now infamous election, Americans were reminded that the federal system allows the individual states to set the electoral rules by which all voters must abide. By design, this system fosters variability while allowing, and perhaps even creating, instances of inequality. The heightened awareness of state power over electoral procedures following the Bush versus Gore election initiated widespread criticism and spurred countless calls for national electoral reform. In the years since, balloting procedures and voting machinery have been closely scrutinized, the availability and convenience of polling places and other voting opportunities have been addressed, and restrictions such as voter identification requirements have been added. In each instance the individual states have been the major political players, shaping the who, when, and where of voting as they see fit.

This system of decentralized rule making by the states is an enduring feature of American politics. Indeed, debates over states' rights and voting laws have colored political conversations since the days of the founding fathers. Yet these laws often are merely the backdrop to electoral politics, influencing the process but not raising eyebrows. The critical aftermath of the 2000 presidential election is one of few exceptions in a very long history. Generally, national tallies are compiled and public figures are elected without much criticism of the process. Yet even when things run smoothly, the states are indisputably important players. Empowered by the federal arrangement, the American states have been able, with few limitations, to actively expand and constrict the electorate through institutional design, and in doing so they have greatly influenced political participation across the nation. This book explores the underpinnings and consequences of electoral federalism over time. I evaluate the numerous state electoral institutions, both restrictive and expansive, that have helped shape American elections and voting behavior throughout the twentieth century—long before the events in Florida put the rules we vote by under a national spotlight.

What Are State Electoral Institutions?

Throughout this book, state electoral institutions are defined as *the laws and procedures governing registration and voting in the American states*. They set the parameters for participation in American elections and effectively mediate the relationship between political actors and political outcomes. They are the rules of the game, and for the most part each state has maintained control over its own institutional profile throughout the twentieth century. Owing to American federalism, there has been great variation in the rules as institutionalized by law, both between states and within states over time. This institutional variation, coupled with and complicated by an assortment of state political histories, leads to a range in participation trends. In short, I posit that institutional effects are conditional on a state's political history, and institutions and political context together have led to varying voter turnout rates in the states and regions throughout the century.

The state electoral institutions I examine here pertain to voting qualifications, voter registration, and voting procedures. These laws are characterized as being either restrictive (rules that aim to limit the vote by restricting participation or making it more costly) or expansive (rules that aim to expand the vote by making participation more convenient or less costly). My expectations about particular state electoral institutions relate to the burden they impose on, or alleviate for, voters in the states where they are implemented—and their effects on state turnout rates are theorized about and assessed accordingly. For example, the most-restrictive electoral institutions that American states enacted during the twentieth century pertained to voting qualifications (e.g., long residency requirements and poll taxes). These limiting institutions are expected, both theoretically and empirically, to decrease voting rates wherever they were implemented. Conversely, later in the century many states enacted expansive reforms to make registration and voting more accessible and convenient. Modern voter registration reforms, especially, sought to reduce the costs associated with registering so as to increase voting.

I contend that examining the boundaries created by both restrictive *and* expansive state electoral institutions is critical to understanding twentieth-century voting and elections. By institutionally easing state electoral processes and fostering a heightened participatory climate through expansive electoral laws, electoral institutions may have changed the status quo. And the restrictive laws implemented over time may have created and perpetuated depressed voting patterns in many American states. The states and regions have differed dramatically in their voting rates throughout the twentieth century, yet there is also a complicated interaction at work between electoral institutions and states' historical legacies that persists even after the institutions have changed. This suggests that while appreciating how state-level electoral institutions evolve over time, we must also try to understand how institutions and social context interact to influence voter turnout. That is, restrictive or expansive laws alone do not explain variation in state voting rates: many high turnout states share some institutional mechanisms, but there is no clear pattern of electoral laws common to all high turnout states in a region. Instead, I posit that the impact of institutions depends on the social context within the state—for example, that the effect of electoral institutions interacts with the racial homogeneity of the state. This dynamic relationship is consequential. Practically speaking, this book demonstrates that if the goal of electoral reform is to increase national participation, we must pay attention to how states' voting histories differ with their institutional profiles. One institutional fix will not uniformly solve problems of low or unequal participation. As long as policy makers ignore this variation, they will be disappointed with the results of electoral reform. Understanding this important relationship—between state electoral institutions, political context, and voter turnout rates from 1920 to 2000—is the focus of this book.

A Historical Vantage Point: Eighty Years Deep

This study begins in 1920—an electoral cut point marking the end of the Progressive Era. Starting in 1920 lets me concentrate on the institutional changes following, but separate from, the electoral reforms initiated during the Populist and Progressive movements in the mid- to late nineteenth century (e.g., women's suffrage, the Australian ballot, the direct election of US senators, ballot initiatives, and referenda). In addition to these institutional changes, voter turnout was quite a bit higher during the nineteenth century than during the twentieth (Bensel 2004; Burnham 1982; Kleppner 1982; Teixeira 1992).[1] As such, the twentieth century emerges as distinct in terms of both voting rules and participation rates, and understanding the changes that occurred during this period is pivotal to understanding the modern American electorate.

The presidential election in 1920 was also the first federal election held after female enfranchisement became national. It thus reflects a moment when the American polity became comparatively inclusive (Kleppner 1982; Rusk and Stucker 1978). It was also a time after the national party system developed, when national elections became more systematic and competitive. Of course there are important exceptions; for example, the restriction of black and minority suffrage within and outside the South and the Democrats' single-party dominance of politics in the southern states during the early twentieth century. I view these specific limitations on participation and electoral competition as by-products of state control over elections and address them directly.

The years since 1920 have been characterized by the evolution, and ultimate removal, of discriminatory voting procedures, especially in the southern states. Restrictive qualifications were generally relaxed during the early years of the century, with a growing emphasis on permanent registration requirements and a modest expansion of the electorate by liberalizing substantive qualifications such as age and duration of residency. The latter half of the century was also marked by growing federal protection of voting rights and increasing federal influence on the administration of elections overall. After the civil rights movement, midcentury electoral reform was directed almost entirely at making participation easier and more convenient, first through registration reform and later through changes in timing and in access to voting opportunities. The book concludes with the remarkably apropos 2000 presidential election, which not only marked the end of the twentieth century but also was punctuated, if not defined, by the power of American federalism to shape national outcomes.

The eighty-year vantage point offered here is unusual. Typically, even in historical accounts, the relationship between electoral institutions and voting behavior has been evaluated over a fairly limited time frame (see, e.g., Franklin and Grier 1997; Kleppner 1987; Lawson 1976, 1985; McGerr 1986, 2003; Rusk 1970, 1974; Rusk and Stucker 1978). And many of the studies on more recent expansive electoral reforms have intentionally limited themselves to the last two decades of the century to "avoid being complicated by the dramatic election law changes of the 1960s" and to "capture the incremental, state-initiated electoral changes taking place in the 1970s, 1980s, and 1990s" (Fitzgerald 2005, 852). Although these temporally bound studies offer a degree of historical appreciation, they tend to contribute institutional snapshots rather than comparative analyses. They thus are incapable of making important comparisons over time and evaluating the evolution of electoral systems throughout the century. By limiting the time frame studied, previous research on electoral reform has ignored the institutional and political changes that have occurred incrementally throughout the history of the United States, failing to recognize the effects of gradual change.

The scope of this book is broader. Examining the progression of American electoral institutions throughout the twentieth century lets me analyze the cumulative effects that changes in electoral institutions have on voting and provides both a historical and a contemporary analysis of twentieth-century political participation in the United States. With its historical breadth, this book not only demonstrates the direct effects that individual electoral laws have on participation, but also explores the important ways a state's collection of electoral laws—its institutional profile—can shape patterns of participation over time. The existing literature does not span space and time in this way and therefore cannot make these macrolevel institutional comparisons.

Chapter Overview

Research on voting and elections in the United States, and voter turnout more specifically, has accounted for a vast amount of the scholarship in political science for decades. There have been at least three distinct trends in research on voting behavior in general and on the relationship between electoral institutions and voter turnout in particular.[2]

First, a great deal of the work has focused on individual-level determinants, typically without discussing how electoral institutions condition voting behavior. Second, most studies that have examined electoral institutions have dealt with a single reform or a handful of reforms. Finally, most of the existing institutional scholarship evaluates the relationship between electoral institutions and voting behavior over a fairly limited time span. This book builds on each aspect of the existing literature.

To begin, chapters 2 through 4 provide the theoretical and empirical basis for understanding the evolution of state electoral institutions and their effects on voter turnout in the American states throughout the twentieth century. These chapters underscore my motivation for the book: that I believe the study of voting and elections should not be confined to individual behavior, and that addressing the institutional variants of state electoral processes—a product of American federalism—is critical to advancing our understanding of voting and electoral reform.

I begin chapter 2 by discussing the importance and exceptionalism of American federalism. Then I situate the contributions of this study within the existing literature on how the costs and determinants of voting relate to twentieth-century voter turnout and within the current literature on state electoral reforms. Ultimately I aim to bolster the link between research on political behavior and research on political institutions. By dealing exclusively with the independent actions of individual voters, a strictly behavioral approach neglects the interactive effects and structural patterns surrounding elections. Instead, I stress the importance of institutional design, and of institutional change over time, in shaping political outcomes while building on previous work about the behavioral norms of political actors. I treat the laws governing elections in the states as the institutional mechanisms that empower citizens or deter them from voting. I focus on the American states, where control over electoral institutions resides, and which are distinct in voter turnout, electoral laws, and political history. This book recognizes the richness of the American federal structure and the dynamic role of electoral institutions in shaping state voting patterns, as is essential to forming conclusions about twentieth-century voter participation.

In chapters 3 and 4 I develop both elements of this picture through an in-depth discussion of state voting rates and state electoral institutions. In chapter 3 I carefully examine voter turnout during presidential and non-presidential election years from 1920 to 2000. I begin by presenting the familiar national trends, then I disaggregate them by region and ultimately by state. This allows us to look at the states' voting rates over time and to classify them as routinely "high" or "low." Regional trends quickly become apparent—especially the perpetually low turnout in southern states, even after the 1964 Civil Rights Act and the 1965 Voting Rights Act, and the consistently high turnout in many midwestern and western states throughout the century. In addition to classifying the states by turnout trends, I assess year-specific state voting patterns and offer a preliminary description of the institutional changes and political events that might have contributed to these trends historically. We can thus see the extensive variation in voting rates at the state level, frequently unnoticed in national-level studies. I also point out the vast difference between turnout rates in the southern states and the nonsouthern states—a distinction that is critical to the empirical analyses and case studies I present in subsequent chapters.

Central to this book is the expectation that the consequences of the rules governing voting in the United States have greatly influenced the political system during the twentieth century. Chapter 4 offers a detailed legislative history of the origins and evolution of an array of prominent electoral institutions—pertaining to voter qualifications, voter registration, and voting procedures—that existed in the American states from 1920 to 2000. For example, most of the rules governing voting qualifications early in the century were very restrictive (or they increased voting costs), such as long residency requirements, property requirements, literacy tests, and poll taxes. Additionally, periodic voter registration and nonvoting purges of registration rolls made registration cumbersome. Conversely, many recent registration and voting reforms are expansive and aim to minimize voting and registration costs, such as mail-in registration, "motor voter" programs, and early voting. This chapter offers a historical chronology of the restrictive and expansive electoral institutions existing in the states over time and of the regional diffusion of specific institutions during particular moments, aided by an original data set I have constructed.

The second half of the book empirically tests the relationship between several restrictive and expansive state electoral institutions and state voting rates from 1920 to 2000. The analyses I present in chapter 5 demonstrate the effect many state electoral laws have had on state participation over time. These results motivate the regional case studies found in chapters 6 and 7.

Chapter 5 begins by describing the original data set, data collection methods, research design, and statistical models I use throughout the empirical chapters of the book. The chapter presents several times-series cross-sectional statistical models to empirically test the primary institutional hypotheses as they relate to the effects each of the restrictive and expansive state electoral institutions had on voter turnout during presidential and nonpresidential election years from 1920 to 2000. It also compares the institutional effects in the southern and nonsouthern states.

The models in chapter 5 demonstrate that a state's electoral environment, as structured by its election laws, creates variation in voting levels, but that electoral institutions do not all affect turnout equally. In fact, the direct effect of many expansive electoral institutions has been minimal, both regionally and over time, whereas the effects of restrictive institutions have been persistent and dramatic. Specifically, restrictions on voting qualifications have produced large and consistently negative effects on turnout in southern and nonsouthern states alike. This runs counter to assumptions that restrictive voting laws—such as long residency requirements, literacy tests, and poll taxes—had little disenfranchising power in the South beyond norms of force, violence, and persuasion (Key 1949; Kousser 1999; Rusk and Stucker 1978). It also points out the prevalence of these provisions in many nonsouthern states, and their equal power to depress the vote. Conversely, the effects of expansive reforms—such as motor voter registration, Election Day registration, and early voting—are modest and vary considerably. Further, by comparing institutional effects in the southern and nonsouthern states, I show that although a few expansive reforms have increased turnout in the nonsouthern states, they have had no effect in the southern states where voting rates are lowest. Further, the magnitudes of the institutional effects on turnout for both the restrictive and expansive reforms are comparable, providing some context for findings about the arguably modest effects of recent expansive reforms.

Chapters 6 and 7 build on the regional results identified in chapter 5 and present two case studies illustrating patterns of institutional effects in the nonsouthern and southern states. Some of the differences may be attributed to varying institutional profiles (state histories of expansiveness or restrictiveness) or to aspects of demographics and culture (racial heterogeneity or civic norms regarding participation). First, in chapter 6 I evaluate the numerous states outside the South—in the Midwest and West especially—that have garnered consistently high voter turnout throughout the twentieth century. As modern reformers search for ways to increase voter participation, it seems fitting to pay close attention to electoral institutions in the states that have had consistently high turnout over time. As this case study reveals, high turnout has no single institutional configuration. There is more variation in these states' electoral institutions than one might expect. This chapter characterizes the institutional arrangements and political climates found in particularly interesting or representative "high turnout" states outside the South, examining the overarching tendencies, institutional and otherwise, that may have heightened participation in these states throughout the century.

Chapter 7 explores the consistently low voter turnout found in the southern states throughout the century, paying close attention to the disenfranchising Jim Crow practices that permeated this region. The dynamic struggle over voting rights in the South is fundamental to understanding the history of political participation in the United States. Despite equalizing electoral reforms later in the century, the southern states have the lowest voting rates in the nation. In this chapter I analyze the historical and institutional mechanisms that account for this consistently depressed turnout and examine how these trends work within a contemporary and historical institutional framework. In doing so I discuss the changes in southern participation rates following the 1964 Civil Rights Act and 1965 Voting Rights Act. I also evaluate the effect of restrictive and expansive electoral institutions on southern voting during two distinct reform periods: from 1920 to 1970, a time marked by the steady implementation of predominately restrictive institutions, and from 1972 to 2000, a time after the civil rights movement when there was a concerted effort to make southern voting laws more inclusive. Finally, I explore the role political competition played in southern elections by examining institutional effects during primary elections from 1920 to 1970—an era of single-party Democratic dominance in the region.

Finally, in chapter 8 I summarize the main findings and contributions of this book and offer some perspective on the limits of electoral reform as we move through the twenty-first century.

PART ONE

The State of Electoral Institutions and Voter Turnout

TWO

Electoral Federalism and Participation in the American States

Democracy, at least in the broadest sense, is defined by representation, and a central facet of political representation requires individuals' participation in government (Hamilton, Madison, and Jay 1961; Lijphart 1997; Pitkin 1967; Piven and Cloward 1988; Verba, Schlozman, and Brady 1995). Accordingly, participation rates are frequently used to measure the success of a democracy. It follows that low voting rates elicit concern about the health of a democratic system (Rosenstone and Hansen 1993; Verba and Nie 1972). For example, elections are the main form of interaction between policy makers and citizens (Mills 1956; Schattschneider 1960), so low voter turnout weakens the relationship between these two groups—at the heart of political governance in the United States—and can exacerbate bias between those who routinely vote and those who do not (Bartels 2008; Citrin, Schickler, and Sides 2003; Fellowes and Rowe 2004; Griffin and Newman 2008; Hajnal 2010; Hill and Leighley 1992). Low voting rates can also have political consequences (Bachrach 1967; Mill 1962; Schattschneider 1960; Verba and Nie 1972). They affect the representativeness and legitimacy of the democratic system and alter the content of the political agenda (Bennett and Resnick 1990; Griffin and Newman 2005; Guinier 1994; Martin 2003; Piven and Cloward 1988; Rosenstone and Hansen 1993; Teixeira 1992; Verba, Schlozman, and Brady 1995; Wolfinger and Rosenstone 1980).[1]

Ultimately, voter turnout offers one metric for evaluating the health of the democratic system: the engagement of the populace and the link between representatives and represented. This is worrisome for observers of modern American politics. Voting rates in the United States were much lower during the twentieth century than during the nineteenth, and although they have fluctuated over time (more if one examines participation at the state rather than the national level), they have been trending downward since midcentury. Federalism is central to this story. The federal system empowers the American states to determine voting structures within their borders. Since all electoral rules "have explicit or implicit political purposes and assumptions" (Burnham 1987, 109), at any moment in history state electoral institutions reflect the type of democracy rule makers sought to design—limiting the vote in some instances and expanding it in others. Within American federalism, electoral institutions—and by extension state governments—are used to define the subset of the public that is, and is not, going to be represented (though admittedly participation is only one aspect of representation). This process has had lasting consequences for the nature of the American democratic system.

The "Turnout Problem" in the United States

The history of electoral politics in the United States is punctuated by changing patterns of participation. The American electorate's propensity for political participation was quite different in the twentieth century than in the nineteenth. Unlike the modern era, the mid- to late nineteenth century is generally described as a period of intense political engagement, heightened partisanship, and high voting rates (Avey 1989; Bensel 2004; Burnham 1987; Key 1966; Kleppner 1982; Mayhew 1986). As the country neared the end of the nineteenth century and moved into the early years of the twentieth, the dynamics governing political participation changed radically. An onslaught of Populist and Progressive reforms—legitimizing the electoral process and stripping power from corrupt political machines—fundamentally changed the electoral landscape (Brody 1978; Burnham 1970; Keyssar 2000; McGerr 1986, 2003; Patterson 2002).

One of the Progressive Era's most pronounced legacies, however, is the dampening of electoral engagement. Turnout rates of the modern American electorate fall well below averages from the previous century (Burnham 1965; Teixeira 1992). Although there has been some ebb and flow in national turnout over time—for example, historians credit the realigning principles of the New Deal for reviving political interest during the 1930s—any vibrancy proved unsustainable. By midcentury the United States witnessed a sizable decline in national voter turnout, and scholars were confronted with a seeming "puzzle of participation" (Brody 1978).

As figure 2.1 shows, national voter turnout in the United States has been low throughout the twentieth century, averaging about 55% during presidential election years and 40% during nonpresidential election years.

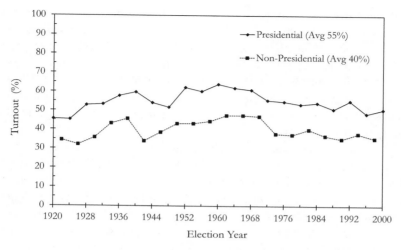

2.1. National voter turnout trends, 1920–2000

National voting rates were not particularly high at any time during this period, and turnout in presidential election years, when just over half the population voted, represents the upper bounds of participation. The low and declining turnout during this time is especially puzzling. Throughout the century there were sizable increases in the median education level, white-collar jobs, and real income—demographic variables that have been theorized, at least at the individual level, to affect turnout positively and should have led to an increase (not a decrease) in voting rates (see, e.g., Burnham 1987; Campbell et al. 1960; Leighly 1995; Rosenstone and Hansen 1993; Rosenstone and Wolfinger 1978; Verba and Nie 1972; Wolfinger and Rosenstone 1980). Further, low turnout does not appear to be caused by increased institutional restrictions, because registration and voting have become less cumbersome over time, especially since the 1960s (Brody 1978; Teixeira 1992). So if demographic characteristics and procedural impediments were the sole barriers keeping people out of the voting booth on Election Day, voter turnout should have systematically increased, not decreased, over the past several decades. This is the heart of the so-called turnout problem in American elections.

Some of the most influential work on voter turnout and electoral reform in American politics is motivated by a national "turnout problem" approach (e.g., Abramson and Aldrich 1982; Gans 1978; McDonald and Popkin 2001; Piven and Cloward 1988; Rosenstone and Hansen 1993; Schattschneider 1960; Teixeira 1992; Wattenberg 1998). Although historical comparisons of United States voting rates during the nineteenth and twentieth centuries are worrisome, the turnout problem is exacerbated by cross-national comparisons. In the canonical portrayal, voter turnout rates from other developed countries are juxtaposed with American national trends (Burnham 1965, 1982; Lijphart 1997; Powell 1986; Verba, Schlozman, and Brady 1995). These cross-national comparisons reveal a startling pattern that characterizes the modern American electorate as essentially nonparticipatory.[2]

Compared with those of other advanced industrial democracies, voting rates in the United States are strikingly low. For example, Powell (1982) lists five countries that stand out for having low voting rates in general elections: "In India, Jamaica, Switzerland, Turkey, and the United States only about two-thirds of the eligible electorate voted in the average national election" (13). Even using presidential turnout rates (the highest rates), comparative analyses reveal that the nation is a participatory laggard. Notably, Powell's impressive comparison of twenty advanced industrialized democracies reveals that "average turnout in presidential elections in the United States as a percentage of the voting-age population was 54% in the period from 1972–80. In the other twenty industrialized democracies, the average turnout was 80%" (1986, 23–24). According to Powell's study, America's national voter participation exceeds that of only one other country—Switzerland. Similar lackluster pictures can be found in Crewe (1981), Dalton (1988), Glass, Squire, and Wolfinger (1984), Jackman (1987), Lijphart (1994), and Verba, Nie, and Kim (1978).

Not only does the United States fall below most of the democratized world in twentieth-century voting rates, the gap is substantial. As Teixeira notes, "Because the highest ranked democracies (Belgium, Austria, and Australia) have turnouts of 90% or more, the gap between the United States and these democracies approaches or exceeds 40 percentage points. Even if one compares the U.S. rate with the average across all twenty democracies (78%), the gap is still 25 points" (1992, 7–8). Further, declining trends in American participation run exactly counter to trends in other countries. While the steady movement in many Western European countries was "toward substantially complete incorporation of the mass public into the political system," the trend in the United States "since about 1900 [has] been a move toward functional disenfranchisement" (Burnham 1982, 122). These patterns have shaped an unflattering global perception of voting in the United States, leading observers of electoral behavior to conclude that a high level of not voting is not only troubling but also characteristically American.

Yet the "turnout problem" in the United States, which is so often de-
cried and analyzed by comparing today with earlier periods in American
history or the United States with other developed countries, actually is an
artificial and somewhat institutionally blind way of understanding turnout.
It is misleading because it does not take into account that United States national turnout actually means average turnout. Since national turnout rates
are typically not recognized as average turnout, the United States is always
treated as a deviant—as if somehow the whole country were weirdly nonparticipatory. This is incorrect in two important ways.

First, the United States is unusual in allowing its subnational units (the
American states) to design their own election procedures, especially for national elections. As such, it is not really comparable to other democratic
polities once we recognize that, in the cross-national perspective, electoral
federalism is unique legally, administratively, and in the number of subnational units involved. This arrangement makes the United States exceptional from that perspective (Ewald 2009; Lipset 1996; Tocqueville 1948).
How many other polities, even federal polities, feature fifty variations of
rules governing turnout for national elections? None. Yet the turnout problem discussion often fails to recognize this essential fact.

Second, by ignoring the importance of electoral federalism in the
United States, both historical and international comparisons of national
voting rates mask the impressive variation across the country both in electoral rules and in turnout rates. The states and regions vary tremendously
in how they structure registration and voting systems and also in how participatory they are. Subnational turnout rates during the twentieth century
have varied not slightly but very considerably. Thus the turnout problem
idea, which has been kicking around for decades and has inspired some of
the most influential scholarship on modern voting habits (such as Burnham 1965; Powell 1986; Piven and Cloward 1988; Rosenstone and Hansen 1993) and even federal reform initiatives (e.g., the 1993 National Voter
Registration Act), misframes twentieth-century voter turnout in the United
States.

This study moves beyond the classic turnout problem approach. I argue
that voting in the United States *is* exceptional, but not because twentieth-
century voting rates were low or because the electorate is oddly deviant
in its tendency not to vote. Instead, it is the electoral environment that
is exceptional. I showcase American federalism as critical to shaping US
voter turnout, and I view electoral federalism as constitutive of the nation's
voter turnout—as fundamental to political participation. To understand
modern voting behavior, we need to explore the federal arrangement in the

states and its effects on subnational voting rates. Participation, as Powell and many others have pointed out, is "facilitated or hindered by the institutional context within which individuals act" (1986, 17); thus the large degree of institutional variation—a by-product of American federalism that leads to variation in state and regional turnout—needs to be evaluated. Further, institutional development casts a very long shadow across the states and regions. Historical analysis is essential for recognizing the slow evolution of state electoral systems and the jurisdictional variation in twentieth-century voter turnout. By examining this relationship subnationally and historically, this book celebrates the developmental and temporal dimensions of American federalism.

Voter Turnout: A Product of American Federalism?

The most impressive responsibility vested in the American states by the federal system is their governance over electoral processes. Since the country's founding, the individual states have created and implemented electoral laws within their borders with minimal federal intervention, essentially creating fifty unique sets of rules. Still today, nearly all electoral institutions originate at the state level. Even the power to determine who is considered qualified to vote—to literally define the electorate—has been delegated to the fifty states. And the way the states have made these determinations, and the basis for them, has varied greatly over time. This individualism was originally justified by the belief that state and local authorities knew their particular circumstances better than outsiders did and could therefore fashion laws that suited their specific needs (even if they did so in normatively objectionable ways). This decentralized electoral system has important ramifications. Variation in state rules about how, or whether, individuals can participate in government affects the political system. By implementing expansive and restrictive electoral institutions throughout the twentieth century, the states have established the limits of participation and shaped American democracy.

Alongside this system of relative state autonomy lay the powerful interests of the federal government. Throughout the twentieth century a tension existed between state and federal perspectives on norms of exclusion and participation within the electoral system. Incongruences have arisen in how easily certain classes of citizens could qualify, register, and ultimately participate in the electoral process. Consequently there were important moments when the federal government was compelled to intervene and supplant state electoral authority in order to establish more uniform and just voting practices. Apart from these important instances of federal action, however, the states have designed and maintained the types of electoral environments they most prefer, anticipating how various electoral rules might affect participation. The evolution of institutional expansion and restriction by the states, coupled with federal involvement, has defined electoral politics in the United States. At its core is the connection between institutional design and anticipated political response. This has had important consequences for the quality of American democracy throughout the twentieth century and before.

I appreciate the importance of the American federal system in this capacity and treat the states as units of analysis. This is a departure from the individual-level framework often used to study American voting behavior (see Leighley 1995 and Lewis-Beck et al. 2008 for a review of this extensive literature).[3] Although our understanding of American voting behavior has benefited greatly from the individual-level behavioral framework, research focusing exclusively on the attributes, characteristics, and demographics of individual voters and nonvoters typically neglects the interactive effects and structural patterns surrounding elections. Political behavior does not occur in a vacuum. We need to evaluate the setting within which political actors are forced to behave (Ewald 2009; Patterson 2002; Rusk 1970, 1974; Thompson 2002; Verba and Nie 1972; Wolfinger and Rosenstone 1980). It is within the institutional dimension that actors' behavior is conditioned. A state's electoral structure directly affects voters' incentive to participate by influencing electoral costs and shaping voting processes. It is often assumed that political institutions have the same effect on everyone and can be largely ignored, but by disregarding the structure of electoral processes, strictly behavioral studies neglect the important institutions that set the limits for American voting. Our understanding of voter turnout requires a better linkage between individual behavior and the specific institutions designed to structure voter participation. This understanding comes from looking at the historical structure of electoral processes in the states and examining how aggregate voting tendencies respond to changing institutional parameters.

This book emphasizes the ability of the fifty states to structure the political environment through institutional design. This is in line with Jerrold Rusk's (1970, 1974) "legal-institutional" theory, which postulates that "the legal-institutionalist properties of the electoral system—ballot and registration systems, voting systems, suffrage requirements, and the like—have important effects in influencing and shaping voting behavior; in essence, they define the conditions and boundaries of decision-making at the polls. Often, though, they are taken for granted, [treated] as 'givens' instead of being probed for their effects on voting behavior" (1974, 1044). This view is also associated with the influential work of Campbell et al. (1960), as well as work by Kelley, Ayers, and Bowen (1967), Kousser (1974), and Rusk and Stucker (1978), all of whom emphasize aspects of electoral law machinery as major determinants of electoral behavior.

I view the boundaries created by state electoral institutions as pivotal. The nature and dynamics of state electoral institutions influence voter participation, and ultimately policy outcomes. It follows that by altering the costs of registering and voting with expansive or restrictive laws, electoral institutions may in fact change the status quo with respect to voting. The institutional independence, incrementalism, and variation present in the states provide a great deal of material for the study of American democracy.

Connecting Electoral Institutions and Voter Turnout in the States

In connecting the effects of various expansive and restrictive electoral institutions with twentieth-century voter turnout, I begin with the Downsian framework. In *An Economic Theory of Democracy* (1957), Anthony Downs formulated a rational choice model of an individual's turnout decision. He posited that when the costs of voting outweigh the benefits, an individual will choose not to vote. Despite many expansive, cost-reducing electoral reforms over time, on the whole the American electoral system places the burden of participation on the individual. For example, a citizen must invest time and energy gathering information about candidates, policies, and the like. She will incur costs from traveling to the polling place on Election Day, in lost wages or time spent in transit—or both. Also, voting is typically inconvenient because of the limited hours most polling places are open, their location, and the fact that most elections take place on weekdays, forcing people to adjust their work schedules in order to vote. Since both politicians and voters realize that the structure of the system makes the individual costs of voting substantial and the rewards minimal, it appears that the electoral process itself creates a disincentive to vote.

In addition to the costs of voting, registration can also be costly (Highton 2004; Kelley, Ayers, and Bowen 1967; Timpone 1998). In fact, many argue that "registration is often more difficult than voting. It may require a longer journey, at a less convenient hour, to complete a more complicated procedure—at a time when interest in the campaign is far from at its peak"

(Rosenstone and Wolfinger 1978, 22). Thus Downs's (1957) conception of voting costs applies during both registration and voting. First eligible voters must decide whether to register, then they must decide whether to vote. At each stage, a cost-benefit analysis will determine whether a person decides to register and then whether he will indeed go to the polls. This suggests, at least in principle, that easing the burdens in the first stage may yield turnout gains in the second, offering hope that electoral reforms that liberalize voter qualifications, lessen registration requirements, and ease voting procedures may in fact increase turnout.[4] This conception, which emphasizes how registration and voting costs affect participation, has framed a great deal of the research on electoral reform.

Much of this research has focused exclusively on the cost of voter registration. Indeed, the uniquely cumbersome registration laws in the United States are frequently identified as a main reason turnout in American elections lags well behind that in most other industrialized democratic countries (see, e.g., Burnham 1965; Gosnell 1930; Kelley, Ayers, Bowen 1967; Piven and Cloward 1988; Powell 1986; Reichley 1987; Squire, Wolfinger, and Glass 1987; Teixeira 1992; Verba, Nie, and Kim 1978; Wolfinger and Rosenstone 1980). Many have argued that adopting less restrictive registration procedures could not only increase voting rates, but also make participation less biased and more inclusive.

Election Day registration has been the single, and in many cases the only, reform to have a substantively significant association with higher voting rates. Although it exists in only a handful of states, countless studies, beginning with Smolka's (1977) work on early-adopting states and Wolfinger and Rosenstone's (1980) classic cross-state analysis, have demonstrated that Election Day registration has a large positive effect on turnout (see, e.g., Brians and Grofman 1999; Fenster 1994; Highton and Wolfinger 1998; Huang and Shields 2000; Knack 2001; Mitchell and Wlezien 1995; Rhine 1996; Teixeira 1992; Timpone 2002; Tolbert et al. 2008). Taken together, these studies suggest that if Election Day registration laws were implemented nationally, voter turnout could increase by 5 to 14 percentage points. Yet findings also suggest that although Election Day registration may increase turnout, especially among the younger and more mobile, it does not necessarily produce a more representative electorate. In particular, racial minorities and the economically disadvantaged may not vote in greater numbers after the adoption of Election Day registration (Brians and Grofman 2001; Fitzgerald 2005; Hanmer 2009; Highton 1997; Knack and White 2000; Rigby and Springer 2011).

Other prominent registration reforms that target how easily people can register, and the time between registration and voting, have considerably more modest effects. For example, motor voter programs, which were adopted by several states before they were mandated nationally under the National Voter Registration Act in 1993, have effects on turnout ranging from basically zero (Brown and Wedeking 2006; Martinez and Hill 1999) to only a few percentage points (Fitzgerald 2005; Franklin and Grier 1997; Highton and Wolfinger 1998; Knack 1995; Rhine 1995). More recently, Hanmer (2009) has shown that effects depend on whether the state adopted motor voter on its own or in response to federal mandate. Additionally, despite a steady loosening of registration deadlines over time (Highton 2004), early registration closing dates seem to pose only a minimal deterrent to voting (Mitchell and Wlezien 1995; Teixeira 1992; Wolfinger and Rosenstone 1980).

Scholarship and reform efforts have recently expanded to making voting easier for those already registered. These increasingly popular convenience reforms (reforms that make voting easier for those that are already registered as opposed to cost-reducing reforms that seek to make registration easier for nonregistrants) include permitting early in-person voting (see Gronke, Galanes-Rosenbaum, and Miller 2008; Hansen 2001; Neeley and Richardson 2001; Richardson and Neely 1996; Rigby and Springer 2011; Stein 1998; Stein and Garcia-Monet 1997), and universal absentee voting (see Dubin and Kaslow 1996; Gronke, Galanes-Rosenbaum, and Miller 2007; Hansen 2001; Karp and Banducci 2001; Oliver 1996; Patterson and Caldeira 1985). Oregon's vote-by-mail system has been studied in depth (see Berinsky 2005; Berinsky, Burns, and Traugott 2001; Karp and Banducci 2000; Kousser and Mullin 2007; Southwell and Burchett 1997, 2000a, 2000b), as has the growing adoption of vote centers (polling places situated throughout a county that allow any registered voter to vote at any location) (Juenke and Shepard 2008; Stein and Vonnahme 2006, 2007). In each instance, however, the general finding is that most convenience electoral laws do little to increase turnout, and they may even have the opposite effect—decreasing turnout and increasing inequality (Berinsky 2005; Burden and Neiheisel 2013; Fitzgerald 2005; Gronke et al. 2008; Hanmer 2009; Tolbert et al. 2008; Traugott 2004).

Although these studies have undoubtedly made important contributions to our understanding of how some electoral institutions affect turnout rates, most of them deal with a single reform or a handful of institutions (e.g., Boyd 1981; Fenster 1994; Franklin and Grier 1997; Gans 1987; Hanmer 2009; Highton 1997; Karp and Banducci 2000; Knack 1995, 2001; Knack and White 2000; Mitchell and Wlezien 1995; Oliver 1996; Piven and

Cloward 1988, 2000; Rhine 1995; Rusk 1970; Smolka 1977; Smolka and Rossotti 1975; Southwell and Burchett 2000a; Stein 1998). This literature also focuses disproportionately on the effects that cost-reducing or convenience electoral reforms—such as motor voter registration, Election Day registration, and early voting—have on state voter turnout (e.g., Brians and Grofman 2001; Fitzgerald 2005; Gronke et al 2008; Highton 2004; Knack 1995; Rhine 1995; Tolbert et al. 2008; Wolfinger and Rosenstone 1980). By dealing exclusively with individual reforms, and especially cost-reducing or convenience reforms, previous work has lacked the scope to comprehensively evaluate the effects of institutional change in American elections. To generate a more complete, fully specified analysis of the effects the electoral process has on participation, especially over time, we must recognize the role (and legacy) of election laws not only in increasing participation but in limiting it as well.

Electoral institutions—both expansive *and* restrictive—have helped structure the vote throughout American history. For decades the states deliberately enacted laws—such as long residency requirements, literacy tests, and poll taxes—to make voting more cumbersome as they actively sought to constrict the electorate. These limiting laws also need to be considered when evaluating the effects of expansive electoral institutions (Rosenstone and Hansen 1993).[5] Examining the entire packages of state election laws together (not one law in isolation) places current registration and voting reforms in their historical context and identifies the electoral institutions—both expansive and restrictive—that have had the most substantial effects on state voter turnout throughout the twentieth century. By exploring a number of electoral institutions over time, I aim to provide a more complete picture of the dynamic evolution of electoral systems across the fifty states and consider the variety of effects these laws have had on participation throughout the nation, identifying both the successes of recent expansive reforms in increasing state turnout and cases where limiting institutions have been used to constrict the electorate.

The Importance of Geographical and Historical Context

Understanding the evolution of twentieth-century voting patterns in the United States is made even more complicated when the trends are disaggregated at the regional and state levels. Arguably, many elements combine to encourage or deter voting, and the particulars of these behavior-inducing arrangements vary geographically and temporally; as such, the typical national-level characterizations of participation in the United States suppress important state and regional variation in both institutional parameters and outcomes. Once national voter turnout trends are disaggregated, however, regional patterns emerge that force us to update our unitary conception of the voting calculation and acknowledge how geographical and historical context shapes the behavior of the modern electorate.[6]

Electoral institutions have undoubtedly influenced state-level turnout throughout the century, even after we control for other factors known to influence voting, such as electoral competition and demographic variables. Given the complexities of the electoral environment, however, they are not the only relevant conditions. Local differences in the voting calculation will produce variation in how state electoral institutions affect turnout rates, particularly in the southern and nonsouthern states. We therefore need to consider the unique political environments where voting occurs. The dominant assumption in the literature is that institutional effects can be generalized from one political context to others (Aldrich 1993; Downs 1957; Riker and Ordeshook 1968; Wolfinger and Rosenstone 1980). I contend, however, that the voting environment, and therefore the voting calculation, is not uniform throughout the nation, so we should expect the effects of particular institutions to vary between states—especially between states in the South and in other regions.

For example, do we expect a citizen in Minnesota to experience voting hurdles in the same way a citizen in Alabama does? Similarly, lowering the costs of voter registration in Wisconsin by enacting a motor voter program might allow some interested citizens to cross the voting threshold, whereas in Louisiana it may not reduce the costs enough to make a difference. Understanding the importance of state and regional variation is critical to inform future policy decisions. Realizing that we cannot just blindly import institutions may encourage more realistic expectations for how electoral reform can influence behavior. Further, exploring the nature and consequences of American federalism implies an appreciation of variation and uniqueness. The cost-benefit framework allows for a twofold story about social circumstances and state norms that affect, and are affected by, electoral rules and ultimately turnout. A state or region's cost-benefit calculus flows from, or at least is related to, its political context and group norms. Whether the state publics are vested in the government or perceive value from voting varies, as do the institutions. This book focuses disproportionately on the institutional aspects as they relate to voting costs.

A state's institutional history will inform and condition the effects of institutional changes. States that have historically welcomed or encouraged voters differ systematically from those that have routinely made voting more difficult. In this sense, institutional history would presumably have a lasting effect on turnout through its effect on political socialization. The states have lasting legacies of restrictiveness or expansiveness that need to be recognized when evaluating the effects of individual reforms. Residents of states outside the South, especially in the Midwest, that have a long history of implementing expansive electoral laws will experience both the realization and the magnitude of institutional change differently than residents of southern states that maintained enormously cost-increasing voting environments for much of the century. The current literature on voting and electoral reform would lead us to expect the largest cost-reducing institutional effects to occur where there is the most to gain—in the South. But it may be that just altering the costs of voting through structural changes—merely making voting and registration more convenient—is not enough to overcome the legacy of Jim Crow.

By foregrounding electoral federalism in the United States, I reveal that there is no "one size fits all" institutional solution for improving voter turnout. Instead, we must consider local costs and benefits within the voting calculation and recognize the great variation that might exist geographically within any single cost-benefit calculation. It also may be that self-imposed, or communally imposed, norms about civic duty influence citizens differently in different places, so that they feel bound to the cultural norms within their state, county, or district. In short, it may be easy or hard to alter norms depending on where the decision on voting takes place. Electoral procedures may influence voting norms differently depending on the local political environment (for a discussion about the adoption of some of these more recent laws, see Hanmer 2009), so we should expect the magnitude of particular reforms to vary regionally—and most dramatically between the states in and outside the South.

Thus we see that electoral institutions matter, but they do not necessarily matter equally. Traditional voting scholarship and the rhetoric often used by political reformers may lead us to expect that every institutional change to reduce the cost of voting will increase turnout, but this has not happened. We need a better understanding of variation in the realization of voting costs. It is clear that, throughout the century, some state and local laws were used to systematically prevent certain types of people from voting. When states with a long history of restricting access to the polls finally ease the barriers to registration and voting, the fit between institutions and the citizenry, at least initially, remains different from the fit in states that have historically promoted participation. This influences the effectiveness of institutional changes both in realization and in magnitude.

At a minimum there may be important theoretical and structural differences between institutional effects in the southern and nonsouthern states. If so, reformers considering potential policy solutions may need to reevaluate their expectations about outcomes and recognize that institutional effects are conditioned, at least in part, by political context and institutional history.

Voting in the United States is unique in the subnational variance that stems from variation in institutions and their historical and geographic context (and presumably their interaction). This makes the effects of institutional reforms less obvious and somewhat conditional. The variation in state participation rates might be due to some blending of institutions and culture. For example, the empirical results presented in chapter 5 suggest that expansive institutions are not a panacea for improving participation when historical conditions are not favorable. This leads to the expectation that historical context is a necessary condition for assessing how electoral institutions affect participation. A state's electoral context is rooted in voting habits and patterns that are due to social circumstances (e.g., racial and social disposition, history and past rules). The central story I am telling concerns the dynamic nature of institutional effects. Each of the American states has a profile that defines past (and perhaps even future) institutions. By examining an array of institutional changes over a century's worth of elections, this book inherently reveals how a process that is both historical and dynamic informs the narrative about incentives and disincentives in American elections.

Conclusion

There are voluminous studies on the behavior, characteristics, and demographics of voters and nonvoters. Since the mid-twentieth century, as concern about the "turnout problem" in the United States grew, attention has been directed to the relationship between electoral institutions and voting rates. Expansive and restrictive institutions have emerged as the cause— and perhaps the remedy—for subpar participation in American elections. And not without reason. Recognizing the link between political institutions and political behavior is critical to understanding voting and elections. Because institutions are malleable, institutional changes may give the latent registrant and latent voter an incentive to participate (Jackman 1987). The underlying assumption is that if registration and voting were easier or cost less, more citizens would register and then vote on Election Day. If so, expansive state electoral institutions could motivate participation and resolve, or at least improve, the turnout problem. Conversely, restrictive or cost-increasing electoral laws may have depressed turnout over time.

The intricate relationship between political institutions and political behavior has shaped the struggle over suffrage rights and election laws throughout American history. The facets of this relationship, particularly in the electoral realm, will continue to be a major characteristic of democratic politics in the United States. I contend that to understand this multifaceted relationship we must appreciate the political environments in which the decision to vote takes place and the regional variation within the changing relationship between political institutions and political outcomes over time—especially between the southern and nonsouthern states. Indeed, we cannot understand the effects of recent cost-reducing reforms on turnout rates, or the policy prescriptions that stem from evaluating these reforms, without seeing how these processes have evolved. By comprehensively evaluating how both expansive and restrictive electoral institutions have affected state turnout during the twentieth century, this book provides an extensive longitudinal analysis of how institutional change has affected voting. It is thus able to identify particularly successful institutional configurations and place contemporary reforms in their historical context.

The state-focused perspective I employ throughout informs our understanding of voting processes in the United States as we decide whether the conclusions drawn from national-level research needs to be modified to explain voting in the states. Additionally, by comparing an array of electoral institutions over an eighty-year span both within states and between states, I offer a comprehensive analysis of the relationship between electoral institutions and political behavior over time. This may help those instituting policies for reforming the electoral process in the United States. To improve political participation and inclusiveness throughout the nation, we must first understand how electoral institutions have affected state and regional voting practices and how these effects have evolved historically. Perhaps the solutions to low voting rates in some states and regions are markedly different from working solutions in other states and regions. If so, understanding why will determine whether we can stimulate or alter political participation.

Chapter 3 will offer an in-depth analysis of national, regional, and state-level voter turnout rates during presidential and nonpresidential election years from 1920 to 2000. If one subscribes to the notion that higher turnout enhances the quality of democracy, then national turnout statistics are worrisome. As figure 2.1 shows, twentieth-century voter turnout in the United States is low despite the efforts of national reform campaigns;

but once the turnout trends are disaggregated, it becomes clear that turn-out has been lower in some states than others throughout the century. The disaggregated turnout rates I present in chapter 3 illuminate the immense regional and state-level variation that motivated this book and lead to an in-depth discussion of the varying institutions that have structured twentieth-century participation in the American states.

THREE

Twentieth-Century Voter Turnout in the United States

Most studies of twentieth-century voting in the United States are motivated by the statistic that only about half of the electorate routinely turns out to vote on Election Day. Although this may be true in the aggregate, once the data are disaggregated by region and then by state, we find much more variation than the national picture conveys. This point, often overlooked in national studies, is central to this book. By examining state participation over several decades, we can develop a finer-grained representation of national trends and better identify when and where the modern electorate began to take shape. Furthermore, disaggregating national turnout by region and state lets us begin to see how institutional configurations, created and enforced at the state level, create variability in participation rates. By offering a close examination of twentieth-century voter turnout in the American states, this chapter presents the first half of the story—variation in state voting rates.

Measuring State-Level Voter Turnout

This study examines trends in state-level voter turnout during presidential election years from 1920 to 2000 and nonpresidential election years from 1922 to 1998.[1] Voter turnout is measured as a percentage calculated by dividing the total number of votes for the highest office on the ballot by the state's voting age population.[2] For presidential election years, I used the total votes cast in the presidential race. For nonpresidential election years I used the total votes cast for a US senator. If no Senate race was held in the state, I used the total votes for governor. In a few instances a seat in the US House of Representatives was the highest office on the ballot.[3] National

Table 3.1 Regional Classification of the American States

			South		
		1	Alabama		
		2	Arkansas		
		3	Florida		
		4	Georgia		
		5	Louisiana		
		6	Mississippi		
		7	North Carolina		
		8	South Carolina		
		9	Tennessee		
		10	Texas		
		11	Virginia		

	Midwest		West		Northeast
1	Illinois	1	Alaska	1	Connecticut
2	Indiana	2	Arizona	2	Delaware
3	Iowa	3	California	3	Maine
4	Kansas	4	Colorado	4	Maryland
5	Kentucky	5	Hawaii	5	Massachusetts
6	Michigan	6	Idaho	6	New Hampshire
7	Minnesota	7	Montana	7	New Jersey
8	Missouri	8	Nevada	8	New York
9	Nebraska	9	New Mexico	9	Pennsylvania
10	North Dakota	10	Oregon	10	Rhode Island
11	Ohio	11	Utah	11	Vermont
12	Oklahoma	12	Washington	12	West Virginia
13	South Dakota	13	Wyoming		
14	Wisconsin				

Note: This table presents the regional classification of the American states used throughout this book. It is also the regional schema employed in the American National Election Survey (ANES). As in Key (1949), in this book the South is defined as the eleven secession states.

figures were constructed by aggregating voting rates across the fifty states. Table 3.1 provides the regional classification I used.

Voter turnout is calculated as a percentage of the state's total voting age population to control for the varying sizes of states' voting age populations. The term voting age population (VAP) refers to the number of individuals who satisfy the national voting age requirement in a state.[4] Although the voting age population statistics could be inflated by including persons who satisfy the age requirement but are ineligible to vote, such as resident aliens and institutionalized citizens (Burnham 1986; McDonald 2002; McDonald and Popkin 2001), they are the most reliable measures for this project, given its eighty-year time span.

First, reliable statistics on the voting eligible population (VEP) do not exist throughout the period I studied, and they were not used in any of the historical work I cite (e.g., Black and Black 1987, 1992; Burnham 1970; Key 1949; Kleppner 1982; Lawson 1976, 1985). Employing them now would make meaningful comparisons with previous historical work difficult, and historical analysis is essential for seeing the jurisdictional variation in turnout. Additionally, the VAP and VEP statistics are highly correlated. During the years for which the VEP statistics are available, the national turnout trends (using VAP or VEP) correlate at .89, and the state-by-state trends correlate at .99. Furthermore, when the statistical models I present in this book were estimated using VEP as the dependent variable instead of VAP (for the years it is available), the findings were robust with those generated from the VAP model. This is consistent with evidence that turnout trends do not vary dramatically based on the denominator used (Patterson 2002; Wattenberg 2002). Because accurate systematic figures on eligible voters are lacking throughout the twentieth century, scholars regularly employ voting age population statistics in contemporary and historical assessments of voter registration and voter turnout (e.g., Althaus and Trautman 2008; Ansolabehere and Konisky 2006; Crocker 1996; Fitzgerald 2005; Gomez, Hansford, and Krause 2007; Knack and Kropf 2003; Teixeira 1992; Whitby 2007), and I follow suit.

Disaggregating National Turnout Trends, 1920–2000

As I noted in chapter 2, most studies of American voting point to national voting figures to demonstrate the "turnout problem" in the United States. In the aggregate, as was shown in figure 2.1, twentieth-century turnout rates appear low compared with statistics from the nineteenth century and also with rates in other industrialized democracies. By focusing solely on these aggregate figures, many conclude that Americans are characteristically nonparticipatory. This is a misleading generalization. In fact, once the national trends are disaggregated by region, as shown in figures 3.1 and 3.2, it is clear that voter turnout varied a lot throughout the century.

In fact, many regions have consistently had voter turnout well above the national average during most of the twentieth century. For example, voting rates in the Midwest were consistently, and impressively, above the national average during *all* election years from 1920 to 2000. Similarly, states in the West and Northeast had reasonably high turnout—above the national average during most of the period and converging with the national average during elections in the late 1970s through 2000. These high turnout regions, especially the Midwest, are particularly noteworthy considering

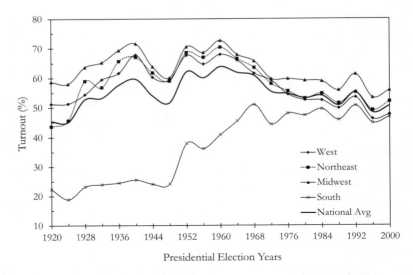

3.1. Presidential election year voter turnout trends by region, 1920–2000. (This graph and all others in this chapter are available in a larger color format at www.press.uchicago.edu/sites/springer/.)

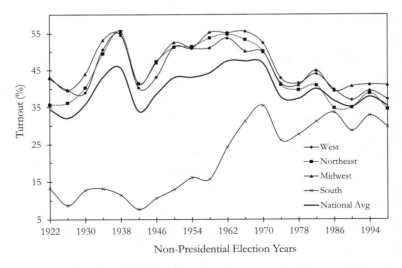

3.2. Nonpresidential election year voter turnout trends by region, 1922–98

the effect high turnout has on political outcomes. Since recent national elections have been decided by increasingly close margins, a region like the Midwest in 2000, with a turnout rate 10 percentage points above the national average, could have a real impact in determining political victories and losses. This distinction is important, yet it is routinely masked by the national figures.

Figures 3.1 and 3.2 also demonstrate that voting levels in the South were below the national average for the *entire* century. Although the regional trends begin to converge over time, narrowing the difference between southern and nonsouthern rates, especially since the late 1960s, after the enactment of the 1964 Civil Rights Act and 1965 Voting Rights Act, there is still a substantial difference between turnout in the southern and nonsouthern states (Burnham 1970; Kousser 1999; McDonald and Popkin 2001; Rusk and Stucker 1978). These figures suggest that southern voting rates have consistently depressed the national trends throughout the period. Of course voting in the South was institutionalized differently than voting in many of the other regions—a connection I will be evaluating throughout this book.

Additionally, since the regions are simply groupings of states, it is not surprising that even more variation appears when the regional trends are further disaggregated. Figures 3.3 through 3.10 illustrate that the voting rates of individual states, even within the same region, vary widely.[5] These

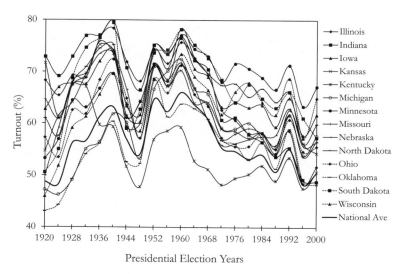

3.3. Midwestern presidential election year voter turnout trends by state, 1920–2000

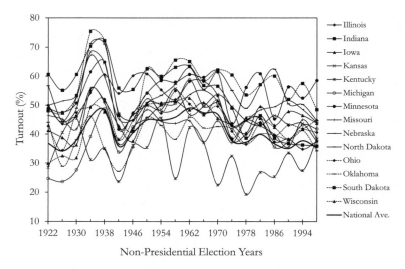

3.4. Midwestern nonpresidential election year voter turnout trends by state, 1922–98

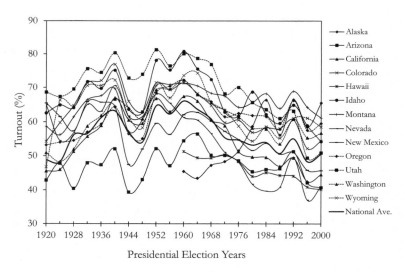

3.5. Western presidential election year voter turnout trends by state, 1920–2000

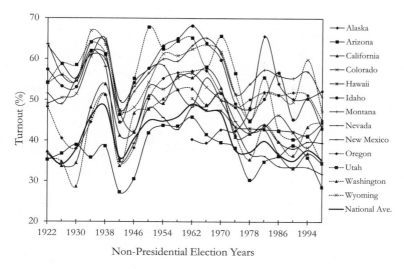

3.6. Western nonpresidential election year voter turnout trends by state, 1922–98

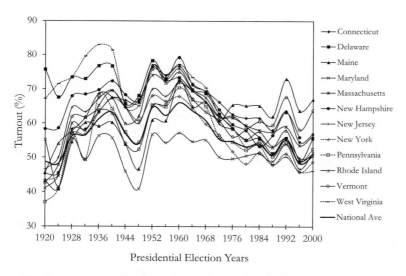

3.7. Northeastern presidential election year voter turnout trends by state, 1920–2000

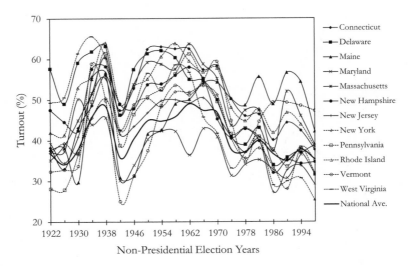

3.8. Northeastern nonpresidential election year voter turnout trends by state, 1922–98

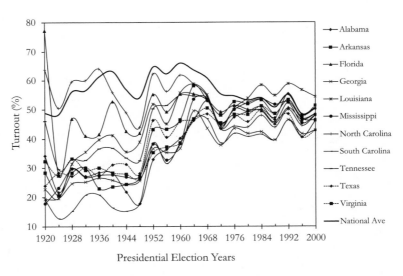

3.9. Southern presidential election year voter turnout trends by state, 1920–2000

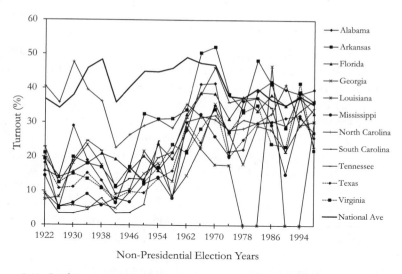

3.10. Southern nonpresidential election year voter turnout trends by state, 1922–98

disaggregated state-level trends provide an underappreciated lens for examining the nature of voting throughout the twentieth century, offering much more detail for our understanding of national turnout rates. These more nuanced trends help us identify similarities and differences between the states in political participation and also aid preliminary theorizing about why state turnout trends look the way they do.

How Do the States Fit into the National Story?

Twentieth-century voting trends have been described a number of ways, but such descriptions typically do not include the histories of individual states. This is unfortunate, since we can learn a great deal from the electoral tendencies of regions and states over time. Considering the nature of political change throughout history among, and within, the American states allows us to further examine the elements fueling political participation. Accordingly, this section situates the voting patterns of individual states within the national story, exposing the chronological boundaries of critical periods during presidential and nonpresidential election years at the state level. By evaluating the national trends from a state perspective, we gain a richer understanding of the norms of twentieth-century participation in the United States.

Presidential Election Years, 1920–2000

The American electoral landscape changed dramatically in 1920 when, after years of organization and protest, the Nineteenth Amendment to the US Constitution was ratified. In the fall of 1920, women across the country were able to vote in national elections. At first this had the unexpected effect of artificially lowering national voting rates as the size of the voting population swelled (the denominator in the turnout equation increased disproportionately to the numerator). The size of the electorate quickly normalized, however, and for the most part voter turnout increased steadily during presidential election years from 1928 to 1940. Notably, in 1928, just two elections after the universal enfranchisement of women, voter turnout increased in all the midwestern, northeastern, and southern states except Texas. In the West, voter turnout increased in all states except Arizona, Idaho, New Mexico, and Wyoming.

Then, in 1944 turnout declined at a striking rate, decreasing in all states except Arkansas, Mississippi, Texas, and Virginia. Many social and political factors may have contributed to this decline: for example, the nation's preoccupation with World War II and its aftermath, widespread internal migration throughout the United States, and perhaps most important, the fact that incumbent Franklin Delano Roosevelt was running for his fourth consecutive term as president. This decrease in voter turnout eventually bottomed out nationally in 1948 at 52%.

In 1952, during the presidential race between Dwight Eisenhower and Adlai Stevenson, voter turnout increased in all fifty states, and Eisenhower won by a landslide in every region but the South. This notable increase of nearly 10 percentage points in turnout in 1952 was likely due to Ike's unprecedented popularity and concerns regarding the Korean War. There is also some chance that turnout increased in 1952 because of the famous election miscall in 1948. Owing to a polling mishap, the headline of an early edition of the *Chicago Daily Tribune* famously read "Dewey Defeats Truman," much to Truman's glee after he won the election by 4.4%.[6] It is possible that the polling fiasco reminded people that actual votes matter more than polls, so more voters were motivated to turn out on Election Day in 1952. It is also worth noting that although at first glance the 1952 national turnout rates look unusually high, this is largely by juxtaposition with the lower than average rates in 1944 and 1948. Those low rates (54% and 52% respectively) are the outliers, not the rates for 1952. When we compare rates in 1940 (60%) with rates in 1952 (62% percent), the high in 1952 looks less striking.

Over the years that followed, participation rates experienced an ebb and flow, generally hovering around 61%, and during the close election between Kennedy and Nixon in 1960, they reached the high for the century with nearly 64% of the voting-age population turning out. In 1960 voter turnout increased in every state except Nevada. Even though many scholars use the 1960 election as a benchmark for gauging the subsequent decline in national turnout, that is somewhat misleading. In reality, the 1960 presidential election garnered the highest turnout in the United States since 1900, so one should expect rates to fall after this unprecedented peak. The 1960 election capped a nearly thirty-six-year rise in turnout and represents an impressive increase over the low points in 1920 and 1924. With the exception of 1944 and 1948, when the nation was preoccupied with World War II and its aftermath, the years between 1928 and 1960 reflect a fairly steady increase in voter turnout.

After the peak in 1960, there was a fairly steady decline in state voting rates. In 1964, the year of Lyndon Johnson's decisive victory over Barry Goldwater, voter turnout decreased in all the midwestern and northeastern states, and in 1968 turnout rates decreased again throughout these regions except in Kansas, Maine, and Maryland. During this period, however, the Civil Rights Act of 1964, the Voting Rights Act of 1965, and the subsequent ratification of the Twenty-Fourth Amendment had a pivotal and relatively swift positive effect on voting rates in the South. Indeed, in 1964, shortly after the federal legislation was implemented, turnout rates increased in ten of the eleven southern states (Alabama, Arkansas, Georgia, Louisiana, Mississippi, South Carolina, Florida, Tennessee, Texas, and Virginia), declining only in North Carolina. Turnout continued to climb in all the southern states during the 1968 election, but it fell throughout the rest of the nation—a trend that continued, more or less, for the rest of the century.

During the 1972 election, in the midst of the Vietnam War and a landslide Republican victory, turnout declined once again, in all states. This was the first election held after the Federal Voting Rights Act of 1970, which outlawed literacy tests, employed as a prerequisite for voting in many states, and also after the ratification in 1971 of the Twenty-Sixth Amendment, lowering the national voting age.[7] In fact, only 55.4% of the voting age population participated in the 1972 election, 54.7% went to the polls in 1976, and only 53.2% turned out in 1980. This marks a decrease of nearly 9 percentage points in national voter turnout since 1964—over the course of just five presidential elections. Notably, however, although turnout declined in most states in 1976, voting rates increased throughout the South, but the following years witnessed a fairly consistent decline. In 1980, 1988, and 1996, turnout was down in most states despite surprising gains in the southern states in 1984. In fact, apart from the anomalous 4% boost in national voter turnout during the 1992 election, when turnout rose in every state but Hawaii, presumably owing to Ross Perot's unprecedented third-party candidacy, and a small national increase in 2000, when states in the Northeast and South had fairly consistent increases, turnout in many states has declined or held steady during the latter part of the century.

Nonpresidential Election Years, 1922–98

Voter turnout typically is lower during nonpresidential election years than during presidential election years—averaging about 40% since 1920. Regional and state patterns are also somewhat harder to detect, given the more local aspect of these races. Although state experiences during nonpresidential election years tend to be more variable, there were a few notable trends throughout the twentieth century. For example, in 1934, amid excitement about the New Deal, voter turnout increased in all the states in the Midwest, Northeast, and West except Kentucky, Maryland, and Arizona. In 1942, during World War II, voter turnout declined in all states except Mississippi—and, conversely, in 1946 turnout rates increased in all states in the Northeast, West, and South except New Hampshire, Colorado, Mississippi, and Florida. Incidentally, in 1946 the Democrats lost a large number of seats in both the House and the Senate. In 1950 turnout rates further increased in all the northeastern, midwestern, and western states apart from Kentucky. In 1962, even before the enactment of federal civil rights and voting antidiscrimination legislation, turnout rates increased throughout the states in the South except Virginia, and in 1966, after the passage of the Civil Rights Act and Voting Rights Act, once again most southern states showed gains in participation. In 1966 voter turnout increased in Alabama, Arkansas, Georgia, Mississippi, South Carolina, Florida, Tennessee, and Virginia and declined in Louisiana, North Carolina, and Texas. In 1970, although voting rates continued to increase in Alabama, Arkansas, Georgia, Florida, South Carolina, Tennessee, Texas, and Virginia, they declined in a handful of other southern states: Louisiana, Mississippi, and North Carolina. Then in 1974, shortly after the national voting age was lowered, voter turnout declined in all states except Kentucky.

From 1978 through 1998, nonpresidential turnout rates varied considerably by state. There were not many consistent regional patterns during this time. For example, in 1982 one-third of the states in each region had increases in turnout, but in 1986 rates varied more substantially, although most of the states in the Northeast and West had declines. Similarly, in 1990 state rates in the Midwest and Northeast varied while turnout was down in all the western states but Arizona and Oregon and all the southern states except North Carolina and Texas. In 1994, turnout rates fluctuated widely outside the South, but they were up in all the southern states except Alabama and North Carolina. Finally, in 1998 regional turnout patterns varied substantially, although turnout in the Northeast was down in all states except Maryland and New Hampshire.

What States Had "High Turnout" or "Low Turnout" throughout the Century?

In this section I present state rankings to determine which states have exhibited consistently "high" or "low" turnout patterns throughout the century. To construct these rankings, I sorted the states according to their presidential and nonpresidential election year turnout, then constructed year-by-year state turnout rankings. The ten states with the highest and lowest turnout rates were identified for each election year from 1920 to 2000. Then these states were sorted based on the number of times, during the twenty-one presidential election years and twenty nonpresidential election years, they appeared in the "highest ten" or "lowest ten." Tables 3.2 and 3.3 present these rankings.

Table 3.2 shows that all the states with the most years in the highest ten category during the twentieth century were located outside the South. Remarkably, 40% of the states with consistently high turnout for 15% or more of the presidential election years from 1920 to 2000 were in the Midwest, and an additional 30% were in the Northeast and West. Further, five out of the eight states with turnout in the "highest ten" for over 50% of the presidential election years were in the Midwest.

The rankings, although similar, vary a bit more during nonpresidential election years. During these less salient elections, the western states dominated the high turnout category, with 40% of the states in the region ranking consistently high during 15% or more of the years. Additionally, 30% of these routinely high-ranking states were in the Northeast and in the West. Notably, almost all the same states were ranked in the highest ten during both presidential and nonpresidential election years. Of these twenty-six overlapping states, 38% were in the West and 31% were in the Midwest and Northeast.

On the other hand, table 3.3 reveals that all eleven southern states consistently dominated the lowest turnout category throughout the century.

Table 3.2 Ranking of States with Consistently High Turnout

State	Region	% of Years with Turnout in Highest Ten
Presidential election years:		
Utah	West	86
South Dakota	Midwest	71
Iowa	Midwest	71
North Dakota	Midwest	67
Indiana	Midwest	62
Idaho	West	57
Minnesota	Midwest	57
West Virginia	Northeast	57
Delaware	Northeast	48
Illinois	Midwest	48
Connecticut	Northeast	43
New Hampshire	Northeast	43
Montana	West	38
Maine	Northeast	33
Wisconsin	Midwest	29
Oregon	West	24
Wyoming	West	24
Alaska	West	19
Nebraska	Midwest	19
Vermont	Northeast	19
Colorado	West	14
Kansas	Midwest	14
Massachusetts	Northeast	10
Missouri	Midwest	10
New Mexico	West	10
Kentucky	Midwest	5
Nevada	West	5
New York	Northeast	5
Ohio	Midwest	5
Rhode Island	Northeast	5
Washington	West	5
Nonpresidential election years:		
Wyoming	West	85
Montana	West	80
South Dakota	Midwest	80
Idaho	West	70
North Dakota	Midwest	65
Utah	West	65
Indiana	Midwest	60
Connecticut	Northeast	50
Delaware	Northeast	40
Minnesota	Midwest	40
Nevada	West	40
Massachusetts	Northeast	35
Alaska	West	30
Maine	Northeast	30
Nebraska	Midwest	30

Oregon	West	30
Rhode Island	Northeast	30
West Virginia	Northeast	25
Illinois	Midwest	20
New Mexico	West	20
Vermont	Northeast	20
Colorado	West	15
Kansas	Midwest	15
California	West	5
New Hampshire	Northeast	5
Pennsylvania	Northeast	5
Washington	West	5
Wisconsin	West	5

Note: States in boldface were ranked in the "highest ten" during both presidential and nonpresidential election years from 1920 to 2000.

Table 3.3 Ranking of States with Consistently Low Turnout

State	Region	% of Pres Years with Turnout in Lowest Ten
Presidential election years:		
Georgia	South	100
South Carolina	South	100
Texas	South	100
Virginia	South	76
Alabama	South	71
Mississippi	South	71
Arkansas	South	67
Tennessee	South	67
Florida	South	62
Louisiana	South	62
Hawaii	West	82
Arizona	West	33
Nevada	West	33
North Carolina	South	33
California	West	24
Alaska	West	27
Kentucky	Midwest	10
New Mexico	West	10
New York	Northeast	10
West Virginia	Northeast	10
Pennsylvania	Northeast	5
Nonpresidential election years:		
Georgia	South	100
Louisiana	South	95
South Carolina	South	95
Texas	South	95
Virginia	South	95

(*continued*)

Table 3.3 (*continued*)

State	Region	% of Pres Years with Turnout in Lowest Ten
Mississippi	South	90
Florida	South	70
Tennessee	South	70
Alabama	South	65
Arkansas	South	50
North Carolina	South	50
Kentucky	Midwest	30
Arizona	West	20
West Virginia	Northeast	20
Maryland	Northeast	15
New Jersey	Northeast	15
Delaware	Northeast	5
Missouri	Midwest	5
Nevada	West	5
New Hampshire	Northeast	5
New York	Northeast	5

Note: States in boldface were ranked in the "lowest ten" during both presidential and nonpresidential election years from 1920 to 2000.

In fact, Georgia was ranked among the lowest ten during all the presidential *and* nonpresidential election years from 1920 to 2000. Similarly, South Carolina and Texas were among the lowest ten during all the presidential election years during this period. Also, a handful of nonsouthern states ranked among the lowest turnout states during several presidential election years. For example, Arizona and Nevada were both in the lowest ten during presidential and nonpresidential election years throughout the period, and so were New York and West Virginia.

State Turnout Trends Compared with the National Average

This section highlights both the consistency of the high and low turnout rankings throughout the century (How often is turnout in the state above or below the national average?) and the magnitude of the classifications (How high and low are state turnout rates comparatively?). Appendix A (available online only: www.press.uchicago.edu/sites/springer/) provides individual state-by-state graphs of state voter turnout compared with the national average from 1920 to 2000. Table 3.4 provides the national average statistics for each election year so that the turnout percentages (compared

Table 3.4 Average National Voter Turnout (%)

Year	Voter Turnout (%)
Presidential election years:	
1920	45.49
1924	45.19
1928	52.77
1932	53.25
1936	57.68
1940	59.65
1944	53.98
1948	51.63
1952	62.13
1956	60.08
1960	63.85
1964	61.86
1968	60.82
1972	55.38
1976	54.67
1980	53.20
1984	53.99
1988	50.73
1992	55.10
1996	48.33
2000	50.51
Nonpresidential election years:	
1922	34.42
1926	32.07
1934	43.17
1938	45.58
1942	33.90
1946	38.50
1950	43.04
1954	43.09
1958	44.28
1962	47.38
1966	47.37
1970	46.83
1974	37.73
1978	37.25
1982	39.96
1986	36.68
1990	35.08
1994	37.76
1998	35.35

with the national average) discussed can be translated into actual turnout statistics.

High Turnout during Presidential Election Years, 1920–2000

As shown in appendix A and summarized in table 3.5, several of the states in the Midwest and West had voter turnout above the national average during *all* the presidential election years from 1920 to 2000. Nine of the fourteen midwestern states had trends above the national average during all presidential election years. Of the thirteen western states, six are in this category. States in the Northeast and South do not fare as well in the high turnout category. In fact, only two northeastern states had high turnout during all presidential election years, and the South had no such states. There are six additional states with turnout trends above the national average in *all but one* of the presidential election years.

It is also important to assess the magnitude of these trends. Aside from having routinely high turnout, most of the midwestern states had particularly high turnout compared with the national average. This is especially true in the nine states listed in table 3.5. For example, appendix A shows that during *all* presidential election years Iowa's turnout ranged from 8% to 22% above the national average, Minnesota's rates were 7% to 17% above, North Dakota's were 5% to 18% above, and South Dakota's rates were 5% to 22% above. The magnitude of these trends demonstrates that not only were voting rates consistently high in the Midwest, they have been substantially higher than the national average during most of the presidential election years throughout the century.

As shown in appendix A, twelve of the thirteen western states had voter turnout above the national average during some subset of presidential election years from 1920 to 2000. Similar to the states in the Midwest, many of the western high turnout states, noted in table 3.5, routinely demonstrated turnout well above the national average. For example, during *all* presidential election years, Colorado's voting rates were 4% to 18% above the national average, and Idaho's rates were 4% to 20% above. Further, Montana's turnout ranged from 8% to 16% above the national average during all presidential years except 1944, and Wyoming's ranged from 4% to 21% above in all years except 1920 and 1980.

As also noted in table 3.5, five northeastern states were in the high turnout category, experiencing rates above the national average during all, or all but one, of the presidential election years from 1920 to 2000. Although the turnout trends in the Northeast vary a bit more in magnitude than those

Table 3.5 High Turnout States Compared with the National Average

Region/State	Presidential Election Years		Nonpresidential Election Years	
	Above National Average All Years	Above National Average All But 1 Year	Above National Average All Years	Above National Average All But 1 Year
Midwest:				
Illinois	X	...	...	X
Indiana	...	X	...	X
Iowa	X	...	...	...
Kansas	X	...	...	X
Kentucky	...	...	...	...
Michigan	...	...	...	...
Minnesota	X	...	X	...
Missouri	X	...	...	...
Nebraska	...	X	X	...
North Dakota	X	...	X	...
Ohio	X	...	...	...
Oklahoma	...	...	...	...
South Dakota	X	...	X	...
Wisconsin	X	...	...	...
West:				
Alaska	...	...	...	...
Arizona	...	...	...	...
California	...	...	...	...
Colorado	X	...	X	...
Hawaii	...	...	X	...
Idaho	X	...	X	...
Montana	X	...	X	...
Nevada	...	...	...	...
New Mexico	...	...	...	X
Oregon	X	...	...	X
Utah	X	...	...	X
Washington	...	X	...	...
Wyoming	X	...	X	...
Northeast:				
Connecticut	...	X	X	...
Delaware	X	...	...	...
Maine	...	...	...	...
Maryland	...	...	...	...
Massachusetts	...	...	X	...
New Hampshire	...	X	...	...
New Jersey	...	X	...	...
New York	...	...	...	...
Pennsylvania	...	...	...	...
Rhode Island	X	...	X	...
Vermont	...	...	...	...
West Virginia	...	...	...	...

Note: States in boldface had "above average" turnout during both presidential and nonpresidential election years from 1920 to 2000. None of the southern states had voter turnout trends warranting inclusion in this table.

in the Midwest or West, the northeastern voting rates tend to be substantially above average throughout the century and are particularly impressive during several presidential election years. For example, Delaware and Rhode Island are the only states in the Northeast with turnout well above the national average during all presidential election years. Notably, turnout in Delaware ranged a striking 7% to 30% above the national average from 1920 to 1972, and Rhode Island's rates ranged from 5% to 15% above from 1924 to 1980.

High Turnout during Nonpresidential Election Years, 1922–98

As shown in table 3.5, many states in the Midwest, West, and Northeast also demonstrated voter turnout well above the national average during *all* the nonpresidential election years from 1922 through 1998. When the classification is expanded to include states with turnout trends above the national average in *all but one* year, the list grows in the Midwest and West. There are no states in the South that can be classified as high turnout during nonpresidential election years from 1922 to 1998. One should also note that many of the high turnout states during nonpresidential election years were also high turnout states during presidential election years. These consistently high turnout states during both types of elections are noted in boldface in table 3.5. The South has no such states.

It is clear that most of the states in the high turnout classification during nonpresidential years are in the Midwest and West: 50% of the midwestern states had voting rates above the national average during nonpresidential election years, and the magnitude of these trends is impressive. For example, during all nonpresidential election years from 1922 to 1998, Minnesota's rates were well above the national average, ranging from 6% to 23% above, and Nebraska's turnout ranged from about 4% to 24% above. North Dakota's and South Dakota's rates also remained above the national average during all nonpresidential years from 1922 to 1998. North Dakota's turnout ranged between 6% and 28% above the national average, and South Dakota's rates were 3% to 32% above.

In addition to the midwestern states, eight of the fourteen western states also displayed voter turnout above the national average during nonpresidential election years from 1922 to 1998. For example, Hawaii's voting rates ranged about 1% to 9% above the national average from 1962, during its first nonpresidential election after gaining statehood, through 1998. And perhaps most striking, during *all* nonpresidential election years, Colorado's rates ranged from 1% to 19% above the national average, Idaho's voter turnout ranged from 8% to 23% above, Montana's rates ranged from 14% to 20% above, and Wyoming's rates ranged from 8% to 24% above.

Last, three of the twelve northeastern states displayed voting rates above the national average during *all* nonpresidential election years. Specifically, Connecticut's turnout ranged from 1% to 20% above the national average, rates in Massachusetts ranged from 1% to 17% above, and Rhode Island's turnout was 3% to 20% above the national average. So it appears that many states in the Northeast, like their western and midwestern counterparts, have been in the high turnout category during nonpresidential election years throughout the century and have had turnout rates substantially above the national average. Furthermore, many of these states displayed rates considerably above the national average during *both* presidential and nonpresidential election years.

Low Turnout during Presidential Election Years, 1920–2000

There is much more variation in states with "low voter turnout" during presidential election years. As shown in table 3.6, only a few states had turnout consistently below the national average during *all* presidential years from 1920 through 2000. In the West, Hawaii consistently experienced below average turnout since gaining statehood in 1959. In the South, seven states are in the low turnout category during *all* presidential election years from 1920 to 2000. Once the definition is expanded to include states with trends below the national average in *all but one* presidential year, four states—three southern and one western—are added to the list. None of the states in the Midwest or Northeast displayed voting rates consistently below the national average during all, or all but one, of the presidential election years.

As shown in table 3.6, only two of the thirteen western states consistently fall into the low turnout category throughout the period. In the West, Arizona's voting rates fell 3% to 15% below the national average during all years except 1924, and Hawaii's rates were 5% to 13% below during the first presidential election after it gained statehood in 1960 and remained low until 2000. The infrequency of low turnout trends in the nonsouthern states underscores the tendency of midwestern, northeastern, and western states to have high, or above average, voter turnout throughout the twentieth century.

The southern states, however, fell disproportionately into the low turnout category, and in most cases their turnout was substantially below the national average. For example, during *all* presidential election years,

Table 3.6 Low Turnout States Compared with the National Average

	Presidential Election Years		Nonpresidential Election Years	
Region/State	Below National Average All Years	Below National Average All But One Year	Below National Average All Years	Below National Average All But One Year
South:				
Alabama	. . .	X	. . .	. . .
Arkansas	X	. . .	. . .	. . .
Florida	X	. . .	. . .	. . .
Georgia	X	. . .	X	. . .
Louisiana	. . .	. . .	. . .	X
Mississippi	. . .	X	X	. . .
North Carolina	X	. . .	. . .	X
South Carolina	X	. . .	. . .	X
Tennessee	X	. . .	. . .	X
Texas	X	. . .	X	. . .
Virginia	. . .	X	. . .	X
West:				
Alaska	. . .	. . .	. . .	. . .
Arizona	. . .	X	. . .	. . .
California	. . .	. . .	. . .	. . .
Colorado	. . .	. . .	. . .	. . .
Hawaii	X	. . .	. . .	. . .
Idaho	. . .	. . .	. . .	. . .
Montana	. . .	. . .	. . .	. . .
Nevada	. . .	. . .	. . .	. . .
New Mexico	. . .	. . .	. . .	. . .
Oregon	. . .	. . .	. . .	. . .
Utah	. . .	. . .	. . .	. . .
Washington	. . .	. . .	. . .	. . .
Wyoming	. . .	. . .	. . .	. . .

Note: States in boldface had "below average" turnout during both presidential and nonpresidential election years from 1920 to 2000. None of the midwestern or northeastern states had voter turnout trends warranting inclusion in this table.

Georgia's turnout ranged from 7% to 42% below the national average, South Carolina's turnout fell 5% to 50% below, and Texas's rates were 4% to 34%. Several other southern states had turnout dramatically below the national average for a subset of years. For example, Arkansas's voting rates fell 10% to 41% below the national average from 1920 to 1964 and 1% to 8% below from 1968 to 2000, and Virginia's turnout fell 2% to 38% below from 1920 to 1992. These trends illustrate that not only was voter turnout in the South remarkably low, especially compared with the rates in most of the midwestern and western states, but the turnout trends are substantially below average throughout the entire presidential series.

Low Turnout during Nonpresidential Election Years, 1922–98

Voter turnout varies more during nonpresidential election years. As shown in table 3.6, only three states—all southern—had voter turnout below the national average during *all* the nonpresidential election years during the twentieth century. During these years, Georgia's turnout ranged from 5% to 42% below the national average, rates in Mississippi were 1% to 43% below, and Texas's rates ranged from 4% to 36% below. When states with trends below the national average in *all but one year* are included, five more states are added. As shown in appendix A, South Carolina's turnout rates ranged from 4% to 41% below the national average and exceeded the national average only once, in 1998. Similarly, Virginia's rates were 4% to 37% below the national average in all years but 1994, and Tennessee's rates ranged from about 1% to 31% below during all nonpresidential election years except 1994. It is worth noting that none of these states surpassed the national average during these election years by 5% or more. Like the presidential election year trends, the nonpresidential patterns illustrate that turnout rates not only are below average in most of the southern states, they are dramatically below average.

Taken together, the state trends described here and presented in appendix A reveal that most of the states have distinct patterns of change relative to the nation. Some start with higher turnout and then merge with the national level. For example, West Virginia begins with turnout higher than the nation and ends the century with below-average turnout, whereas some states like Utah and South Dakota are consistently higher than the nation. It also illustrates that the South's negative deviation from the national average throughout the twentieth century was far greater than the positive deviations in the Midwest and West. Many expect voter turnout in the South to be low, but appendix A demonstrates how severe the difference was. The following chapters aim to determine the extent to which changes in electoral rules versus population characteristics versus electoral competitiveness can account for the divergent patterns of state turnout relative to national turnout.

Conclusion

This chapter has shown the importance of studying variation in voter turnout across the American states, rather than only national trends, and of using a historical perspective to understand twentieth-century voting patterns. Most of the previous scholarship on voter turnout in the United States has focused on the national level, offering little information on how the states are distinctive within the national trends. This is a vital omission. As this chapter has demonstrated, a great deal of variation exists within regional and state-level turnout patterns; this variation has been masked by studies conducted at the aggregate level. When we disaggregate these trends it becomes clear that two radically opposed trends persisted throughout the century: the consistently high turnout rates in the nonsouthern states—especially in the Midwest—and the remarkably low turnout rates in the southern states during both presidential and nonpresidential election years. The components fueling this variation demand further analysis. The variation in turnout rates between the southern and nonsouthern regions, and the seeming consistency of high and low turnout tendencies within many individual states could be associated with several aspects of state and electoral politics. High or low turnout could be attributed to electoral institutions, political competition, mobilization, or—most realistically—some combination of these elements. This study focuses on the effects of political institutions and evaluates how they might have influenced participation in the states over time and contributed to the state-level variation this chapter illuminates.

Of course, we can make a preliminary assessment of the relationship between state turnout trends and electoral institutions. As this chapter has shown, most states with voter turnout consistently, and usually substantially, above the national average are in the midwestern and western United States. This tendency warrants further investigation. If the high turnout states in the Midwest and West tend to have disproportionately expansive voting laws, then perhaps there is a link between electoral institutions and participation rates.[8] Further, this chapter has demonstrated that the only states with consistently low turnout during all presidential and nonpresidential elections are in the South. This does not seem accidental. The southern tendency to discriminate against and disenfranchise blacks, and in many cases poor whites, was broad and relentless. Jim Crow laws in the South, particularly those relating to voting rights, surely affected political participation in the region. Accordingly, we might expect voter turnout to be disproportionately lower in the southern states because of racist disenfranchising rules that made voting exorbitantly costly for some citizens; and one might contend that turnout rates are higher in the western and midwestern states because voting laws there have been historically expansive, so that the costs of voting are comparatively low and a commitment to voting is high. Although these connections are speculative at this point, even a sweeping institutional characterization of voting laws and norms in these regions seems to connect with the observed voting patterns presented throughout this chapter. At a minimum, they warrant further investigation.

Chapter 4 examines the origin and historical evolution of a variety of restrictive and expansive electoral institutions that have structured voting and elections within individual states. This in-depth discussion character- izes state electoral institutions independent of participation trends, chroni- cles how dramatically state registration and voting processes have changed throughout the century, and frames the empirical analyses of the effects of state electoral institutions on state turnout presented in later chapters.

FOUR

A History of Twentieth-Century State Electoral Institutions

The balance of state versus federal power has ebbed and flowed over the course of American political development. Either body's expansion into new areas of policy making has been highly contested and uneven. Many policy domains that were once exclusively in the hands of the states no longer are. But one domain in which state control has remained particularly strong is electoral administration. Many observers find the degree of electoral decentralization in the United States surprising, since elections and their principles are vastly important to both the explicit and the implicit meaning of citizenship and are the underpinnings of representation within the American democratic system. Yet the states, presumed to have a greater sense of what their local citizenry needs from its republican operations, have dominated this critical area. Over time, however, tension has existed between state preferences and national objectives related to equality and democratic representation in voting. The struggle between the principles of American federalism and pressure for electoral reform has greatly influenced the character of state electoral institutions and institutional change throughout the twentieth century and before.

Electoral reform has changed the electoral landscape dramatically over the twentieth century. Accordingly, this chapter surveys the expansive and restrictive rules—pertaining to state voting qualifications, voter registration processes, and voting procedures—that regulated voting in the United States throughout the century. I describe the origin and evolution of many state-initiated laws and also of reforms mandated by federal legislation. This historical account underscores the dynamic processes that shaped voting and elections during an earlier era—one often unfamiliar to readers drawing from their experiences with present-day election laws—and also explores contemporary electoral reforms.[1]

Voting Qualifications

Elections are central to representative democracy. Given their importance in principle and in practice, and despite rhetoric championing the "right to vote," many people are surprised to learn that the US Constitution does not guarantee anyone the right to vote or establish any of the voting or registration processes that structure this fundamental act. In practice, the right to vote is not a vested, natural right (see Keyssar 2000 for more on this). Voting is treated more as "a privilege for which individuals must demonstrate their worthiness" (Burnham 1987, 109). Under the federal system, the states guard access to this privilege. They grant (or deny) participation to citizens who possess (or lack) certain constitutional qualifications (which are also determined by the states). Of course the Constitution has been amended over time to prevent the states from denying certain classes of citizens the right to vote. Ultimately, however, the power to determine who is a qualified elector—to define the electorate—has been delegated to each of the fifty states.

This decentralized governance over the electoral system has meant that access to the vote is highly varied. In some states individuals have been excluded for reasons that appear arbitrary, whereas in other states the franchise has long been inclusive. This has important repercussions for the American democratic system. If a large number of citizens cannot exercise the right to vote, then the democratic character, openness, and responsiveness of the government are challenged. Further, the creation of these laws and subsequent changes to them are inherently political acts. It is no mistake that those who benefit from a limited or an expansive franchise are typically the same people who construct the laws. History teaches us that knowing who made such determinations, and the basis on which they were made, is of great importance.

In examining twentieth-century voting rules, we see that the democratic notion of universal suffrage has often been incongruent with electoral practices in many of the states. This is particularly true for laws on voting qualifications, which have tended to be the most-restrictive electoral institutions enacted by the states. The qualifications I evaluate include property requirements, literacy tests, poll taxes, and long residency requirements, which were typically found in state constitutions and, depending on state law, could typically be changed or removed only by constitutional amendment.[2] These restrictive institutions were designed to limit participation and imposed a distinct burden on would-be voters in the states where they operated.

Although restrictive voting qualifications are typically thought to have existed only in the Jim Crow South, in reality they were much more widespread. Table 4.1 identifies the states that implemented restrictive voting qualifications throughout the first several decades of the century. The table identifies sixteen nonsouthern states in addition to all eleven southern states. Incidentally, many of these nonsouthern states are in the West and Northeast and tend to have high immigration rates. Not only does this imply that these states tried to control their comparatively diverse electorates, archival research suggests that their motivation for adopting these

Table 4.1 State Voting Qualifications, by First Election Year after Elimination

State*	Property Requirement	Literacy Test	Poll Tax
Alabama	1966	1966	1968
Alaska	. . .	1970	. . .
Arizona	. . .	1972	. . .
Arkansas	. . .	. . .	1964
California	. . .	1972	. . .
Connecticut	. . .	1972	. . .
Delaware	. . .	1970	. . .
Florida	. . .	. . .	1942
Georgia	1966	1966	1946
Hawaii	. . .	1970	. . .
Louisiana	1966	1966	1936
Maine	. . .	1972	1956
Massachusetts	. . .	1972	1964
Mississippi	. . .	1966	1964
Nevada	. . .	. . .	1966
New Hampshire	. . .	1970	. . .
New York**	. . .	1970	. . .
North Carolina	. . .	1972	1922
Oregon**	. . .	1970	. . .
Pennsylvania	. . .	. . .	1938
Rhode Island	1950	. . .	1952
South Carolina	1966	1966	1952
Tennessee	. . .	. . .	1954
Texas	. . .	. . .	1968
Virginia	. . .	1966	1966
Washington	. . .	1970	. . .
Wyoming	. . .	1970	. . .

Source: This is an original data set I constructed from the official state codebooks and state session laws. Where there was ambiguity, I contacted state election officials.

Note: "Residency requirements" is also classified as a voting qualification in this study; however, it is measured as a continuous variable and is not suitable for inclusion in this table. Discussion of this variable is found in the text, and descriptive statistics are available in appendixes C and D.

*States that did not have any of these voting qualification provisions from 1920 to 2000 were omitted from the table. Southern states are noted in boldface.

**Unless otherwise noted, the states entered the study in 1920 with the provision. There were two exceptions: New York adopted a literacy test in 1922, and Oregon did so in 1924.

restrictive laws was similar to the racially charged justifications prevalent in the South. Outside the South, however, these restrictive laws were largely directed at minority groups other that blacks. For example, literacy tests in Arizona were aimed at disenfranchising Native Americans, and in California they were directed at Mexican and Japanese residents (Bolinger and Gaylord 1977). For example, Oregon's 1920 electoral code reads, "No negro, Chinaman, or mulatto shall have the right of suffrage" (Oregon Laws 1920, article 2, section 2). Looking at the states' historical patterns redefines the usual characterization of restrictive voting qualifications as strictly southern and reveals restrictive rules outside the South. The following sections will discuss how each of these restrictive voting qualifications has been used across the nation.[3]

Property Requirements

Owning property was once a fundamental qualification for taking part in American elections, although that is often forgotten today. Unlike some of the other voting qualifications I examine, owning property was a common prerequisite to voting in the nineteenth century (see Keyssar 2000), but I include it in this study because of its prominence during the first half of the twentieth century and the way it restricted the right to vote for individuals not owning property. Property requirements have long been regarded as tactics used by the states to disenfranchise minorities and the poor—who were often the same people, especially in the South. Property requirements aimed to ensure that early American voters would be mainly white, landowning males. Over time, however, property requirements became rarer. By the early 1920s these laws, once widespread in the southern and northeastern states, had been largely eradicated. As shown in table 4.1, during the twentieth century only four southern states—Alabama, Georgia, Louisiana, and South Carolina—and one nonsouthern state—Rhode Island—had property requirements for voting in general elections.

The specific parameters of the property requirements varied from state to state, but generally voters had to own a nontrivial amount of land in the state and live on it or hold real estate or personal taxable worth in the state, in order to vote. For example, to qualify to register and vote in Alabama in 1923, a man (or his wife) needed to "own forty acres of land and reside on it, or own real estate of a taxable value of $300 or more, or own personal property of the taxable value of $300 or more" (Code of Alabama 1923, section 312). Similarly, a 1920 Rhode Island law stipulated that "who is really and truly possessed in his own right of real estate of a value of $134 over and above all encumbrances, or which shall rent for $7 over and above any rent reserved or the interest of any encumbrances thereon, may qualify to vote" (Public Laws of the State of Rhode Island 1920). By mid-century, however, as the civil rights movement gained momentum, property requirements were among the first to be abolished. Their removal was made permanent under the 1965 Voting Rights Act, which mandated that no state could set property requirements for voting in national elections.[4]

Literacy Tests

Literacy tests were not used as widely as poll taxes to restrict the vote, but they were popular nonetheless. As table 4.1 shows, they were implemented in twenty southern, western, and northeastern states during the years following Reconstruction, and they persisted into the early 1970s. Such tests typically were designed to be very difficult and constituted an effective disenfranchising mechanism. The state election code usually specified how the test was supposed to be conducted, though specific test-giving practices varied by state, ranging from writing and reciting parts of the US Constitution to answering a series of difficult trivia-like questions.[5] Most commonly, however, states with literacy tests required that, except in cases of disability, applicants be able to sign their names without assistance and read a paragraph from any printed text in a manner that showed he was not reciting the passage from memory. Typically the registrar selected the text. Most states used passages from the US Constitution, the state constitution, or a section from the state statutes.

The test was supposed to be administered as fairly and systematically as possible, and its format was typically outlined in great detail in the state election code. For example, the 1920 McKinney's Consolidated Laws of New York Annotated stipulated,

> There shall be in the place of registration one hundred extracts from the constitution of this state, of approximately fifty words each, which extracts shall be selected by the Secretary of State. Such extracts shall be printed in English on uniform paste-board slips in double small pica type, and the slips shall be kept by the inspectors in a box so constructed as to conceal the slips from view. The new voter, if required to prove his ability to read and write English, shall draw out at random one of such slips and read aloud intelligibly all of the matter printed thereon and shall then write legibly in English ten words of the matter on such slip, to be selected by an inspector. Each slip shall be returned to the box immediately after each test and the contents of the

box shall be shaken up by an inspector before another drawing. (McKinney's Consolidated Laws of New York Annotated 1920, Book 17)

Although many states attempted, at least on the surface, to administer literacy tests impartially, there were fairly clear regional divides in the way they were constructed and employed. Generally, states in the South forced individuals to prove much more than plain literacy, and assessing their performance was much more subjective. Of the twenty states that imposed literacy tests during the twentieth century, Alabama, Georgia, Louisiana, and Mississippi all required individuals to demonstrate far more than reading and writing ability. For example, to qualify to vote in Alabama before 1946, an applicant had to "read and write any article of the Constitution of the United States in the English language" (Acts of the General Assembly of Alabama 1900); however, after the adoption of the Boswell Amendment in 1946, they had to prove much more. In particular, the state constitution was amended to require applicants to understand and explain any article of the US Constitution, to be of good character, and to prove they understood the duties and obligations of good citizenship under a republican form of government (General Laws and Joint Resolutions of the Legislature of Alabama 1945, 336). The third requirement was usually assessed by forcing applicants to answer questions on Alabama state law or federal law and by evaluating their interpretation of selected constitutional sections.[6]

Similarly, to pass a literacy test in Georgia, applicants had to either read or write a selected constitutional section and pass an oral test showing their good moral character and understanding of the duties and obligations of citizenship under a republican form of government (1949 Temporary Supplement of the Code of Georgia Annotated, 34–617). The oral exam in Georgia required applicants to correctly answer ten of thirty questions. The exam often consisted of questions such as Who is the president? What is the president's term of office? May the president be legally elected for a second term? If the president dies in office, who will succeed him? How many groups compose the Congress? How many senators are there from Georgia? What is a senator's term? Who are the Georgia senators? Who is the governor? Who is the lieutenant governor? Who is the chief justice of the Georgia supreme court? In what city are the laws of the United States made? Who is the commander in chief? In what congressional district do you live? (1949 Temporary Supplement of the Code of Georgia Annotated). If applicants could not answer at least ten of the questions correctly, their applications for voter registration were immediately rejected. Similarly, literacy tests in Louisiana and Mississippi required applicants to satisfactorily fill out a detailed form, write sections of the Preamble to the US Constitution from dictation, read and interpret any section of the US Constitution or the state's constitution, and answer questions constituting a citizenship test.

Although the logistics of these tests varied from state to state, their existence dramatically limited voting where they were imposed, especially for those who were poor or were racially targeted. States that required applicants to satisfactorily read a section of the Constitution disenfranchised thousands of otherwise qualified citizens. Inadequacies in public education generated by a long history of racism and segregation, particularly in the South, made passing any test of literacy or comprehension an unfair prerequisite for voting. In effect, literacy tests would, as one delegate to the 1965 US Commission on Civil Rights noted, "take advantage of the fact that in Mississippi at least 10% of the white and 60% of the colored population can neither read nor write" (US Commission on Civil Rights 1965, 4). Furthermore, literacy tests gave county registrars extremely broad discretion in determining applicants' qualifications. Registrars alone determined whether applicants were of good moral character, had demonstrated a reasonable understanding of the duties and obligations of citizenship under a constitutional form of government, and had properly interpreted a section of the Constitution.

The power given to registrars was questionable, since most state statutes did not prescribe any standards to control or guide them in making these determinations, and registrars (who are political officials) generally appeared far from impartial. As noted in an expansive report on California election laws, "fear and hatred played a significant role in the passage of the literacy requirement" (Bolinger and Gaylord 1977, 59). For example, at the discretion of registrars the literacy test "was not enforced among the Italians of San Francisco in the first decades of this century nor against Yiddish-speaking Los Angeles Jews in the years after 1920, nor even against the newly naturalized Issei Japanese after 1952. The sole enforcement, and that largely sporadic, seems to have been against a group more native than the nativists themselves: the Spanish-speaking Mexican-Americans" (Bolinger and Gaylord 1977, 59–60). In practice, even outside the South, the understanding and interpretation clauses embedded in many literacy tests seemed designed to furnish a loophole by which the registrar could favor some applicants over others.

Though many champions of literacy tests throughout the 1950s and 1960s and into the early 1970s attested that they helped ensure a more engaged and civic-minded electorate, the racist and classist motivations and ramifications of these tests could not be ignored. Their existence directly impeded American democracy. This sentiment was expressed in an impassioned 1967 speech by Commissioner Charles Kirkpatrick of the President's Commission on Registration and Voting Participation, dealing with the persistence of literacy tests in New York. Throughout his speech, Kirkpatrick chastised state representatives for perpetuating the unjust institution and attested that

> a democratic system rests ultimately on the belief that each man is the best judge of his own interests and that he should have, through the ballot box, a voice in choosing those who govern him. On what grounds should we deny to the person who has not learned to read the rights we accord to others? That he cannot read the ballot? Then shall we also disenfranchise the blind? That he cannot read newspapers? Then shall we disenfranchise the deaf because they cannot hear radio or television? That he will not be an "informed" voter? Then shall we require that each voter pass a test in current events? The arguments for a literacy requirement lack cogency; their superficial merits vanish under scrutiny. (Kirkpatrick 1967, i)

Kirkpatrick added that

> literate men are not equally well-informed, nor equally rational, nor equally moral, nor equally rich, nor equally devoted to their country. Neither are the illiterate. Who would argue that the political judgment of a literate man of doubtful morality or patriotism is better than that of an honest but illiterate patriot? Literacy tests are a remnant of class discrimination. They discriminate against the poor, the aged, and rural inhabitants. It is not the wealthy who can neither read nor write. It is the poor and the dispossessed. Literacy tests have no more place in a modern democracy than property tests, which have long since been abandoned. (1967, ii)

In light of the persuasive and persistent pleas of reformers and civil rights activists, by the late 1960s it was clear that whatever merit literacy tests might once have had was no longer valid or tolerable. It was concluded that employing literacy tests as a prerequisite to registering and voting placed an onerous burden on those in states where they were implemented, particularly in the South, and that such tests denied the right to vote to many otherwise qualified individuals. To ensure that voting rights were more equally maintained, literacy tests were voided in jurisdictions covered by section 4 of the Voting Rights Act in 1965, and in all states for five years under the act's reauthorization in 1970.[7] The US Supreme Court eventually upheld the 1970 ban in *Oregon v. Mitchell* (1970), which was made permanent for all states in 1975.

Poll Taxes

Poll taxes restricted voting in many states for more than half of the twentieth century and before. In the sixteen states where poll taxes were assessed, they imposed an explicit and undeniable burden on individuals. Historically, paying a poll tax as a prerequisite for voting is often perceived as strictly an element of the Jim Crow South, but poll or head taxes were also levied in many nonsouthern states. Table 4.1 lists the states that imposed poll taxes throughout the twentieth century. Although these laws were predominately found in the South, a handful of states in the West and Northeast also made people pay in order to vote.

Although the specific features of these laws varied, poll taxes presented a real hurdle for potential voters. Generally, early state constitutions required poll taxes as a voting qualification in the same way they specified age, citizenship, and residency. For example, in 1908 the Nevada state constitution stated: "The legislature shall provide by law for the payment of an annual poll tax, of not less than two nor exceeding four dollars, from each male person resident in the state between the ages of 21–60 years (uncivilized American Indians excepted), to be expended for the maintenance and betterment of the public roads" (Nevada Compiled Laws 1929). Similarly, a 1936 Georgia law stipulated that "no person shall be qualified to vote unless he shall have paid all poll taxes due at least six months before the same, except when said election is held within six months from the expiration of the time fixed by law for the payment of said taxes" (Georgia State Constitution 1936). The constitutional requirement in Georgia also noted that "all taxes be paid as a prerequisite right to register and vote, and municipal taxes are not excluded from the category of 'all' taxes" (Georgia State Constitution 1936).

In many ways, poll taxes were treated like any other state or local tax. People paid their poll taxes to the county tax collector. Payment records were compiled and submitted to election officials, who used the payment list as a makeshift registration roster on Election Day. The state electoral codes were usually very specific about how this would be undertaken. For example, the 1926 Texas State Constitution specified:

Each commissioner's court before the first day of October every year shall furnish the tax collector a blank book for each voting precinct. Then, the county tax collector shall deliver to the board that is charged with the duty of furnishing election supplies separate certified lists of the citizens in each precinct who have paid their poll taxes. Said board shall furnish each presiding judge of a precinct the certified list and supplemental list of the voters in his precinct at the time when he furnishes other election supplies. (Vernon's Annotated Texas Statutes 1926, chapter 5, article 2970)

Similarly, the 1908 state constitution in Georgia required that

the tax collector of each county should, before the 20th day of April of each year, prepare and file with the county registrars a complete list of all persons living in the county on April 10 of that year, who appear to be disqualified from voting by reason of nonpayment of poll taxes, or by reason of idiocy, insanity, or conviction of crime whose penalty is disenfranchisement, unless such convict has been pardoned and the right of suffrage restored to him; and said list shall also show the race of such person—that is to say, whether white or colored. (Georgia State Constitution 1908)

At first poll taxes seemed relatively benign. State officials claimed their use was largely motivated, or at least justified, by the need to grow local economies and to systematically monitor the size of the expanding electorate. But as state voter registration procedures became more formalized, poll tax rosters and proxy registration lists became less necessary, and the motivation for such laws became more questionable. The proclaimed benefits of the taxes rapidly lost credibility once the character of the electorate and the limiting effect such laws had on participation were scrutinized.

By the 1950s, the preponderance of restrictive voting laws in the South could not be ignored, and the racial motivations for assessing poll taxes were exposed. In 1965 various civil rights commissions were established to investigate unfair voting practices in the South, especially the use and consequences of the poll tax. Since the Fifteenth Amendment prohibited an express denial of the franchise to African Americans, the commission began to scrutinize other seemingly neutral voting qualifications that could accomplish the same result. The first device closely examined by the 1965 US Commission on Civil Rights was the two dollar poll tax in the state of Mississippi. The commission concluded that "although the poll tax receipts were designated for educational purposes, it [was] clear that the primary purpose of the tax was to restrict the franchise" (US Commission on

Civil Rights 1965, 10). According to one individual's testimony before the commission, the poll tax was adopted because "the leaders of the black counties were eventually able to persuade the convention that education and property qualifications, with the addition of a poll tax, would be the best means of eliminating the negro vote" (68). The 1965 commission also noted that

> the poverty of Mississippi Negroes affects their ability to comply with Mississippi voting laws. A Negro desiring to qualify to vote for the first time must pay $4.00 in poll taxes (a $2.00 poll tax must be paid for the two years preceding the election). At the wage rates prevailing in the Delta, many Negroes would need a day or more of labor to earn this amount. Payment of the tax for each adult would constitute a significant expenditure for a family whose yearly income is less than $1,000. (US Commission on Civil Rights 1965, 33)

On hearing this, a member of the 1965 commission observed, "The very idea of a poll tax qualification is tantamount to the State of Mississippi saying to the Negro: 'We will give you two dollars not to vote'" (69). After the commission's investigation concluded, it was clear that the poll tax was unnecessary in light of more systematic registration procedures, placed a great burden on those it was imposed on, and, most notably, was being used by state officials to selectively disenfranchise particular groups.

As the nation began paying more attention to the various criteria states used to define the electorate, some southern states were compelled to defend themselves against accusations of racism. For example, a long introduction to Vernon's Annotated 1952 Texas Statutes, concerning the ratification of an amendment to article 6, section 2 of the state constitution in 1902, which made the payment of a poll tax a prerequisite of voting, states:

> Contrary to general opinion now, this amendment was not the result of racial prejudice, but was sponsored by the reform element in the Democratic Party and the Prohibitionists as an election law reform. It was the repeated charge of these groups that the "big interests" and the "liquor interests" controlled thousands of negro and Latin American voters through paid "fluence" men. The poll tax amendment was designed to decrease this controlled vote. It also provided an automatic system of mandatory registration of voters without the use of the hated phrase calculated to stir bitter memories of the Reconstruction. (Vernon's Annotated Texas Statutes 1952, XXII)

Similarly, in 1958 Alabama defended itself against accusations of racism pertaining to the payment of poll taxes by noting in the state election code that "the obligation to pay a poll tax is not an obligation that may be enforced by legal process or otherwise, but it is to be performed voluntarily as a test of good citizenship, leaving the question of qualification under this section to each individual" (Code of Alabama Recompiled 1958).

Despite state attempts to justify and preserve the legality of poll taxes, the federal government was compelled to take action against this infringement of voting rights. It was clear that in the absence of a federal mandate, the states would continue to enforce these seemingly undemocratic practices. Eventually, in January 1964, the Twenty-Fourth Amendment to the US Constitution prohibited the poll tax as a requirement for voting in national elections.[8] At the time of the amendment's ratification, Alabama, Arkansas, Massachusetts, Mississippi, Nevada, Texas, and Virginia still required paying the poll tax as a qualification for voting.[9]

Residency Requirements

Requiring long residency also served as a restrictive condition for voting in nearly all the American states throughout most the twentieth century; such requirements existed at the state, county, and district level. For example, in the southern states the average requirement was living in one's state for just over ten months in order to vote, although the time ranged from zero to 730 days throughout the century. One had to live in one's county about four months, and in one's district nearly two months, though these requirements ranged from zero to 365 days throughout the period. Outside the South, the average state residency requirement was nearly seven months, though it ranged from zero to 730 days from 1920 to 2000. The average county requirement was about a month and a half, and the district requirement was just under one month, though these requirements ranged from zero to 180 days.

In the early years, reformers touted long residency requirements as a way to create a more informed and stable electorate and let voters become acquainted with political issues and candidates. They also made the administration of elections easier, since precinct officers would know that the people who showed up at the polls were who they claimed to be and were entitled to vote. They also helped election officials better prepare for elections by having enough ballots printed, prepare registers of voters for precinct officials, and the like (Keyssar 2000). Yet long residency requirements also had social and political repercussions, and in practice they were not as benign as early reformers suggested they were meant to be. They proved costly to voters and, in effect, disenfranchised a large part of the increasingly mobile population throughout the century.

Indeed, long residency requirements had direct political effects. For example, in California, Bolinger and Gaylord noted, "As in the case of the English literacy requirement, the Democratic Party activists saw challenges over the issue of residency as a device used by Republicans to unfairly disenfranchise large numbers of their supporters, particularly since Democrats were likely to be more mobile than Republicans" (1977, 76). Additionally, in the southern states it appeared that the lawmakers' motives may have not been as pure as their rhetoric suggested. For example, a report by the US Commission on Civil Rights observed that "the requirement of long residency [in Mississippi], two years in the state and one year in the election district, was aimed at the supposed 'disposition of young Negroes to change their homes and precincts every year'" (1965, 8). So it seems that despite the professed, and perhaps superficial, good intentions of early reformers, long residency requirements may have done more harm than good. By formally limiting voting to those who had fulfilled their quota of residential stability, long residency requirements made voting costly and in many ways inaccessible to much of the mobile public.

As with all the restrictive voting qualifications discussed above, the federal government eventually forced the states to ease their most egregious requirements. In 1970 the federal Voting Rights Act amendments required all states to implement a "fair and reasonable" residency requirement for presidential elections. In the states this was largely interpreted to mean zero to sixty days, but many states instituted a zero to thirty-day requirement. Since adherence to this act was inconsistent nationally, in *Dunn v. Blumstein* (1972) the Supreme Court declared that long residency requirements for voting in state and local elections were unconstitutional and firmly limited state requirements to no more than thirty days. However, some states resisted this ruling and have continued to impose longer residency requirements at the county or district levels.

Voter Registration Laws

In many ways the voting qualifications discussed above can also be construed as qualifications to register, since registration has been a prerequisite for voting in most states throughout the century.[10] Voter registration in the United States establishes that a person is a citizen, a resident, and a qualified voter at the address from which she registers. Throughout the twentieth century, no person whose name was not on the registration rolls in her state was permitted to vote in any election. Voter registration can thus be regarded as the first official step toward the exercise of the franchise. Although participation in this first step is broad, it is far from universal. The registration laws implemented throughout the United States are considered among the world's most demanding. In Europe, by contrast, there is typically no registration burden on individual voters; voter registration is handled automatically by the government. Prospective voters in the United States, however, face a double hurdle for participation, and the burdens of registration fall primarily on the voters themselves. Electoral reformers have regularly targeted costly voter registration procedures for expansive reforms. Their rationale is that once state registration requirements are made more inclusive, more individuals will register and ultimately vote on Election Day (see Highton 2004). The following sections describe the striking variation in states' approaches to pursuing registration reform and establishing systematic voter registration systems.

Periodic and Permanent Voter Registration Systems

Most formal voter registration laws in the United States were passed between the end of Reconstruction and the onset of World War I. Before this, most states adopted informal registration procedures that were radically different from modern ones. Early in the century American communities were smaller and populations were more stable, so voter registration was not a major concern. Most people knew their neighbors, and residents were easily identified, even if election officials did not know them personally. Yet as populations grew, often through immigration, and especially in urban areas, concerns about voting fraud also grew. To quell these concerns, it became necessary to determine voters' eligibility in advance of elections to keep unqualified persons from voting; and so the first modern voter registration systems emerged.

Most states sought to make matters more systematic by adopting periodic voter registration. Periodic registration was an amalgam of some of the earlier informal systems. It assumed that it was desirable to prepare a completely new list of eligible voters before each major election or at frequent intervals stipulated by state law. This meant individuals had to reregister every one, two, or four years depending on their states' provisions. Periodic systems, although more systematic, were very cumbersome for individuals. Would-be voters had to assume the start-up costs of registering to vote not only once but repeatedly. Further, voters often were unaware that they needed to reregister and were turned away on Election Day because their registration was no longer valid.

In practice, periodic registration systems made it harder for people to participate, and they were widely criticized. In their study on voter registration laws, Smolka and Rossotti noted that the early periodic system "was attacked by civic groups such as the National Municipal League and election scholars, such as Joseph P. Harris, because it was both inconvenient for the voters and very expensive" (1975, 2). The system proved cumbersome to voters, failed to function efficiently, and was not an effective solution to election fraud, especially in big cities, as the influence of political machines grew. Reformers loudly urged that the periodic voter registration systems be replaced with permanent registration.

Under a permanent voter registration system, registrants would remain on the rolls until they died, moved away, changed their names, or were otherwise disqualified from voting. Permanent systems also provided for registration throughout the year at a central location; under periodic systems, precinct registration was available only for a few days before a general election. These new permanent systems were comparatively efficient and economical. In January 1927 the National Municipal League, a civic organization that had been in the forefront of the municipal reform movement, published "A Model Registration System" as a supplement to its monthly magazine, the *National Municipal Review*. This article, which touted the benefits of permanent registration, was very influential in promoting its widespread adoption by the states over the following years. Advocates argued that permanent voter registration systems were far superior to periodic registration, especially in easing the burdens associated with the earlier systems. An important advantage was their cost-reducing properties—their convenience to voters.

Although Boston in 1896, Milwaukee and Omaha in 1912, and Oregon in 1915 are credited with pioneering permanent registration, the real diffusion of the reform did not begin until the late 1920s, when states began adopting the system in rapid succession. Generally, states in the Midwest and West adopted permanent registration early in the century, while states in the South tended to be laggards. Over time, however, permanent registration completely replaced periodic and informal systems, and today that is how virtually every American voter registers to vote for state and national elections. The only exception is North Dakota, where registration has not been required since 1951, and some cities that require periodic registration for infrequent municipal elections.

After the widespread adoption of permanent registration systems, the public became less preoccupied with vote fraud and more concerned with the effect registration procedures had on voter turnout and voter bias. To onlookers and scholars, it did not seem coincidental that national turnout dropped steadily during the period when registration systems became more elaborate. Indeed, throughout the second half of the twentieth century, registration laws were regarded as a major obstacle to voting. Further, numerous studies have revealed that less restrictive registration procedures may increase voter turnout (e.g., Brians and Grofman 2001; Highton 1997, 2004; Knack 1995, 2001; Mitchell and Wlezien 1995; Rhine 1995; Wolfinger and Rosenstone 1980). In response, Congress and the state governments have adopted several electoral reforms to ease the burdens of voter registration. At the federal level, Congress enacted the National Voter Registration Act in 1993. This legislation was especially popular for its "motor voter" provision, which mandated that states allow individuals to register, or reregister, at state Department of Motor Vehicles offices and various other public agencies. Then, in 2002 Congress passed the Help America Vote Act, which—among other features—attempted to remedy registration-related problems on Election Day by allowing provisional voting for voters whose names mistakenly did not appear on the rolls. Many states also acted independently throughout the century to liberalize their registration requirements.

Even though differences in registration procedures no longer center on the general type of system the state employs (periodic versus permanent), a vast amount of variation in permanent registration systems has existed throughout the century. In particular, state nonvoting purge rules, the ease and availability of registration, and closing dates for registration have been targets of reform. The following sections examine how these processes have evolved in the states and discuss a variety of national and state-initiated reforms aimed at increasing American participation by expanding voter registration.

Nonvoting Purges

Although the widespread enactment of permanent voter registration decreased the burdens associated with the periodic system, permanent voter registration was far from cost-free, and its permanency varied. In practice, the "permanency" of registration systems is directly related to state election law on nonvoting purges. In states that implemented nonvoting purges, the registration rolls were routinely reviewed, and individuals who had not voted for a stipulated number of years were purged from the lists. This entailed reverting, at least implicitly, to a pseudoperiodic system. Some states purged every two years, whereas other states never purged for not voting, although they often verified their lists. Nonvoting purges were common in the states throughout the century. From 1920 to 2000, purge periods ranged from two to ten years of not voting before a registrant was purged from the state rolls. In the nonsouthern states the average time was three years of not voting before one was purged, and in the southern states it was four years.

Even though nonvoting purges were desirable insofar as they kept registration lists fairly current, the states that removed people from the registration lists for failing to vote within a short time frame had not really moved far from the periodic system. Although nonvoting purges eliminated registrants who had died, had moved, or were no longer qualified to vote for one reason or another, they also invariably removed many people who were still qualified to vote but failed to do so for various reasons. Further, individuals who were purged often were not immediately notified and could have turned out to vote on Election Day only to find that they no longer qualified. This suggests that in many ways nonvoting purge rules were costly to individuals in the same way as periodic registration systems but on a more limited scale, since only nonvoters, not the entire registered electorate, were purged. In response to these concerns, state purge periods have become longer on average, and over time many states eliminated the nonvoting purge out of concerns about fairness and the costliness of re-registration. Nonvoting purges finally were formally outlawed for covered states in 1993 under the National Voter Registration Act.

Mail-in Voter Registration

As permanent voter registration became more widespread, the accessibility of registration became more relevant. Additionally, as the United States became increasingly engaged in conflict overseas, concerns about the voting rights and registration opportunities of displaced servicemen became more salient. So it is not surprising that many of the first registration reforms centered on increasing accessibility and convenience. In the 1930s and 1940s, mail-in voter registration systems were touted for being more convenient and for preventing citizens abroad from being disenfranchised. It was argued that "short of a system of election day registration, potentially the most convenient system of voter registration is one involving registration by mail depending, of course, upon how readily available are the mail forms" (Bolinger and Gaylord 1977, 111).

Until mail-in voter registration systems were adopted, the convenience of registration in most states depended almost entirely on the availability of deputy registrars, so there was considerable variation from county to county in how easily a person could register to vote. For example, a 1960 California survey of county practices showed that

> twenty-two counties did not appoint volunteer deputies, only eight counties conducted a door-to-door canvass for unregistered voters, twelve would not allow their deputies to rove from place to place in search of unregistered voters, seventeen did not ordinarily appoint deputies to register voters in places where large numbers of people congregated, and eighteen did not provide for reimbursement of deputies, the remainder paying from 5 cents to 25 cents per registration. (Bolinger and Gaylord 1977, 99)

After mail-in voter registration was adopted the importance of these deputies naturally diminished.

Mail-in registration also made voter registration much more convenient. The county recorder would supply a registration form without charge to any qualified person who requested one. The county recorder would also distribute state mail-in registration forms throughout the county at government offices, fire stations, libraries, and other locations open to the public. At first many states required citizens to justify their need to register by mail—to provide a reason, or essentially qualify for doing so. Possible justifications included serving in the military; being out of state or otherwise absent on business; illness, hospitalization, or disability; being a student or confined; religious reasons; or having official duties on Election Day. State rules varied on the number of justifications needed to qualify for mail-in registration, and in some cases an oath was required. Once an exception was granted, the person could register by mail.

Over time, states expanded the inclusiveness of mail-in registration. Many states adopted universal mail-in provisions, allowing every qualified state resident who was not already registered to apply to register by mail without giving a cause. As shown in table 4.2, universal mail-in voter registration was first adopted by Kentucky in 1924 and, at least in the beginning, existed primarily in rural areas. Over time it spread widely across the country—particularly after 1942, when federal law permitted members of the armed forces to register by mail and vote by absentee ballot. Over the century, all but three states adopted universal mail-in voter registration. New Hampshire and Wyoming did not do so during the period under study, and North Dakota did not have mail-in registration before eradicating the

Table 4.2 Voter Registration Laws, by First Election Year after Adoption

State*	Universal Mail-In Registration	Motor Voter Registration	Election Day Registration
Alabama	1994	1996	. . .
Alaska	1976	1994	. . .
Arizona	1992	1984	. . .
Arkansas	1996	1996	. . .
California	1976	1996	. . .
Colorado	1996	1986	. . .
Connecticut	1988	1992	. . .
Delaware	1982	1994	. . .
Florida	1996	1996	. . .
Georgia	1996	1996	. . .
Hawaii	1988	1990	. . .
Idaho	1996	1992–94	1994
Illinois	1996	1996	. . .
Indiana	1996	1996	. . .
Iowa	1976	1990	. . .
Kansas	1972	1994	. . .
Kentucky	1924	1996	. . .
Louisiana	1996	1990	. . .
Maine	1984	1996	1974
Maryland	1974	1988	. . .
Massachusetts	1994	1994	. . .
Michigan	1996	1976	. . .
Minnesota	1974	1978	1974
Mississippi	1992	1992	. . .
Missouri	1996	1996	. . .
Montana	1972	1992	. . .
Nebraska	1986	1994	. . .
Nevada	1992	1988	. . .
New Hampshire	. . .	. . .	1994
New Jersey	1974	1996	. . .
New Mexico	1994	1992	. . .
New York	1976	1996	. . .
North Carolina	1996	1984	. . .
North Dakota**	. . .	. . .	. . .
Ohio	1978	1984	. . .
Oklahoma	1996	1996	. . .
Oregon	1976	1984	1920–26; 1976–84
Pennsylvania	1976	1996	. . .
Rhode Island	1996	1996	. . .
South Carolina	1986	1996	. . .
South Dakota	1996	1996	. . .
Tennessee	1972	1996	. . .
Texas	1966	1996	. . .
Utah	1976	1996	. . .
Vermont	1998	1998	. . .
Virginia	1996	1996	. . .
Washington	1994	1990	. . .
West Virginia	1984	1992	. . .
Wisconsin	1976	. . .	1976
Wyoming	. . .	. . .	1994

Source: This is an original data set I constructed from the official state codebooks and state session laws. Where there was ambiguity, I contacted state election officials.

Note: "Frequency of periodic registration," "nonvoting purge period," and "registration closing date" were also classified as voter registration laws in this study; however, they are continuous variables and were not suitable for inclusion in this table. These variables are discussed in the text, and descriptive statistics are available in appendixes C and D.

*Unless otherwise noted, states have had the specified law for the entire period evaluated in this study. Southern states are noted in boldface.

**North Dakota eliminated its voter registration requirement in 1951.

state's registration requirement in 1951. The adoption of universal mail-in registration across the country was the first step toward more convenient and less costly voter registration.

Motor Voter Registration

Motor voter programs—allowing voter registration at state Department of Motor Vehicles offices—aimed to make voter registration more accessible and convenient. As illustrated in table 4.2, motor voter registration became popular in some of the midwestern and western states beginning in 1976. For example, Michigan and Minnesota adopted the program in the late 1970s; Arizona, Colorado, Maryland, Nevada, North Carolina, Ohio, and Oregon did so in the late 1980s; and many more states followed in the early 1990s. The states that waited longest to adopt motor voter programs were located mostly in the South.

Based on the seeming successes of early-adopting states, reformers professed that lowering the costs of registration even minimally—by allowing motor voter registration—could be an incentive to latent registrants and positively influence turnout (see Piven and Cloward 1988, 2000). In 1993 the National Voter Registration Act, well known for its motor voter provision, aimed to accomplish just that. The NVRA required all nonexempt states to implement motor voter registration before the 1996 presidential election.[11] Six states (Idaho, Minnesota, New Hampshire, North Dakota, Wisconsin, and Wyoming) were formally exempt from the 1993 NVRA, including its section on motor voter registration; but as noted in table 4.2, Idaho and Minnesota adopted motor voter programs anyway. Despite the federal legislation, there was a lot of regional and temporal variation in the accessibility of voter registration throughout the century, but the programs' effects on voter turnout have proved modest at best (Brown and Wedeking 2006; Fitzgerald 2005; Franklin and Grier 1997; Hanmer 2009; Knack 1995; Martinez and Hill 1999; Rhine 1995).

Registration Closing Date and Election Day Registration

From the 1940s through the early 1960s, there were several congressional hearings on state voting practices and voter registration. Although the hearings held during the 1960s primarily concerned the lack of voting by minority groups—specifically the obstruction of voting among blacks in the southern states—the laws generated from these hearings helped liberalize many state rules on voting qualifications and voter registration. In addition to discussions about disenfranchising laws (e.g., literacy tests, poll taxes), the time afforded for voter registration was scrutinized. It was argued that because voters' interest in elections builds progressively toward Election Day, closing voter registration too early—weeks and even months before the election—posed a formidable obstacle to registration. Indeed, the report of the President's Commission on Registration and Voting Participation in 1963 recommended that "registration should not close more than three to four weeks before the election date" (Bolinger and Gaylord 1977, 106).

In response, several national and state proposals during the latter part of the century called for later registration closing dates. In nonsouthern states from 1920 to 2000, closing dates ranged from zero days before an election, in states with Election Day registration, to 180 days before. In the southern states, closing dates ranged from 10 days to 180 days before Election Day. Throughout the period, the average closing date in the nonsouthern states was 25 days, and the average in the southern states was 37 days. Over time, in light of reform efforts, state registration rolls closed later and later, with most current state closing dates fixed at about 30 days or less before the general election.

Many reform proponents have also advocated eliminating the period between registration and voting. Indeed, Election Day registration is often touted as the electoral institution most capable of generating substantial changes in state turnout (see, e.g., Brians and Grofman 1999, 2001; Cain, Donovan, and Tolbert 2008; Hanmer 2009; Mitchell and Wlezien 1995; Rhine 1996; Teixeira 1992; Wolfinger and Rosenstone 1980). Despite the expectation that Election Day registration could dramatically increase voting rates, it exists in only a handful of states. Table 4.2 shows that by the 2000 presidential election, six nonsouthern states (Idaho, Maine, Minnesota, New Hampshire, Wisconsin, and Wyoming) allowed Election Day registration. Additionally, Oregon implemented Election Day registration from 1920 to 1926 and again from 1976 to 1985. It did not exist in any of the southern states during the twentieth century.

Of course, Election Day registration also has potential drawbacks. For example, in his study on the early experiences of Election Day registration in Minnesota and Wisconsin, Smolka cautioned that "although Election Day registration probably contributed to a marginal increase in voter turnout, about 1 to 2 percentage points in both Minnesota and Wisconsin; it also encouraged many voters to wait until Election Day to register. This caused confusion and long lines at the polls, and errors were made that permitted hundreds of voters to vote in the wrong precincts or wards"

(1977, 68). In many ways the fears illustrated by Smolka's example are bolstered by the warnings politicians advance in response to reformers' pleas for more widespread adoption of Election Day registration. Perhaps the potential for electoral fraud and confusion at the polls are more likely to occur under an Election Day registration system, but reformers continue to maintain that, with conscientious implementation and instruction from the states that have successfully used it for decades, it could be the most effective way of eliminating one of the most costly elements of the registration and voting process.

Voting Procedures

Of all of the electoral institutions explored in this chapter, the laws governing voting procedures—such as the number of hours the polls are open on Election Day or whether the state allows people to vote early or by absentee ballot—have the most direct influence on the ease of voting. Their influence on turnout is fairly objective; if the procedures are structured in a way that is expansive and clear, then voting is inherently less cumbersome. To date, most of the scholarship on voter turnout and electoral institutions demonstrates that election administration does affect participation to some degree.[12]

Poll Hours

How long the polls are open on Election Day is important in determining how many people will be able to vote. Presumably, the longer the polls are open, the more opportunity people have to cast their votes. Over the years, poll hours have become progressively longer; however, during the first half of the century, especially in many predominately rural states, the polls opened very early to accommodate farmers and typically closed by midafternoon. Yet catering to the American farmer has become less and less important over time, even in rural areas. For example, even a 1957 report on election laws in Kentucky noted that "some farmers may still vote early, but the almost universal use of the automobile makes it less necessary that they have the opportunity" (Research Staff of the Legislative Research Commission 1957, 49). Most states thus have increasingly adopted a norm by which the polls open early enough to accommodate people on their way to work, between 7:00 a.m. and 8:00 a.m., and close just after dusk.

Although it seems benign at first glance, the expansiveness of poll hours can have real effects on participation. Opening hours skewed toward the morning make it harder for younger voters and working-class voters to get to the polls, and poll hours skewed toward the evening make it harder for older people and upper-class voters to turn out (Hansen 2001). Recently some have suggested that uniform poll opening and closing times (adjusted across time zones) should be established nationally to curb voter apathy as news of vote totals and electoral victories flows from the East Coast to the West Coast on election night. This sort of reform could have significant ramifications. As noted in the 2001 report of the Task Force on the Federal Election System, compared with the current decentralized system, a nationwide law regulating poll opening times would reduce the morning voting hours in the eastern states, presumably dampening voter turnout among people who are older, white-collar, and white. Furthermore, a uniform poll-closing law would reduce the number of evening voting hours in the western states and perhaps dampen turnout most among workers who are young, blue-collar, and Latino (Hansen 2001). Although it is impossible to know how many of the people who now vote between 8:00 a.m. and 9:00 a.m. on the East Coast would not vote at all if the polls opened at 10:00 a.m., or how many westerners who now vote between 7:00 p.m. and 8:00 p.m. would not vote at all if the polls closed at 6:00 p.m., the number would almost certainly not be trivial, especially with increasingly close presidential vote margins and variable regional turnout rates.

Early Voting and Absentee Voting

Apart from expanding the number of hours people can vote on Election Day, reformers have become enthusiastic about letting voters cast their ballots early. In-person early voting and universal absentee voting laws allow citizens to cast their ballots well before Election Day at several government offices and other public locations, and even from home. By providing a larger window of time to participate and expanding the availability of polling locations, both these programs offer an easy way to vote before Election Day.

Although early voting was virtually nonexistent two decades ago, by the 2000 election several states allowed registered voters to cast their ballots before Election Day. As shown in table 4.3, nineteen states adopted in-person early voting provisions allowing citizens to vote at community centers, fire stations, libraries, and other government agencies before Election Day. Additionally, from 1920 to 2000, nineteen states created universal absentee voting provisions allowing citizens to vote by absentee ballot for any reason. In contrast to the "universal" provision, some states have

Table 4.3 Voting Procedures, by First Election Year after Adoption

State*	In-Person Early Voting	Universal Absentee Voting
Alaska	1996	1996
Arizona	1994	1992
Arkansas	1996	. . .
California	1998	1978
Colorado	1992	1992
Hawaii	1994	1994
Idaho	1994	1994
Kansas	1996	1996
Maine	2000	2000
Montana	2000	2000
Nebraska	2000	2000
Nevada	1994	1992
New Mexico	2000	1990
North Carolina	2000	2000
North Dakota	. . .	1998
Oklahoma	1992	1992
Oregon	. . .	1980
Tennessee	1994	. . .
Texas	1988	. . .
Washington	1998	1974
Wisconsin	2000	2000
Wyoming	. . .	1992

Source: This is an original data set I constructed from the official state codebooks and state session laws. Where there was ambiguity, I contacted state election officials.

Note: "Hours polls are open" was also classified as a voting procedure in this study; however, it is a continuous variable and was not suitable for inclusion in this table. Discussion of this variable is found in the text, and descriptive statistics are available in appendixes C and D.

*States that did not have any of these voting qualification provisions from 1920 to 2000 were omitted from the table. Southern states are noted in boldface.

required people to justify their need for absentee ballots. For example, in some states they must verify their military status or demonstrate that they are students or would be hospitalized, disabled, or out of the country on Election Day. Universal provisions, on the other hand, allow *all* citizens in the state the right to vote by absentee ballot without justifying it.

By the latter part of the twentieth century, many states instituted both of these provisions. Most of them are in the West and Midwest, but these convenient voting procedures are becoming widespread across the nation. Although these voting provisions are fairly new, preliminary studies reveal that in-person early voting can have a positive, though fairly minimal, impact on turnout (Gronke, Galanes-Rosenbaum, and Miller 2007, 2008; Hansen 2001; Richardson and Neeley 1996; Stein 1998; Stein and Garcia-

Monet 1997). Research on how unrestricted absentee voting affects turn-out is generally inconclusive, however. Often research in this vein addresses who votes by absentee ballot and how it affects campaigns rather than whether the institution itself increases overall turnout (Gronke, Galanes-Rosenbaum, and Miller 2007, 2008; Hansen 2001; Oliver 1996). Even though these processes are still rather new and their effects have yet to be fully realized, by allowing individuals a larger span of voting time and the unrestricted ability to vote before Election Day, early in-person voting and universal absentee voting are unmatched at making voting convenient.

Institutional Implications

In principle, American citizens have a constitutionally protected right to participate in elections equally with other citizens in the same jurisdiction; yet, as I have demonstrated throughout this chapter, the "equal right to vote" is not absolute across the states. Access to the ballot and the burdens associated with the electoral process have varied substantially throughout the century. This is a product of federalism, under which the states can impose their own voting qualifications and registration procedures and can regulate access to the franchise in many other ways. As shown in ta-ble 4.4—which displays the total number of states that had each electoral law in 1920, in 2000, and at any given point in time during the century—state approaches to structuring electoral institutions have evolved tremen-dously throughout the century, with an overarching trend toward increas-ing expansiveness.

To characterize the institutional variation abounding in the states, this chapter has explored the historical evolution of a wide array of state elec-toral institutions throughout the twentieth century. Most striking, this his-torical evaluation illustrates that state political institutions and electoral mechanisms are dynamic, not static. It also reveals substantial, though not absolute, regional differences in the electoral rules of the game imple-mented over the century. Although many restrictive electoral laws on voter qualifications existed in the nonsouthern states, overall electoral laws, even those governing registration and voting procedures, have been more restric-tive in the South. Conversely, electoral institutions in a vast majority of the nonsouthern states, especially in the Midwest, have been consistently ex-pansive. This distinction is important for our understanding of twentieth-century voter turnout. As Verba and Nie noted, "We must examine not only the individual citizen but also the conditions that the citizen encounters when he or she participates politically" (1972, 56). Indeed, this book aims

Table 4.4 Total Number of States with Various Electoral Laws over Time

Electoral Law	Year (No. of States)		
	1920	2000	Anytime
Voting qualifications:			
Property requirements	5	0	5
Literacy test	16	0	20
Poll tax	15	0	16
Long residency requirement	36	0	38
Voter registration:			
Permanent registration	22	50	50
Nonvoting purge	4	3	48
Universal mail-in	0	47	47
Motor voter	0	45	46
Late closing date	32	26	38
EDR	1	6	7
Voting procedures:			
Long poll hours	29	45	45
Early voting	0	19	19
Absentee voting	0	19	19

Source: This table was constructed using an original data set I collected from the official state code-books and state session laws. Where there was ambiguity, I contacted state election officials.
Note: "Anytime" reflects the total number of states that had the law at any given time between 1920 and 2000. Long residency requirement reflects the number of states whose "most restrictive residency requirement" is 227 days or more (at or exceeding the mean). Late closing date reflects the number of states that close their registration rolls 28 days or less before Election Day (at or exceeding the mean). Long poll hours reflects the number of states that keep their polls open for eleven hours or more on Election Day (at or exceeding the mean).

to relate these institutional patterns to the state turnout trends presented in chapter 3—arguing that electoral institutions, in their ability to structure the voting process, affect voting patterns. Further, the expansiveness or restrictiveness of voting laws will lead to variation in institutional effects. Specifically, southern norms of electoral restriction may have created and perpetuated consistently low voting rates, while the expansiveness of the voting rules found outside the South may have influenced the perpetually high turnout these states experienced throughout the century.

This regional characterization raises important questions about how the pervasiveness, persistence, and implications of restrictive and expansive state electoral institutions have affected participation. First we must consider whether institutional voting constraints mean different things, or produce different effects, in the southern and nonsouthern states. Further, we might speculate on why such voting constraints have existed at all. In practice, groups can successfully adopt and implement restrictive laws only if the majority of people in the state allow it, or at least cannot effectively oppose it. So perhaps the evolution of voting laws reflects a divergent political history of the way various regions and states respond to "otherness" or how the dominant society in the states has responded to issues of "otherness" throughout the century. It is also important to consider whether the nature of electoral institutions is the same in all states, and particularly whether the same comparisons can be made between states in and outside the South. It also raises questions about whether the meaning of institutional change differs over time. For example, is a state's decision to remove the poll tax in 1920, when other restrictive institutions impede the vote, fundamentally different from the decision to remove it in 1960? The context of the institutions seems to be somewhat fluid over time. Furthermore, how long state electoral laws are expansive or restrictive may have variable consequences for turnout rates and the voting culture in the state.

On the surface, when restrictive qualification requirements are removed and more expansive institutions are adopted, we may expect voter turnout to increase; but the legacy of costly institutions may affect the voting culture in a state well after the law has changed. Similarly, one might expect that voting rates will be depressed in a state with restrictive registration laws and will increase if the state adopts a more expansive registration process. Yet there could be an implicit difference in the institutional effect between a state that never had the restrictive institution and a state that had it and then changed the rules. If so, the voting culture might be different in these two states, which may yield different observable institutional effects. Understanding this dynamic relationship requires in-depth systematic analysis focused on regional and state variation over time in both institutional costs and voting rates. This relationship between state electoral institutions and state voting rates during presidential and nonpresidential elections from 1920 to 2000 will be examined empirically in the next three chapters.

PART TWO

State and Regional Analyses

Exploring the Effect of Electoral Institutions on Twentieth-Century Voter Turnout in the American States

Low national voting rates have concerned observers of American politics for decades. Not only can they affect election outcomes, partisan electoral advantages, and public policy, but from a normative standpoint they challenge the theoretical underpinnings of democracy. Yet one is hard-pressed to find an effective solution. Over time, reformers have turned to electoral institutions as the cause of—and perhaps also the remedy for—low voter turnout. Indeed, restrictive electoral laws during the first half of the twentieth century may have created and perpetuated a depressed voting cycle in many states. In response, reformers have argued that by easing registration and voting processes, and by fostering a climate that heightens participation, expansive electoral institutions may change the status quo. During the latter part of the century this reasoning resulted in an onslaught of state and national reforms—such as motor voter registration, Election Day registration, and early voting—aimed at reducing the costs of registration and voting in order to increase participation.

Of course, institutional change takes time, and the behavioral effects of reform are often slow to materialize. To appreciate the role of institutions in shaping twentieth-century voting patterns, we need a broad scope. Exploring past effects and linking both expansive and restrictive institutions to turnout trends over time may, in turn, guide reform decisions in the future. For example, if the restrictiveness or expansiveness of electoral institutions has generated an observable change in state participation rates throughout the twentieth century, then it could be that by making voting laws more expansive, electoral institutions may boost voter turnout in the states where it is waning. Further, if the structure of elections has consequences for voter participation, then we need to identify the institutions that have generated the most sizable impact on turnout in either direction—and also isolate where these effects have been most realized over time.

This chapter engages these issues empirically by analyzing, first, whether a variety of expansive and restrictive state electoral institutions have had an effect on political behavior at the state level beyond state demographics and levels of electoral competition, and second, the extent to which specific institutions are determinative. I present extensive time-series cross-sectional analyses, systematically testing the effects of several restrictive and expansive electoral institutions on voter turnout in the American states during presidential and nonpresidential election years from 1920 to 2000, and I compare results from the southern and nonsouthern states. This informs a discussion about where the states have been and where they are going in terms of political participation, as related to the characteristics of their electoral institutions. If the main objective of electoral reform is to alter state and even national voting rates, then we must recognize how the states and their voting histories have differed throughout the century and incorporate a broad perspective into our analyses. Evaluating the effects of an array of restrictive and expansive laws together is the first step.

Model Specification

This book suggests that changes in a variety of institutional variables affect the decision to turn out on Election Day, and changes in the distribution of these variables are expected to map onto varying state turnout levels over time. To examine this relationship empirically, I pooled data across the fifty American states and over the forty-one biennial election years from 1920 to 2000.[1] There are twenty-one observations of voter turnout in each state during presidential election years and twenty during nonpresidential election years.[2] The first election year used in this analysis is 1920—a year marking the culmination of the Progressive movement, after the national enfranchisement of women and amid a nationalized party system, but before the enactment of many important state and federal electoral reforms pertaining to registration and voting in the states.[3] Since this study focuses on changes during the twentieth century, 2000 is the last election year included in the analysis. Appendix C presents descriptive statistics for all the variables during presidential election years from 1920 to 2000, and appendix D presents the descriptive statistics during nonpresidential election years from 1922 to 1998. Both appendix C and appendix D also include sources for the data used in the analyses.

To model the effects of a number of state electoral institutions governing voting qualifications, voter registration, and voting procedures on state-level turnout over time, extensive multivariate regression models were estimated. The general specification is as follows :

$$T_{it} = \beta_0 + \beta_1 Q_{it} + \beta_2 R_{it} + \beta_3 P_{it} + \beta_4 D_{it} + \beta_5 E_{it} + \delta Y_t + \mu_i + \varepsilon_{it},$$

where i indexes states, t indexes years, T is voter turnout, Q is a vector of requirements pertaining to voting qualifications, R is a vector of voter registration laws, P is a vector of voting procedures, D is a vector of demographic variables, E is a vector of Election Year indicators, Y is a vector of year dummy variables, μ are state-level fixed effects, and ε is a stochastic error term.

Pooled time-series cross-sectional models with state and year fixed effects, also known as least squares dummy variable (LSDV) models, are frequently used in the literature on state electoral reform, and in much of the work on over-time policy making in the states (see, e.g., Fitzgerald 2005; Knack 1995; Teixeira 1992; Tolbert and Smith 2005). Given my focus on American states over eighty years, this modeling approach is more appropriate than cross-sectional analyses of single election years, pooled models without unit and time controls, or random effects models.[4] State and year fixed effects were included in the models to control for any unmeasured or time-invariant state-level or year-specific factors that might influence voter turnout (for more on this see Achen 1986; Ansolabehere and Konisky 2006; Hanmer 2009). When we include fixed effects, the institutional coefficients are able to pick up the impact of the electoral laws themselves rather than adding in the influence of any unmeasured variables—that is, any unmeasured effects that are specific to the individual states or to particular years.

Including state fixed effects also helps circumvent the endogeneity that may exist between state rule makers and the type of electoral laws found in a given state. This sort of endogeneity could occur if we assume that the unobservable factors affecting the selection of election laws are unrelated to the unobservable factors that affect turnout; however, unobserved attitudes toward political participation could play a role in the adoption of the set of laws as well as in an individual's decision whether to vote (Achen 1986; Hanmer 2009). When the factors leading to the selection of a particular law are not taken into account, estimates of the effect can be biased upward. Including state fixed effects in the model helps reduce, if not eliminate, such bias by capturing any time-invariant unobserved attitudes toward participation.

There are, however, two substantial disadvantages to estimating these models with state and year fixed effects. First, there is a loss of efficiency, since many degrees of freedom are used when estimating the unit and time dummy variables. Second, there is an attenuation of total variance, since the between-unit variance is assigned to the fixed effects (Stimson 1985). In practice, including state fixed effects allows the model to compute the "within" estimator, which uses only variation within individual states for identification. As a result, the analyses I present here make comparisons within states, not between states. Note that both of these issues make it harder, rather than easier, to detect institutional effects. In fact, for variables that change very slowly over time (like state electoral laws), the lack of sub-stantial within-unit variance makes fixed effects analysis perhaps too strong a test for institutional effects, although single cross-sectional tests are too weak. This suggests that including the fixed effects may risk underestimat-ing the effects of institutions on state turnout rates. Without the fixed ef-fects, however, one risks exaggerating the effect of institutions, which seems even less desirable. The trade-off is essentially between potentially biasing the institutional effects upward or biasing them downward, and the mod-els I present reflect the more conservative downward approach. In addition to the attractiveness of a conservative modeling approach, including state and year fixed effects makes good sense, since the study deals with fifty unique states over eighty unique years.

In addition to the issues outlined above, combining cross-sectional and time-series data also risks encountering heteroskedasticity, autocorrelation, and cross-sectional correlation, which suggest that parameter estimates may be biased and inefficient (Stimson 1985). This is a problem, since one of the key assumptions in the classic linear model is that no autocorrela-tion or serial correlation between the disturbances enters into the popula-tion regression function; that is, the disturbances in the current time period (t) are not linearly related to the disturbance term in the previous time pe-riod ($t - 1$). This concern is particularly relevant to this study, since voting rates may not be independent from one election to the next (e.g., higher turnout during one election could be related to higher turnout in the next election).

Indeed, the presence of a first-order autoregressive error process, AR(1), was detected within the cross-sectional units. The autocorrelation was re-moved from the models, specifying that within panels there is AR(1) and that the coefficient of the AR(1) process is common to all panels (An-solabehere and Konisky 2006; Beck and Katz 1995; Stimson 1985). The autocorrelation was removed from the models using the Prais-Winsten transformation. Alternatively, a lagged dependent variable could have been added to the models to remove it. Although one can often remove autocorrelation by adding a lag term, it has been shown that doing so in a model with fixed effects and panel-corrected standard errors can lead to biased and inconsistent estimates of the coefficients and standard errors (Kristensen and Wawro 2003). After removing the AR(1), the time-series cross-sectional models were estimated using panel-corrected standard errors (PCSE). Panel-corrected standard errors were used to correct for panel heteroskedasticity and contemporaneous correlation (Beck and Katz 1995, 1996). The key motivation for using PCSEs is to improve the inferences made from the time-series cross-sectional data by taking into account the complexity of the error process in a way that does not ask too much of the data (Beck 2000; Beck and Katz 1995, 1996).[5]

Measurement

The dependent variable in each model is state-level voter turnout during presidential election years from 1920 to 2000, or nonpresidential election years from 1922 to 1998. As I noted earlier, voter turnout is measured as a percentage calculated by dividing the total number of votes for the highest office on the ballot by the state's voting age population (VAP). During presidential election years I used the total votes cast in the presidential race. During nonpresidential election years I used the total votes cast for a US senator. If no Senate race was held in the state, I used the total votes for governor. In a few instances a seat in the US House of Representatives was the highest office on the ballot. Voter turnout is calculated as a percentage of the state's total voting age population to control for the varying sizes of that population (see chapter 3 for a complete discussion of turnout measurement).

State Electoral Institutions

As I demonstrated in chapter 4, the electoral landscape has changed dramatically throughout the twentieth century. Although states regularly adopted restrictive reforms during the early part of the century, many recent reform efforts have stressed adopting expansive electoral institutions. Variation in the type of electoral institutions governing voting is expected to generate specific effects on voter turnout. The following section will outline these directional expectations more concretely. Given the eighty-year time span of this project, no data exist on the implementation of state electoral institutions. As a result, this book focuses on state adoption and elimination years, assuming that the laws are enforced in accordance with the statutory provisions. The possibility that these laws may be applied unevenly is a certain but unavoidable limitation of this study (see Bassi, Morton, and Trounstine 2013; Burden and Neiheisel 2013; Hanmer 2009; Piven and Cloward 1988).

Voting Qualifications

As I discussed throughout chapter 4, every state's constitution establishes its preconditions, or qualifications, for voting. The most-restrictive electoral institutions enacted in the American states during the twentieth century pertained to voting qualifications. In the statistical models, dummy variables indicate the adoption of three prominent qualifications limiting voting—property requirements, literacy tests, and poll taxes. Of course, although these provisions were prevalent in the southern states, they were by no means confined to the South. Many of these institutions existed in the nonsouthern states as well. Apart from being implicitly racist tactics, all of these institutions are theorized to limit participation and decrease turnout owing to their associated restrictiveness, their actual and figurative costliness, and the enormous burden they placed on potential voters.

Additionally, long residency requirements also served as restrictive preconditions for voting in nearly all the states throughout most the twentieth century. In practice, these requirements had to be satisfied at the state, county, and district level. In the statistical models, residency requirement is coded as a continuous variable, measured in days, capturing the length of a state's most restrictive residency requirement, since voters would need to satisfy all the residency requirements at any level of abstraction (state, county, district) in order to participate. For example, if residents were required to live in the state for one year, in the county for thirty days, and in the district for ten days before being allowed to vote, the variable was coded as the longest requirement in days (e.g., 365 days). Long residency requirements proved cumbersome for voters, especially the increasing mobile population. As the length of a state's most restrictive residency requirement increases, voter turnout is expected to decrease.

Voter Registration

Voter registration has been a prerequisite for voting in most states throughout the twentieth century. Although permanent voter registration systems currently exist in all but one of the American states, this was not always the case.[6] As I discussed in chapter 4, early periodic voter registration systems, forcing voters to reregister after a fixed time as specified by state law, were very common throughout nearly half of the century. They operated under the assumption that it was necessary, and even desirable, to prepare a completely new registration roster for each major election, or at frequent intervals as stipulated by state law. In the models, frequency of periodic registration is coded as a continuous variable capturing the number of years before mandatory reregistration under the state's periodic registration system. States with a permanent voter registration system were assigned a value of one hundred. These systems were widely criticized for being inefficient and cumbersome. Given the burdens associated with periodic voter registration systems, they are expected to affect voter turnout negatively. A periodic registration system's effect on turnout, however, was closely connected to the frequency of the state's mandatory reregistration stipulation. This is captured in the models: as the number of years between mandatory reregistration under a periodic system increased (individuals had to reregister less frequently), voter turnout is expected to increase.

Registration reforms have also addressed the permanency of one's registration status. Before they were formally outlawed for covered states under the National Voter Registration Act in 1993, many states employed nonvoting purges. These states routinely reviewed their voter rolls and purged registrants who had not voted for a stipulated number of years. Although nonvoting purges had the desirable quality of keeping voter lists current by eliminating people who had died or moved, they may have also erroneously eliminated viable registered voters who did not vote for their own reasons. In the models, nonvoting purge period indicates the number of years an individual could not vote before being purged from the state's registration rolls. States without a nonvoting purge are assigned a value of one hundred. This is a substantially long period of time, indicating that individuals will be purged only if they fail to vote for one hundred years (which is not bound to happen). As the number of years of not voting before a registrant is purged increases (and registration remains intact longer) voter turnout is expected to increase.

As states replaced periodic voter registration with permanent registration systems, the details of the registration laws themselves were scrutinized (Burden and Neiheisel 2013; Hansen 2001; Highton 2004; Timpone 1998). Amid growing concern that onerous registration processes posed a major obstacle to voting, many states adopted expansive, cost-reducing institutions that stressed easing the burdens of voter registration (see Knack 1995; Mitchell and Wlezien 1995; Piven and Cloward 1988; Rhine 1995;

Wolfinger and Rosenstone 1980). For example, in the 1930s and 1940s mail-in voter registration systems were touted for their convenience and for keeping citizens abroad from being disenfranchised. At first many states required citizens to justify their need to register by mail, but more and more states adopted universal mail-in provisions allowing qualified state electors to apply for registration by mail without limitation or cause. In the models, universal mail-in registration is coded as a dummy variable indicating whether the state allowed universal mail-in voter registration without justification. Given the added convenience associated with this reform, states that allow universal mail-in registration are expected to have higher turnout than states that do not.

Motor voter registration—allowing registration at state motor vehicle offices—was also aimed at making voter registration more accessible and convenient. In 1993, the National Voter Registration Act, well known for its "motor voter" provision, required all states to implement motor voter registration before the 1996 presidential election. As shown in the chapter 4, despite federal intervention there was quite a bit of variation in the adoption of motor voter registration programs across the nation. Despite this variation, motor voter registration is coded as a dummy variable indicating whether the state allowed people to register at state Department of Motor Vehicles offices.[7] States with motor voter programs are expected to have higher levels of voter turnout than states that do not.

The window of time afforded to complete voter registration has also been the subject of many reform discussions. Because voters' interest in elections builds progressively until Election Day, early registration closing poses a formidable obstacle to registration and subsequent voting. Over time, in light of reform efforts, state registration rolls have closed later and later, and many have advocated eliminating the time lag between registration and voting. In the models, registration closing date is a continuous variable measuring the number of days between the close of voter registration and Election Day. The variable ranges from zero days—in states with Election Day registration—to 180 days. Presumably, early closing dates—those that occur long before Election Day—will exclude voters who do not become interested until shortly before Election Day. Conversely, late closing dates—closing registration very near to Election Day—may allow participation by those who just became interested in the election. Accordingly, in the statistical models, as the number of days between the closing of registration and Election Day increases (creating a larger lag time between registration and actual voting), voter turnout is expected to decrease.

Along these lines, in the models a dummy variable also captures states with Election Day registration—allowing voters in the state the maximum time to register before casting their vote and essentially creating one-stop registration and voting.[8] Election Day registration is often touted as the electoral institution most capable of generating substantial changes to state turnout and is expected to be associated with higher turnout rates.

Voting Procedures

Finally, laws governing voting procedures influence how easily voters participate in the electoral process. For example, the number of hours the polls are open on Election Day affects how many will be able to vote. Presumably, the longer the polls are open, the greater the opportunity to vote, especially for those who work long hours, have multiple jobs, or must travel a great distance to the polls. Hours the polls are open is a continuous variable measuring the total number of hours the polls are open in a state on Election Day. It is expected that as the time the polls are open increases, giving greater access, voter turnout will also increase.

Recently reformers have also become enthusiastic about allowing voters to cast their ballots before Election Day. By 2000, over twenty states had adopted in-person early voting or universal absentee voting, or both. In-person early voting is a dummy variable indicating whether a state explicitly allows in-person early voting, where voters can cast their ballots at voting centers, community centers, fire stations, libraries, and some government agencies well before an election. Additionally, universal absentee voting identifies states that allow all voters to vote by absentee ballot without justifying their need to do so. By increasing the window of time on, or even before, Election Day when people can vote, states that allow either in-person early voting or unrestricted absentee ballots are expected to have increased turnout.[9]

Electoral Calendar

Many noninstitutional factors can also affect state voting rates. For example, characteristics of the electoral calendar are important, since participation may be influenced by the level of public discussion, interest, and mass mobilization surrounding particular races, issues, or campaigns (Boyd 1986, 1989; Patterson and Caldeira 1983; Rosenstone and Hansen 1993; Verba, Schlozman, and Brady 1995). Accordingly, dummy variables were included to identify years when there was a concurrent gubernatorial race or Senate race that might increase turnout. Having a large number of congressional seats up for grabs may also raise voter turnout. Contested House seats is included to control for the percentage of congressional seats contested by the two major parties during a congressional election year. The number of initiatives on the ballot was also included, since Smith and Tolbert (2007) and Tolbert and Smith (2005) have shown that initiatives may increase electoral interest and turnout. This is a continuous measure reflecting the number of initiatives on the ballot in a particular state during a given election year.

Finally, vote margin was included because the amount of electoral competition is important in shaping participation rates, particularly during the period being studied, and especially in the South (Key 1949; Kim, Petrocik, and Enokson 1975; Shachar and Nalebuff 1999). Lack of electoral competition may decrease voter turnout. Vote margin measures the difference in the number of votes garnered by the winner and loser of the highest race on the ballot (e.g., president, senator, governor, US House member). As the vote margin between the candidates increases—making victory more secure and reflecting less competition—interest in the election and mobilization efforts decrease, and turnout is also expected to decrease.

State Demographics

Since national social scientific surveys began to flourish in the 1950s, scholars have theorized about the relationship between various demographic indicators and the likelihood that an individual will vote. This is arguably the most extensive area of research on individual-level political participation in the United States. Several demographic variables, such as education, per capita income, racial composition, and age, prove to be highly correlated with individual-level voter turnout (see, e.g., Campbell et al. 1960; Leighley 1995; Lewis-Beck et al. 2008; Miller and Shanks 1996; Verba and Nie 1972; Wolfinger and Rosenstone 1980). It seems reasonable to expect these variables to influence voter turnout in the states as well.[10]

The models include five key variables related to state demographics: education, per capita income, black population, other population, and age. Higher education and wealth are often associated with increased registration and voting (Filer, Kenny, and Morton 1993; Nie, Junn, and Stehlik-Barry 1996; Rosenstone and Hansen 1993; Teixeira 1992; Wolfinger and Rosenstone 1980). In the statistical models, education is measured as the percentage of a state's residents age twenty-five and older who graduated from high school in a given year, and per capita income in 2000 dollars[11] captures movement in the average per capita income in $1,000 increments within a state. Being a racial minority is often associated with decreased participation, particularly in the southern states and states with large immigrant populations (Rosenstone and Hansen 1993; Teixeira 1992; Wolfinger and Rosenstone 1980). To measure the effects of race on turnout, I included two variables in the statistical models. The first variable, black population, controls for the percentage of a state's total black population, and the second, other population, controls for the percentage of a state's total "other" population, where "other" is defined as neither white nor black. Finally, age is a variable long theorized to be positively correlated with voter turnout, particularly among the senior age cohorts (Campbell 2003; Rosenstone and Hansen 1993; Teixeira 1992; Wolfinger and Rosenstone 1980). In these models, age 45 or above is measured as the percentage of a state's total population forty-five and older.[12]

Empirical Results

The statistical analyses presented in this book examine the effects of several state electoral institutions, electoral calendar indicators, and key state demographic variables on state voter turnout from 1920 to 2000.[13] Despite the historical appeal of an aggregate study spanning all forty-one election years, there is reason to believe that important differences exist between voter turnout trends during presidential and nonpresidential election years.[14] Indeed, many studies on electoral reform have examined their effects separately because of the substantially higher turnout during presidential elections across states and the expectation that institutional effects may vary depending on the salience of the election being held (Fitzgerald 2005; Jackson 1997; Knack 1995; Smith 2001; Tolbert et al. 2008). I also conducted separate analyses during presidential and nonpresidential election years. Table 5.1 presents the results for the twenty-one presidential election years from 1920 to 2000, and table 5.3 presents the results for the twenty nonpresidential election years from 1922 to 1998.[15]

In both tables, model 1 provides the results for all fifty states. One of the key patterns identified in the examination of state turnout patterns and the character of state electoral institutions (their expansiveness or restrictiveness) presented in earlier chapters is the important differences between the southern and nonsouthern states. Their varying approaches to setting limits on voting are integral to understanding state voting patterns throughout the century. Because significant structural and substantive differences exist between the states in and outside the South, models for these regions were estimated separately.[16] Model 2 presents the results for the thirty-nine nonsouthern states, and model 3 provides results for the eleven southern states. State and year dummy coefficients are not shown in the tables to save space, but their inclusion is noted. None of the state or year variables were dropped due to perfect multicollinearity.[17] Many of the state and year dummy variables were statistically significant at the $p \leq .05$ significance level or higher.[18] Overall, the influence of electoral institutions on voter turnout is evident and robust. Even when controlling for many important state demographic and election-specific variables, several electoral institutions appear to have had a significant, albeit variable, effect on voter turnout in the states throughout the century.

Presidential Election Years, 1920–2000

The results presented in table 5.1 reveal that most of the restrictive voting qualifications implemented in the states during the twentieth century had a substantial negative effect on state turnout during presidential election years from 1920 to 2000. Specifically, long residency requirements, which were theorized to negatively affect voter turnout by effectively disenfranchising the mobile population, had a statistically significant negative effect on turnout rates in the southern states. Although the magnitude of the effect appears quite small at first, since the variable is coded in days, the negative coefficient suggests that as the number of days electors were required to reside in their state, county, or district before Election Day increased, they were less likely to vote. Specifically, as the state's most restrictive residency requirement increased by one hundred days, southern voter turnout decreased by nearly 1 percentage point. The mean residency requirement in the southern states during the period was just under one year (306 days), which corresponds to a 2.16 percentage point decrease in turnout after the adoption of a residency requirement in states with an average requirement. Throughout the century, the effect of these requirements on southern turnout ranged from a minimum of zero (in states with no residency requirements) to about 5 percentage points (in states with residency requirements of two years, the longest during the period). This finding lends support to state and national reforms targeting excessively long residency requirements and the plight of the mobile electorate as they attempt to reduce, or abandon, these restrictions, especially in the southern states, where they appeared to have a real effect in depressing participation.

As expected, property requirements, which were theorized to decrease turnout in the few states that employed them, depressed voting rates by 4.6 percentage points during presidential election years in model 1. This

Table 5.1 State-Level Voter Turnout during Presidential Election Years, 1920–2000

Variable	Model 1: All States		Model 2: Nonsouthern		Model 3: Southern	
Voting qualifications:						
Property requirement	−4.599**	(1.318)	−6.461**	(2.000)	−3.824**	(1.299)
Literacy test	−4.689**	(0.917)	−3.662**	(0.841)	0.299	(2.085)
Poll tax	−5.753**	(0.819)	−0.277	(1.089)	−7.866**	(1.199)
Residency requirement	−0.002	(0.002)	0.003	(0.002)	−0.007**	(0.002)
Voter registration:						
Frequency of periodic registration	0.005	(0.005)	−0.006	(0.005)	0.017	(0.011)
Nonvoting purge period	0.003	(0.004)	0.009*	(0.004)	0.006	(0.012)
Universal mail-in registration	0.545	(0.546)	0.131	(0.575)	−0.729	(1.318)
Motor voter registration	0.469	(0.622)	0.666	(0.621)	−3.481	(2.268)
Registration closing date	−0.021**	(0.007)	−0.014	(0.011)	−0.045**	(0.013)
Election Day registration	2.980**	(1.008)	4.843**	(1.060)	. . .	. . .
Voting procedures:						
Hours polls are open	1.111	(0.862)	2.453**	(0.909)	−3.848	(2.453)
Hours polls are open squared	−0.080	(0.041)	−0.119**	(0.043)	0.121	(0.133)
In-person early voting	1.575	(0.949)	0.369	(0.995)	−1.115	(1.718)
Universal absentee voting	−0.383	(1.007)	1.784	(0.946)	−1.353	(5.694)
Electoral calendar:						
Gubernatorial race	−1.821**	(0.469)	−1.994**	(0.444)	1.186	(0.989)
Senate race	0.339**	(0.124)	0.360**	(0.147)	0.298	(0.432)
Contested House seats	0.049**	(0.010)	0.031**	(0.011)	−0.002	(0.013)
Initiatives on ballot	0.132*	(0.057)	0.152**	(0.060)	0.053	(0.282)
Vote margin	−0.084**	(0.013)	−0.062**	(0.011)	−0.057**	(0.022)
State demographics:						
Education	0.343**	(0.120)	0.356**	(0.113)	0.322	(0.256)
Per capita income	0.370*	(0.160)	0.140	(0.175)	−0.490	(0.383)
Black population	−0.679**	(0.112)	0.228	(0.138)	−0.149	(0.180)
Other population	−0.213*	(0.101)	−0.220*	(0.099)	−0.429	(0.256)
Age 45 or above	0.675**	(0.097)	0.508**	(0.106)	−0.176	(0.335)
Constant	40.798**	(7.415)	26.419**	(7.966)	64.955**	(15.259)
State fixed effects	Yes		Yes		Yes	
Year fixed effects	Yes		Yes		Yes	
N	1,030		799		231	
R^2	0.832		0.775		0.919	

Note: Panel-corrected standard errors are in parentheses.

*$p < .05$

**$p < .01$

negative effect also existed in the southern and nonsouthern comparison. They were shown to decrease turnout by nearly 4 percentage points in the southern states that implemented them (Alabama, Georgia, Louisiana, and South Carolina) and by over 6 percentage points in Rhode Island—the only nonsouthern state to have a property requirement during the period.[19] Incidentally, Rhode Island's presidential election year turnout increased dramatically after property requirements were eradicated in 1950. Before the property requirement was removed, presidential turnout averaged about 60% in the state, but over the five elections after its eradication (1952–68), turnout averaged over 70%. Voter turnout trends in Rhode Island are examined further in chapter 6.

Literacy tests were arguably the most severe and notorious restrictive electoral institutions used in the states throughout the century; yet, surprisingly, they had significant but somewhat inconsistent effects on turnout during the period. Results show that, overall, literacy tests decreased voting rates in model 1 by about 4.7 percentage points during presidential election years, and in the thirteen nonsouthern states that implemented them, voter turnout declined by over 3 percentage points. This suggests that in one-third of the nonsouthern states, the increased costs associated with the literacy test created a nontrivial deterrent to voting, one that is rarely recognized in this region.

At least five of the nonsouthern states (Alaska, Arizona, California, Hawaii, and New York) that implemented literacy tests also had sizable immigrant populations and, as I said earlier, cited curbing participation among these new groups as a reason for adopting literacy tests (Bolinger and Gaylord 1977). Further, as shown in chapter 3, these states also routinely had some of the lowest voting rates in the nation. Even now, the racist way literacy tests were implemented in the southern states evokes the familiar characterization of Jim Crow. So it is curious that, as shown in table 5.1, literacy tests did not have a statistically significant effect on turnout in the South (model 3). This finding, though unsatisfying at first glance, could arise because many of the southern states that required literacy tests also assessed poll taxes; as a result, the independent effect of the literacy test may be overwhelmed by the effect of the poll tax,[20] or it could be attributed to the smaller sample size in the South. The discrepancy could also reflect the indirect nature of the laws' effect on southern voting: the effect of the literacy test in the southern states may have been mitigated by the size of the states' black population.

Indeed, the link between literacy tests and race, particularly in the South, was steadfast. Even Justice Hugo Black, writing the Supreme Court's opinion for *Oregon v. Mitchell* (1970), cited the "long history of the discriminatory use of literacy tests to disenfranchise voters on account of their race" as the reason for the judicial decision. Table 5.2 presents interactive results testing this dynamic relationship, and reveals that the effect of a literacy test on state voter turnout during a presidential election appears to be related to the state's racial heterogeneity.[21] The literacy test did not have a statistically significant effect on southern turnout rates in the original model (model 1), but once the interaction term was included to capture the relationship between the implementation of a literacy test and the size of state's black population (model 2), the literacy test coefficient and the interaction term both became statistically significant. This suggests that the effect of having a literacy test intervenes in the direct effect between the size of a state's black population and southern voting rates; in other words, although a literacy test does not seem to directly affect state turnout, there is a moderating effect between race, the literacy test, and southern turnout.

As shown in model 2, once the interaction term is included in the analysis the literacy test variable effectively measures the influence of the test on turnout in a state with zero blacks. Although this scenario is implausible, the model suggests that the literacy test would have a very large (15.2) positive effect on turnout rates in such a state. The interaction term indicates, however, that the effect of the size of a state's black population on turnout is negative (−0.48) when the state has a literacy test. That is, the effect of literacy test, once the interaction is included, is large and positive, but it decreases somewhat as the size of the state's black population increases. To illustrate this relationship, consider that in a state where 12% of the population is black (the minimum in the southern states during the period), the adoption of a literacy test would create a sizable 15.13 percentage point increase in voter turnout; however, in a state with a 27% black population (the average in the southern states during the period), literacy tests provide a (slightly smaller) 15.06 percentage point boost. Finally, in states where 52% percent of the population is black (the maximum population in the southern states during the period), there is a 14.94 percentage point increase (even smaller). Overall, once the interactive effect of race is considered, these results suggest that the literacy test had a surprising positive effect on turnout in the southern states, but the magnitude of the positive effect decreases to some degree as the size of the state's black population increases.

Table 5.2 also presents interactive results for the literacy test and the size of a state's white population (model 3). It seems that the effect of a state's white population size on voter turnout in states with a literacy test is

Table 5.2 Southern Voter Turnout during Presidential Election Years, 1920–2000

Variable	Coefficients					
	Model 1		Model 2		Model 3	
Voting qualifications:						
Property requirement	−3.824**	(1.299)	−3.833**	(1.287)	−3.949**	(1.288)
Literacy test	0.299	(2.085)	15.190**	(5.031)	−32.123**	(10.079)
Literacy test × black population	. . .	. . .	−0.484**	(0.144)	. . .	. . .
Literacy test × white population	. . .	. . .	. . .	. . .	0.471**	(0.145)
Poll tax	−7.866**	(1.199)	−8.594**	(1.190)	−8.587**	(1.194)
Residency requirement	−0.007**	(0.002)	−0.007**	(0.002)	−0.007**	(0.002)
Voter registration:						
Frequency of periodic registration	0.017	(0.011)	0.003	(0.012)	0.003	(0.012)
Nonvoting purge period	0.006	(0.012)	0.003	(0.012)	0.003	(0.012)
Universal mail-in registration	−0.729	(1.318)	−1.675	(1.308)	−1.639	(1.308)
Motor voter registration	−3.481	(2.268)	−3.837	(2.244)	−3.860	(2.248)
Registration closing date	−0.045**	(0.013)	−0.034**	(0.013)	−0.035**	(0.013)
Election Day registration	. . .	. . .	. . .	. . .	. . .	. . .
Voting procedures:						
Hours polls are open	−3.848	(2.453)	−5.688*	(2.512)	−5.700*	(2.520)
Hours polls are open squared	0.121	(0.133)	0.224	(0.136)	0.224	(0.136)
In-person early voting	−1.115	(1.718)	−0.639	(1.771)	−0.652	(1.769)
Universal absentee voting	−1.353	(5.694)	−1.485	(5.828)	−1.551	(5.833)
Gubernatorial race	1.186	(0.989)	0.981	(0.945)	1.019	(0.948)
Senate race	0.298	(0.432)	0.270	(0.410)	0.270	(0.412)
Contested House seats	−0.002	(0.013)	−0.008	(0.013)	−0.008	(0.013)
Initiatives on ballot	0.053	(0.282)	0.071	(0.289)	0.071	(0.288)
Vote margin	−0.057**	(0.022)	−0.045*	(0.020)	−0.045*	(0.020)
State demographics:						
Education	0.322	(0.256)	0.420	(0.250)	0.415	(0.251)
Per capita income	−0.490	(0.383)	−0.069	(0.370)	−0.075	(0.373)
Black population	−0.149	(0.180)	0.360	(0.225)	0.619*	(0.292)
Other population	−0.429	(0.256)	−0.268	(0.244)	. . .	. . .
White population	. . .	. . .	. . .	. . .	0.278	(0.245)
Age 45 or above	−0.176	(0.335)	0.187	(0.317)	0.163	(0.320)
Constant	64.955**	(15.259)	52.239**	(14.881)	25.473	(22.855)
State fixed effects	Yes		Yes		Yes	
Year fixed effects	Yes		Yes		Yes	
N	231		231		231	
R^2	0.919		0.926		0.925	

Note: Panel-corrected standard errors are in parentheses.
*$p < .05$
**$p < .01$

positive (0.47) and statistically significant. This does not mean that the literacy test increases turnout—only that it increases the effect (or size of the association) between the state's white population size and voter turnout. In fact, the direct effect of a literacy test is very large and negative (-32.1), but the magnitude of the effect decreases to some degree as the number of whites in the state increases. For example, in a state where 48% of the population is white (the minimum in the southern states during the period), instituting a literacy test created a 31.9 percentage point decrease in turnout, whereas in a state with a 72% white population (the average white population in the southern states during this period), there is a 31.8 percentage point decrease. Finally, in a state where 87% of the population is white (the maximum in the southern states during the period), the literacy test created a decrease of 31.7 percentage points. So it seems that the negative effect on turnout associated with a literacy test is (slightly) smaller in states with large white populations. Overall, these interactive results indicate that a state's racial heterogeneity mitigated the effects of literacy tests on turnout in the South. I will pursue this complicated finding further in the case study of the southern states in chapter 7.

Besides literacy tests, poll taxes were arguably the most significant impediment to voting in the Jim Crow South. As expected, table 5.1 reveals that poll taxes had a sizable effect on presidential election year voting rates, depressing turnout in the full model (model 1) by nearly 6 percentage points. Of course all eleven southern states required the payment of a poll tax, typically six to twelve months before the general election. In the South the poll tax appears to have depressed turnout by nearly 8 percentage points. This is a substantial finding–nearly twice the decrease associated with the property requirement and far exceeding any other institutional effect in the region. According to the results, however, poll taxes did not significantly depress turnout in the handful of nonsouthern states that adopted them. There is some sense that the amount of the southern poll taxes in relation to the local economies, and the southern states' frequent stipulation that voters must first pay back taxes to qualify, created a burden for individuals that was not felt as severely outside the South. Further, the southern states assessed poll taxes much longer than their nonsouthern counterparts, suggesting that their effect might be felt more substantially in one region than in the other.

By the late twentieth century, permanent voter registration had become commonplace in the American states. Since then, most reform discussion has centered on easing the burdens of registration and making it more convenient. Late registration closing dates and Election Day registration, especially, are frequently touted for adding flexibility and expansiveness. The results presented here validate their potential for shaping participation rates. For example, as shown in table 5.1, early registration closing dates have affected voter turnout in interesting ways in both the southern and nonsouthern states. Specifically, as the time between the close of voter registration and Election Day increased by ten days, turnout decreased by a modest 0.2 percentage points in all states (model 1) and by about 0.5 percentage points in the South. This suggests that, depending on the timing of a state's closing date, the associated effects range from a 0.45 percentage point decrease in southern turnout in states with closing dates ten days before the election (the minimum during the period) to a sizable 8.10 percentage point decrease in states with closing dates 180 days before the election (the maximum during the period). This finding supports claims that early registration closing dates suppress voter turnout, particularly in the South.

In light of this finding, it is tempting to infer that moving closing dates substantially closer to Election Day—even adopting Election Day registration—could affect turnout positively. Indeed, consistent with previous research, this study demonstrates the increasing effects associated with the adoption of Election Day registration (Fenster 1994; Fitzgerald 2005; Hanmer 2009; Highton 1997; Knack 1995, 2001; Mitchell and Wlezien 1995; Teixeira 1992; Tolbert et al. 2008). Specifically, Election Day registration increased voter turnout by nearly 3 percentage points during presidential election years in model 1, and by nearly 5 percentage points in the nonsouthern states. This is a substantial institutional effect, the largest in the model. Incidentally, Election Day registration is a reform adopted entirely at the discretion of the individual states, not because of a federal mandate (Hanmer 2009). It also tends to be adopted by states with highly participatory populations (e.g., Idaho, Minnesota, and Wyoming), which I will discuss further in the nonsouthern case study in chapter 6. None of the southern states adopted Election Day registration between 1920 and 2000.

Neither the frequency of periodic registration nor universal mail-in registration had a statistically significant effect on southern or nonsouthern voter turnout during the twentieth century. Additionally, and perhaps most notably, motor voter, which was mandated by the federal government under the 1993 National Voter Registration Act and was expected to radically stimulate registration and voting throughout the United States, did not have statistically significant effects on state-level turnout in any of the states during the period.[22] This is consistent with previous studies that have evaluated the effects of the motor voter reform (and other registration reforms) and found only a minimal effect at best (Crocker 1996; Fitzgerald 2005; Franklin and Grier 1997; Highton and Wolfinger 1998; Knack 1995; Martinez and Hill 1999; Rhine 1995; Teixeira 1992). However, the act also mandated that covered states remove their nonvoting purge provisions. As shown in table 5.1, this appeared to have a significant, albeit small, positive effect on turnout in the nonsouthern states. Since states that eliminated the purge were assigned 100, results suggest that eliminating the purge corresponded to a nearly 1 percentage point increase in nonsouthern voter turnout.

Taken together, these findings are important, since much of the motivation for the 1993 National Voter Registration Act was to ease the costs of voting for disadvantaged individuals, especially those who suffer socioeconomically. Although the data used in this analysis cannot provide information about the characteristics of the individual voters affected by motor voter or the nonvoting purge, the results do reveal that motor voter was largely ineffective at increasing voting rates in southern and nonsouthern states alike; and the removal of the nonvoting purge affected nonsouthern turnout only marginally. This finding validates concerns that easing registration processes may do little to increase actual voting (Timpone 1998) and suggests that perhaps the legacy of the National Voter Registration Act was not to increase turnout but to loosen the long-observed empirical ties between registration and voting (Erikson 1981; Brown and Wedeking 2006). The weaker effects of the registration reforms on turnout could be evidence that over time such reforms are succeeding by making registration less predictive of voting and therefore less of a politically manipulated barrier to voting (Berinsky 2005; Hanmer 2009; Highton 2004).

Finally, table 5.1 presents some interesting results about the effects of voting procedures on state voting rates. Although the literature is generally mixed on the effects of in-person early voting and universal absentee voting (Fitzgerald 2005; Gronke, Galanes-Rosenbaum, and Miller 2007; Gronke et al. 2008; Hansen 2001; Oliver 1996; Richardson and Neeley 1996; Stein 1998; Stein and Garcia-Monet 1997; Stein, Leighley, and Owens 2005), these reforms, particularly in-person early voting, are growing in popularity across the nation. This study shows that neither reform had a statistically significant effect on voter turnout during the period. Of course these laws are comparatively new, and it might take longer to realize their effects.

The total number of hours the polls are open on Election Day, however, exhibited an interesting curvilinear relationship with presidential election year turnout in the nonsouthern states (model 2). When the marginal effects of the poll hours and poll hours squared terms are calculated, it appears that longer poll hours always predict increased turnout (Wolfinger and Rosenstone 1980; Wolfinger, Highton, and Mullin 2005). The real difference is between states with short polling windows (e.g., four to five hours) and those that keep their polls open for nine to ten hours. Keeping the polls open longer seems to have little additional effect, and there may even be a downturn after eleven hours. This suggests that there is a point (around ten hours) at which state turnout rates are maximized (i.e., the number of potential voters who are going to vote have voted), and keeping the polls open an additional hour will not generate higher turnout.

Noninstitutional Effects

Thus far, state electoral institutions have been shown to have a real but rather modest effect on presidential election year turnout throughout the twentieth century; yet we must also consider the political environment in which elections take place and the effect of important demographic variables.

First, several of the electoral calendar measures had a statistically significant effect on twentieth-century voting rates, particularly in the nonsouthern states (model 2). As shown in table 5.1, concurrent Senate races and contested House seats both generated modest increases in turnout. Also, consistent with previous findings (Smith and Tolbert 2007; Tolbert and Smith 2005), ballot initiatives positively affected nonsouthern turnout rates by 0.15 percentage points. The results also suggest that gubernatorial races decreased nonsouthern turnout by nearly 2 percentage points. Typically, gubernatorial elections coincide with congressional midterm elections, so the negative result during presidential election years may be an artifact of the variable's infrequency during the presidential analysis. Although this finding is consistent with previous research (Patterson and Caldeira 1983), there is no clear-cut reason to believe that gubernatorial elections in themselves depress turnout. Note that none of these election-specific variables had a statistically significant effect on voting rates in the South.

Political competition is also an important aspect of electoral politics and participation in American elections. Accordingly, findings suggest that decreased competition (or larger vote margins) is associated with declining turnout. Specifically, as the difference between the winner's and loser's vote margin increased—generating less electoral competition and a safer victory—turnout declined by about 0.06 percentage points in both the southern and nonsouthern states. This result is consistent with many who have argued that competitive political environments can induce civic participation, whereas limited competition may depress turnout (Cassel 1979; Dye 1984; Hofstetter 1973; Key 1949; Patterson and Caldeira 1983; Rosenstone and Hansen 1993).

This is a particularly interesting finding given Key's (1949) hypothesis that a lack of electoral competition, not restrictive electoral institutions, depressed southern voting rates. Of course it is clear that these factors are interrelated. For example, if there is no viable electoral contest, interest in the election may wane, and voters will not bother to confront procedural voting hurdles; however, the results in this chapter suggest that variation in state and regional participation rates cannot be entirely explained either by competition or by institutions. Indeed, even if they have had a small effect, many electoral institutions have, in fact, altered turnout rates even after controlling for electoral competition within and outside the South. The institutional focus of this book, however, does not dismiss the competition argument but reveals that many electoral institutions have altered voting rates even after controlling for competition.[23] The effect of electoral competition in relation to electoral institutions will be pursued further in the following chapters.

Despite the inclusion of state and year fixed effects, which can swamp the explanatory power of aggregate demographic variables, many important classic state demographic indicators also generated significant results in the models. In particular, education and age each boosted nonsouthern turnout by about 0.4 percentage points. The finding regarding age, in particular, underscores the important role a state's older population may have had on voting rates throughout much of the century. Over time this suggests that they have a disproportionate effect on the content of the policy agenda and the nature of representation, as Campbell (2003) has suggested. Additionally, racial heterogeneity had a small negative effect on nonsouthern turnout. None of the state demographic variables were statistically significant in the southern states.

Evaluating Institutional Effects over Time

The results in table 5.1 examined the direct effect that a number of electoral laws had on twentieth-century state turnout. In this section I present an additional analysis evaluating whether institutional effects evolve over time. I aim to determine whether, for example, the decrease in turnout after the introduction of a restrictive voting law occurs after several elections as behavioral responses to these laws adapt, or if the change is more immediate (and thus, ostensibly, more of a direct institutional effect). The analysis is focused on those institutions that had the largest and most robust effects in the models presented in table 5.1. Count variables were constructed for each of the electoral institution variables. These new count variables measured the number of years the state had a given law (e.g., the state was assigned a 1 for the first year it had the law, a 2 in the second election year with the policy, a 3 in the next, and so on); a transformed version of this variable (squared) was also included to test for nonlinear effects where indicated. Overall, the previous results were supported when the number of years since enactment was considered, but there were a few notable findings.

First, outside the South, Election Day registration continued to have a positive linear effect on voter turnout even when modeled as a count variable. In adopting states, Election Day registration increased turnout by 1.35 percentage points every year the state had the policy.[24] The effects associated with the literacy test, however, were curvilinear and varied depending on the number of years the state employed the restriction.[25] As shown in figure 5.1, the predicted marginal effects of the literacy test on nonsouthern voting rates suggest that turnout decreases steadily for the first few years the state has the restriction, but after some time (around the six-year mark) the negative effects begin to taper off and the literacy test begins to have a

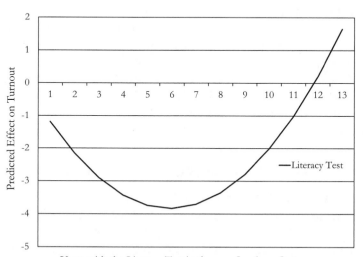

Years with the Literacy Test in the non-Southern States

5.1. Timing of literacy test effects in the nonsouthern states

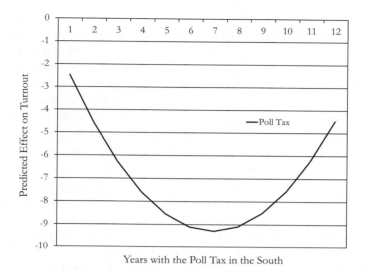

Years with the Poll Tax in the South

5.2. Timing of poll tax effects in the southern states

slightly smaller negative effect on voting rates—and perhaps even a slight positive effect. Additionally, in the South the poll tax exhibited an interesting effect on turnout over time. As shown in figure 5.2, the relationship is curvilinear. The poll tax appears to decrease southern turnout steadily over the first seven years after the restriction is adopted, then, during years eight through twelve, the negative effect becomes less pronounced.

Taken together, the results from this additional analysis suggest that, when they occur, the effects of expansive reforms—or at least Election Day registration—continue to increase steadily the longer the state has the institution. In contrast, the effects associated with restrictive laws—such as the literacy test outside the South and the poll tax in the southern states—negatively affect participation, but the effects seem to taper off over time. Further work might aim to illuminate the basis for the variation in effects over time—to determine, for example, whether the tapering off of effects associated with restrictive laws is due to voter learning or to varying partisan mobilization (or demobilization) strategies.

Discussion

Overall, the analysis of presidential voter turnout rates—typically the nation's highest—confirms that the influence twentieth-century electoral institutions have had on voting has been exceptionally diverse. Although the results suggest that these institutions have affected state turnout even after controlling for demographic and election-specific influences, an asymmetry exists in the effects of expansive and restrictive institutions. It seems that the institutions that yielded the largest and most consistent effects on turnout are restrictive (cost-increasing), not expansive (cost-decreasing), reforms. This runs contrary to the expectation of reformers, who have argued that in the absence of an initiative to dramatically ease the costs of participation, turnout suffers. In fact, as I have demonstrated throughout this chapter, electoral institutions do not all affect voter turnout equally.

Findings suggest that restrictive electoral institutions, especially those pertaining to voting qualifications, have consistently depressed state turnout throughout the century, while expansive, or cost-reducing reforms, demonstrate more variable effects. Though at first the findings about restrictive institutions may seem inconsequential in an era of convenience reform initiatives, restrictive electoral institutions are not uncommon, especially since many states continue to adopt restrictive voter identification laws and also require proof of citizenship.

For example, in 2006 Georgia enacted cost-increasing legislation requiring voters to show one of seven forms of government-issued photo identification when voting. Although Georgia is one of several states that now require voters to provide photo identification, the formats of the new laws are particularly restrictive. Previously, voters in Georgia could show one of seventeen forms of identification, including nonphoto identification such as birth certificates, Social Security cards, utility bills, payroll checks, and other documents bearing a name and address. The new photo identification requirement, however, is costly to individuals who are fully eligible, registered, and qualified to vote but who do not have a Georgia driver's license, passport, employer identification card, or other forms of photo identification issued by the state or federal government. To comply with the new legislation, those lacking one of the approved documents must pay twenty to thirty-five dollars for a state-issued identification card, in addition to their travel costs to get one. This process is particularly costly, since only 56 of Georgia's 159 counties offer the cards, at a handful of state agencies. Accordingly, some opponents of this legislation have referred to it as a modern-day poll tax of sorts and argued that it disproportionately affects blacks, the poor, the sick, and the elderly by making it harder to vote. This type of restrictive law, as I have demonstrated throughout this chapter, is bound to have real consequences for already low turnout rates in Georgia and the other adopting states.

In addition to demonstrating asymmetry in effects, this study's historical focus can also inform our expectations about how institutional changes affect turnout rates. Examining restrictive and expansive reforms together over eighty years emphasizes the importance of these institutions and provides historical context for understanding the effects of institutional change. Generally it is unreasonable to think one can alter an electoral institution and produce a 20% increase in voter turnout. In fact, the results presented here reveal that the gains generated by expansive reforms, where they exist, are modest and incremental; yet this study has also shown that small percentages are far from trivial. The magnitudes of many of the effects of expansive reforms are comparable to those of the early restrictive measures. For example, the adoption of Election Day registration increased turnout in all states by almost half as much as poll taxes depressed them— and outside the South, Election Day registration increased voting rates by nearly twice as much as literacy tests decreased them. When we analyze results throughout the century and compare them with earlier reforms, we find that the tendency of cost-reducing reforms to alter voting rates is more variable than that of restrictive laws; but when they do generate effects, they are comparable in size to those of other institutional changes. This has been overlooked in more limited studies.

Finally, and perhaps most striking, this analysis has revealed important differences between the effects of electoral institutions in the southern and nonsouthern states, especially with regard to expansive reforms. Although we might expect the largest institutional effects to occur in places where there is the most to gain (those with the lowest voting rates), like the southern states, the analysis presented in this chapter demonstrates that expansive reforms have increased turnout only in the nonsouthern states. Taken together, these findings raise several important questions. Why do some electoral institutions affect turnout while others do not? How much does location matter? Are the regional effects driven by state-specific effects? Do these state and regional relationships change over time? There are a number of possible answers to these questions; each necessitates further investigation into the comparative state dynamics in these two regions, the focus of the case studies in the following chapters.

Nonpresidential Election Years, 1922–98

Let me briefly discuss institutional effects during nonpresidential election years from 1922 to 1998, which are less salient and have lower participation than years with a presidential election. As shown in table 5.3, many of

Table 5.3 State-Level Voter Turnout during Nonpresidential Election Years, 1922–98

Variable	Model 1: All States		Model 2: Nonsouthern		Model 3: Southern	
	Coefficients					
Voting qualifications:						
Property requirement	−4.940**	(1.581)	−0.570	(2.430)	−5.122**	(1.818)
Literacy test	−2.392**	(0.861)	−1.599	(0.933)	1.386	(1.932)
Poll tax	−6.282**	(1.262)	−3.224	(1.668)	−6.278**	(1.418)
Residency requirement	0.002	(0.003)	0.001	(0.004)	−0.002	(0.003)
Voter registration:						
Frequency of periodic registration	0.001	(0.009)	−0.001	(0.010)	−0.016	(0.018)
Nonvoting purge period	−0.002	(0.006)	0.006	(0.006)	−0.001	(0.013)
Universal mail-in registration	0.369	(0.710)	0.313	(0.806)	−1.004	(1.450)
Motor voter registration	−0.014	(1.146)	0.726	(1.025)	−0.603	(2.197)
Registration closing date	0.003	(0.009)	−0.014	(0.014)	0.005	(0.014)
Election Day registration	3.014*	(1.311)	4.236**	(1.360)	. . .	. . .
Voting procedures:						
Hours polls are open	1.055	(1.303)	1.917	(1.246)	−0.436	(2.858)
Hours polls are open squared	−0.052	(0.061)	−0.067	(0.061)	−0.018	(0.148)
In-person early voting	2.215	(1.474)	−0.193	(1.648)	0.589	(2.492)
Universal absentee voting	−0.749	(1.512)	1.566	(1.487)	. . .	. . .
Electoral calendar:						
Gubernatorial race	2.613*	(1.231)	0.217	(1.300)	4.875*	(2.355)
Senate race	1.587**	(0.280)	1.396**	(0.309)	1.984**	(0.543)
Contested House seats	0.057**	(0.012)	0.034*	(0.015)	0.023	(0.017)
Initiatives on ballot	0.319**	(0.088)	0.292**	(0.095)	−0.109	(0.578)
Vote margin	−0.109**	(0.011)	−0.087**	(0.012)	−0.111**	(0.015)
State demographics:						
Education	0.593**	(0.131)	0.460**	(0.140)	0.224	(0.299)
Per capita income	−0.055	(0.202)	−0.130	(0.248)	−0.720	(0.440)
Black population	−0.359**	(0.143)	0.156	(0.224)	0.230	(0.219)
Other population	−0.037	(0.115)	−0.150	(0.128)	0.118	(0.283)
Age 45 or above	0.660**	(0.104)	0.378**	(0.140)	0.644	(0.362)
Constant	17.148	(9.539)	18.658	(9.761)	9.981	(17.750)
State fixed effects	Yes		Yes		Yes	
Year fixed effects	Yes		Yes		Yes	
N	976		760		216	
R^2	0.801		0.691		0.878	

Note: Panel-corrected standard errors are in parentheses.

*$p < .05$

**$p < .01$

the restrictive voting qualifications that depressed turnout during presidential election years also constrained voting during nonpresidential election years. For example, property requirements were associated with a nearly 5 percentage point decrease in turnout for all states (model 1) and a decline of over 5 percentage points in the southern states (model 3). This reflects an increase of nearly 2 percentage points from the effects noted in the southern states during presidential election years. Additionally, similar to the findings during presidential election years, literacy tests depressed turnout in all states by over 2 percentage points—about half the magnitude they had during presidential election years. They did not, however, have a statistically significant effect on turnout in the southern and nonsouthern comparison. Finally, poll taxes decreased turnout by over 6 percentage points both in all states (model 1) and in the southern states (model 3) during nonpresidential election years. These results are similar in magnitude to the effects presented in the presidential model.

Like the presidential election year models, voter registration reforms continued to have a minimal effect on voting rates during nonpresidential election years. In fact, only Election Day registration increased voter turnout by over 3 percentage points in all states (model 1), and by over 4 percentage points in the nonsouthern states (model 2). Additionally, unlike the presidential models, where the total number of hours the polls are open on Election Day had a statistically significant effect on nonsouthern turnout, none of the convenient voting procedures examined in this study influenced voter turnout during nonpresidential election years.

Beyond institutional effects, electoral environment seemed to really influence nonpresidential turnout. For example, gubernatorial races increased southern turnout by a substantial 5 percentage points, whereas concurrent Senate races positively affected turnout in both the southern and nonsouthern states by over 1 percentage point. Contested House seats and ballot initiatives also increased turnout outside the South. Finally, vote margin seemed to play a big role in shaping turnout during nonpresidential election years. As the vote margin between the winner and loser of the highest race on the ballot increased by one hundred votes (a less competitive race), turnout declined by about 1 percentage point across all of the modeling specifications (all states, nonsouthern states, and southern states).

Finally, similar to the presidential models, state demographic variables had an effect on turnout in the nonsouthern states during nonpresidential election years. For example, both education *and* age increased turnout outside the South. Racial heterogeneity also seemed to play a role in model 1; specifically, as the black population in a state increased, turnout declined, but the variable was not statistically significant in the regional comparison. In fact, like the model during presidential election years, none of the demographic variables were statistically significant in the southern states during nonpresidential election years.

The comparison between institutional, election-specific, and demographic effects during presidential and nonpresidential election years reinforces a fairly persistent finding in studies examining the effects of reforms on aggregate turnout rates: that different patterns of political behavior exist across different types of elections (Fitzgerald 2005; Knack 1995; Tolbert et al. 2008). It appears that electoral institutions—of any sort, but predominately expansive institutions—affect state turnout less during nonpresidential election years than during presidential election years. This is presumably due, at least in part, to the salience of the election. Because nonpresidential elections garner comparatively less interest, mobilization efforts, and engagement than presidential elections, the motivating effects of expansive institutions in particular are tapered. In short, it seems that simply making voting or registration more convenient is not enough to motivate voters to participate during less salient elections—especially in the southern states where turnout has suffered the most.

Conclusion

Because electoral institutions are adaptable, they hold—at least in theory—remarkable potential as mechanisms for change in political participation. The main goal of this chapter has been to demonstrate empirically that a robust relationship has existed between expansive and restrictive state electoral institutions and state turnout throughout the twentieth century. The analysis presented here has revealed an asymmetry between the effects associated with expansive institutions and with restrictive institutions. The statistical models demonstrate that restrictive electoral laws routinely depress participation, whereas expansive reform initiatives typically do not produce substantial increases in voter turnout. Yet this does not necessarily mean electoral reform has failed (Berinsky 2005; Gronke et al. 2008; Hammer 2009; Traugott 2004); instead, perhaps we have been unrealistic in expecting any single reform to induce people to participate. Additionally, we must appreciate the hand of history in shaping state participation patterns. In fact, although the analyses reveal that restrictive laws consistently depressed turnout where they were implemented, history has generally led to these laws' being abandoned. If we considered the absence of the restrictive law rather than its presence, we would see large positive reform effects over time. Indeed, this suggests that removing burdens to voting greatly expands the proportion of the population who vote, while measures to make voting easier for those already inclined to go to the polls increase turnout only moderately (which makes sense, if the latter reform affects only those with a high propensity to vote).

So where does this leave us? Rather than offering a pessimistic verdict about the limitations of institutional change for altering political behavior, this study reveals that we must modify our expectations and strive to identify where and when institutional changes might be most necessary and successful. Although policy makers have routinely assumed that electoral reforms would produce equivalent effects wherever they are implemented, regardless of geography or political history, there is no "one size fits all" institutional solution for altering voter turnout in the United States. Although cost-reducing reforms might increase voter turnout in the nonsouthern states, given their history of expansiveness, the southern states, steeped in a longer history of restrictiveness, may not respond the same way. The history of restricted voting in the southern states might require a different type of reform. It could be that to truly overcome the social and economic legacy of disenfranchisement, inclusion and electoral commitment must be felt, and practiced, more fully in that region. This might necessitate socioeconomic initiatives in addition to electoral reforms.

At a minimum, recognizing both regional and state variation in twentieth-century institutional effects and electoral history is critical to informing future policy decisions about reform at both the state and the federal levels. It may also help us establish more realistic expectations about how electoral reform can affect behavior as we move through the twenty-first century. The analyses presented in this chapter demonstrate that electoral institutions have some effect (though perhaps smaller than expected) on voting rates, as do political competition and state demographics—but to varying degrees. Further, they affect turnout in a somewhat counterintuitive way. In states that have high rates of electoral participation (for reasons having nothing to do with institutions), institutions promote voting more than they do in states where rates are low (for reasons having nothing to do with institutions). By the same token, in states—particularly southern states—that have long histories of restricting suffrage, expansive electoral institutions do much less to increase turnout than they do in nonsouthern states that are already highly participatory. This underscores that an inherently dynamic process is at work, and that political development casts a very long shadow across states and regions. That idea animates the central premise of this book—that recognizing the developmental and temporal dimension of electoral federalism is essential for understanding voting in the United States.

The following chapters focus directly on these regional dynamics. The region-specific analyses in chapters 6 and 7 are motivated by the differing effects that exist between the southern and nonsouthern states. They aim to discover what else might be going on to complicate institutional effects, highlighting the dynamic nature of the electoral process. As shown in these case studies, some of the differences may be attributed to varying institutional profiles (histories of expansiveness or restrictiveness) or aspects of demographics and culture (e.g., racial heterogeneity, civic norms regarding participation). Chapter 6 evaluates several high turnout states outside the South, paying particular attention to the Midwest. Generally turnout in the Midwest has been well above the national average throughout the twentieth century, so the chapter will assess the particularities of the electoral laws and voting culture throughout this region. Since many of the states outside the South did not enact any of the restrictive voting qualifications but were early adopters of many of the expansive electoral reforms, the chapter will explore the effect expansive electoral laws have in the absence of restrictive laws. It will examine whether the high turnout in some nonsouthern states is promoted by, or associated with, a longer history of expansive electoral rules. Then chapter 7 examines the consistently low turnout in the southern states and further explores the historical relationship between voting and electoral institutions in the South given its long history of limiting participation and the unique political environment that constrained electoral competition for much of the century.

SIX

Where Are the High Turnout States?

The American federal system infuses geographical boundaries with political substance. The division between state and national politics, broadly, and among independent actors within the states more specifically, has political consequences. Federalism allows the states to foster local interests by adopting policies that suit the preferences of their citizens. As Key observed,

> The creation of a federal system implies the existence of territorial differences among people of the nation. To some degree these geographical political cleavages solve themselves by the division of powers between the national and state governments. So long as a sphere of action remains solely in the hands of the states, the people of New York cannot, through the national government, impose their views about a matter within that sphere upon the people of Texas or vice versa. (1956, 21)

Among other things, the states have the power to create a variety of electoral environments. As I have demonstrated throughout this book, the way the states have managed their electoral processes during the twentieth century has often been independent from other states and, in many cases, from the federal government. Federalism has allowed the states to create fifty unique electoral processes tailor-made to fit their publics.

Given the importance of elections in the American political system and the impressive power the states historically have had in structuring voting processes, one would expect varying institutional structures to generate political consequences. As I demonstrated in chapter 5, the nature of state electoral institutions—how expansive or restrictive they are—can alter voter participation to varying degrees. And regional differences in both the quality of electoral institutions and their effects have emerged throughout the twentieth century. Most apparent are the distinct differences between voter turnout and electoral institutions in the nonsouthern states and the southern states. More generally, as Onuf noted in his discussion of regionalism, "The most powerful explanation for sectional difference was to be found in the divergent development of Northerners and Southerners" (1996, 11). Over and over, it appears that voting rates are consistently high, or at least significantly above the national average, in many midwestern and western and even some northeastern states, while voter turnout in the southern states is routinely low. My aim in this book has been to link these state turnout patterns with the adoption or removal of varying restrictive or expansive electoral laws.

This chapter presents in-depth state investigations of the nonsouthern states that have routinely had high voting rates during the twentieth century. I selected the sample based on norms pertaining to case study analysis as established in the literature on qualitative and quantitative methods (e.g., Eckstein 1975; Geering 2004, 2007; George and Bennett 2004; King, Keohane, and Verba 1994, 1995; Lazarsfeld and Barton 1951; Mahoney and Goertz 2006; Munck 1998; Pierson 2004). The rationale for focusing on these states is that if the high turnout states in the Midwest, West, and Northeast have similarly expansive voting laws or exhibit similar patterns in adopting particular laws, that may add substance and specificity to the claim that electoral institutions have influenced participation. Additionally, it could be that high turnout patterns originate from early institutional changes and are nurtured by a longer expansive electoral history. As shown in chapter 4, many of the midwestern states, at least, tended to adopt more expansive voting laws before other states throughout the nation. Perhaps states with consistently high turnout throughout the century have had longer histories of being expansive than states in other regions and possibly even within the same region. To explore the institutional adoption patterns of distinctively high turnout states, I begin this chapter by evaluating whether a state's unique institutional history appears to directly condition the effects of institutional change on turnout.

Although low turnout in the southern states is easily conceived as a predominately institutional story (the steady and long-standing implementation of restrictive electoral laws under Jim Crow), the consistently high turnout in many of the nonsouthern states from 1920 to 2000 is somewhat harder to explain. In many ways the high turnout states outside the South exhibit an amalgam of qualities that could affect their turnout rates beyond the effects of electoral institutions. Thus this chapter begins to explore some of the most distinctive aspects of these states, evaluating the nature of their electoral institutions. It also looks at other noninstitutional aspects of the states' political environments that may contribute to their high participation rates. In doing so it evaluates a variety of potential turnout-boosting aspects of the voting culture and voting environments in these high turnout states. In particular, it explores the states' institutional tendencies and patterns of electoral expansiveness, evaluates their racial and ethnic homogeneity and perspective on "otherness" as they relate to the enactment of restrictive or expansive electoral laws, characterizes their political culture, and discusses the influences of heightened electoral competition, party activity, mobilization, and the overall strength of political partisanship on participation patterns.

Classifying High Turnout States outside the South

As shown in chapter 3, there are distinct regional patterns in state voter turnout throughout the twentieth century. Overall, the states in the Midwest exhibited consistently high turnout over time, followed closely by many states in the West and in some cases the Northeast. Within these regional patterns, individual states have repeatedly experienced high, or above average, turnout throughout the century. Accordingly, this analysis of nonsouthern states focuses on those states with exceptionally and consistently high turnout within their regions. To evaluate the electoral environments—institutional and otherwise—that are common in the "high turnout" states, we must first identify which states should be considered high turnout. To discover which midwestern, western, and northeastern states routinely exhibited high turnout throughout the century, I evaluated each state in terms of the consistency (How frequently does it exhibit turnout above the national average?) and magnitude (How high are its turnout rates throughout the century?) of its turnout during presidential and nonpresidential election years from 1920 to 2000. Tables 6.1, 6.2, and 6.3 identify the states with turnout rates consistently above the national average during all (or all but one) presidential or nonpresidential election years during the period and note whether they had the highest turnout (in magnitude) in the region for 50% or more of those years. This evaluation allowed me to classify "high turnout" states within each nonsouthern region.

As shown in table 6.1, of the fourteen midwestern states, five are clas-

Table 6.1 Identifying "High Turnout" States in the Midwest, 1920–2000

| Midwestern States | Turnout Rates above the National Average | | | | Ranked with Highest Turnout for 50% (or More) of Series | |
| | Presidential Years | | Nonpresidential Years | | | |
	During All	During All But One	During All	During All But One	During Presidential Years	During Non-presidential Years
Illinois	X	. . .	. . .	X	. . .	. . .
Indiana	. . .	X	. . .	X	X	X
Iowa	X	. . .	. . .	. . .	X	. . .
Kansas	X	. . .	. . .	X	. . .	. . .
Kentucky	. . .	. . .	. . .	. . .	. . .	. . .
Michigan	. . .	. . .	. . .	. . .	. . .	. . .
Minnesota	X	. . .	X	. . .	X	. . .
Missouri	X	. . .	. . .	. . .	. . .	. . .
Nebraska	. . .	X	X	. . .	. . .	. . .
North Dakota	X	. . .	X	. . .	X	X
Ohio	X	. . .	. . .	. . .	. . .	. . .
Oklahoma	. . .	. . .	. . .	. . .	. . .	. . .
South Dakota	X	. . .	X	. . .	X	X
Wisconsin	X	. . .	. . .	. . .	. . .	. . .

Note: States in boldface are classified as "high turnout states" in the region and are the focus of the discussion throughout the chapter.

sified as high turnout during the twentieth century: Illinois, Indiana, Minnesota, North Dakota, and South Dakota. Figures 6.1 and 6.2 present the presidential and nonpresidential election year voting rates for these states. Impressively, Minnesota, North Dakota, and South Dakota each had turnout above the national average during all presidential and all nonpresidential election years from 1920 to 2000. The magnitudes of their turnout, compared with other states in the region, were also substantial. As shown previously in table 3.1, South Dakota had one of the top ten highest rates for 71% of presidential election years during the period and for 80% of nonpresidential election years; and North Dakota was ranked in the top ten for 67% of presidential and 65% of nonpresidential election years. Minnesota also ranked high; it was in the top ten for 57% of presidential and 40% of nonpresidential election years. Indiana also exhibited turnout above the national average during all but one presidential election year and all but one nonpresidential election year. It was also ranked in the top ten during 62% of presidential election years in the series and 60% of nonpresidential election years. Finally, Illinois had turnout above the national

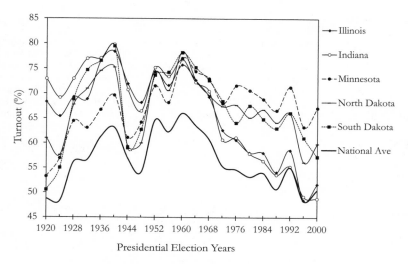

6.1. Turnout in the "high turnout" midwestern states, 1920–2000

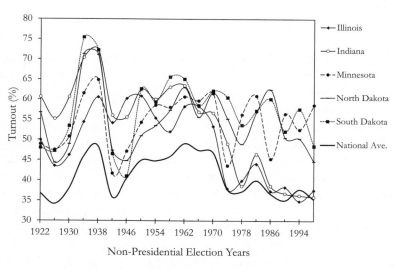

6.2. Turnout in the "high turnout" midwestern states, 1922–98

Table 6.2 Identifying "High Turnout" States in the West, 1920–2000

Western States	Turnout Rates above the National Average				Ranked with Highest Turnout for 50% or More) of Series	
	Presidential Years		Nonpresidential Years		During Presidential Years	During Nonpresidential Years
	During All	During All But One	During All	During All But One		
Alaska	. . .	. . .	. . .	. . .	. . .	. . .
Arizona	. . .	. . .	. . .	. . .	. . .	. . .
California	. . .	. . .	. . .	. . .	. . .	. . .
Colorado	X	. . .	X	. . .	. . .	. . .
Hawaii	. . .	. . .	X	. . .	. . .	. . .
Idaho	X	. . .	X	. . .	X	X
Montana	X	. . .	X	. . .	. . .	X
Nevada	. . .	. . .	. . .	. . .	. . .	. . .
New Mexico	. . .	. . .	. . .	X	. . .	. . .
Oregon	X	. . .	. . .	X	. . .	. . .
Utah	X	. . .	. . .	X	X	X
Washington	. . .	X	. . .	. . .	. . .	. . .
Wyoming	X	. . .	X	. . .	. . .	X

Note: States in boldface are classified as "high turnout states" in the region and are the focus of the discussion throughout the chapter.

average during all presidential election years from 1920 to 2000 and all but one nonpresidential election years from 1922 to 1998. Voting rates were also fairly high in Illinois, ranking in the top ten for 48% of presidential and 20% of nonpresidential election years.

As shown in table 6.2, five of the thirteen western states are classified as high turnout states during the twentieth century: Colorado, Idaho, Montana, Utah, and Wyoming. Figures 6.3 and 6.4 present the presidential and nonpresidential election year voting rates for these states. Impressively, turnout in Colorado, Idaho, Montana, and Wyoming was above the national average during all presidential and all nonpresidential election years from 1920 to 2000; however, the magnitude of the rates varies. Idaho exhibited top ten turnout during 57% of the presidential election years and 70% of the nonpresidential election years. Additionally, Utah displayed higher than average turnout during all presidential and all but one nonpresidential election years. The magnitude of Utah's turnout rates is notable. It ranked in the top ten during 86% of the presidential election years in the study and 65% of the nonpresidential election years. The other states' rankings are a bit more variable: Colorado was in the top ten during

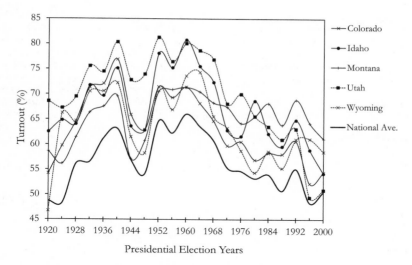

6.3. Turnout in the "high turnout" western states, 1920–2000

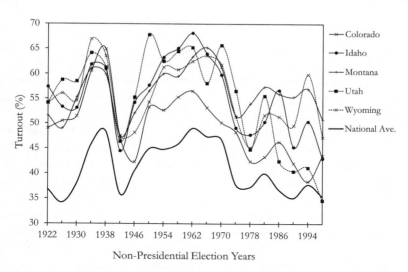

6.4. Turnout in the "high turnout" western states, 1922–98

Table 6.3 Identifying "High Turnout" States in the Northeast, 1920–2000

Northeastern States	Turnout Rates above the National Average				Ranked with Highest Turnout for 50% or More) of Series	
	Presidential Years		Nonpresidential Years		During Presidential Years	During Nonpresidential Years
	During All	During All But One	During All	During All But One		
Connecticut	. . .	X	X	. . .	. . .	X
Delaware	X	. . .	. . .	. . .	. . .	. . .
Maine	. . .	. . .	. . .	. . .	. . .	. . .
Maryland	. . .	. . .	. . .	. . .	. . .	. . .
Massachusetts	. . .	. . .	X	. . .	. . .	. . .
New Hampshire	. . .	X	. . .	. . .	. . .	. . .
New Jersey	. . .	X	. . .	. . .	. . .	. . .
New York	. . .	. . .	. . .	. . .	. . .	. . .
Pennsylvania	. . .	. . .	. . .	. . .	. . .	. . .
Rhode Island	X	. . .	X	. . .	. . .	. . .
Vermont	. . .	X	. . .	. . .	. . .	. . .
West Virginia	. . .	. . .	. . .	. . .	X	. . .

Note: States in boldface are classified as "high turnout states" in the region and are the focus of the discussion throughout the chapter.

14% of presidential and 15% of nonpresidential election years; Montana was in the top ten during 38% of presidential and 80% of nonpresidential election years; and Wyoming was in the top ten during 24% of presidential and 85% of nonpresidential election years.

Finally, table 6.3 presents the two northeastern states classified as high turnout during the twentieth century: Connecticut and Rhode Island. Figures 6.5 and 6.6 show the presidential and nonpresidential election year voting rates for these states. Rhode Island is the only northeastern state that consistently had turnout above the national average during all presidential and all nonpresidential election years from 1920 to 2000, but the magnitudes of these rates vary. Rhode Island's turnout was ranked in the top ten for only 5% of presidential election years during the century and 30% of nonpresidential election years. Additionally, Connecticut had turnout above the national average during all but one presidential election and all nonpresidential elections throughout the period. The magnitude of Connecticut's turnout is comparatively high, ranking in the top ten during 43% of presidential and 40% of nonpresidential election years. These "high turnout" nonsouthern states will be the focus of the rest of the chapter.

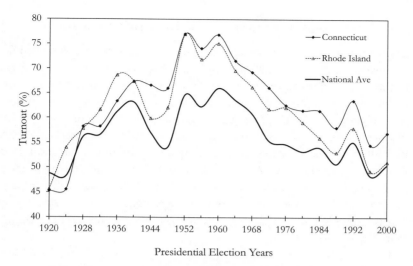

6.5. Turnout in the "high turnout" northeastern states, 1920–2000

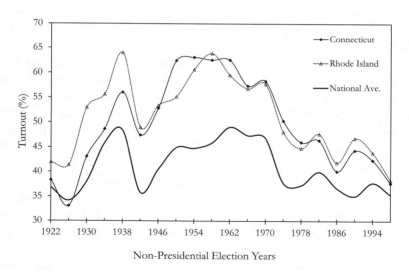

6.6. Turnout in the "high turnout" northeastern states, 1922–98

Electoral Institutions in the High Turnout States

Although the empirical analysis in chapter 5 demonstrated that several restrictive and expansive electoral institutions had an effect on voter turnout
in the nonsouthern states throughout the twentieth century, it remains to
be shown how individual institutions map onto states with disproportionately high turnout. For example, it would be useful to understand the
distinct properties of electoral institutions within these consistently high
turnout areas: Do the states with regularly high turnout share institutional
similarities? And how different are they institutionally from the other states
in the same region? To address these questions, this section will compare
the types of electoral institutions that have been adopted in the states with
consistently high turnout during presidential and nonpresidential election
years from 1920 to 2000.

Overall, the high turnout midwestern states—Illinois, Indiana, Minnesota, North Dakota, and South Dakota—implemented the most expansive electoral laws compared with states in the other regions. Perhaps most
significant, unlike many of the American states throughout the twentieth
century, none of the states in the Midwest—high turnout or otherwise—
imposed property requirements, administered literacy tests, or assessed
poll taxes as a qualification for voting. As a result, none of these states have
a history, or legacy, of the overt restrictiveness and disenfranchisement that
occurred in some of the other nonsouthern states (and obviously in the
South). On the other hand, each of these states had fairly long residency
requirements until the early 1970s, when the federal government inter-
vened. On average, the most restrictive residency requirement in the high
turnout midwestern states was 193 days, whereas the average length in the
other midwestern states was 184 days.

The midwestern states were also reasonably expansive with regard to
voter registration procedures throughout the century. Most of these states
adopted permanent registration systems early in the period, and of course
North Dakota eliminated voter registration from 1951 onward. Additionally, the registration closing dates in these states were generally liberal and
close to Election Day. The average closing date in the high turnout states
throughout the period was just eighteen days before the election, whereas
the average closing date in the other midwestern states was thirty days. In
1974 Minnesota enacted one of the most liberal voter registration policies
by instituting an Election Day registration program. Most of these states,
however, adopted motor voter early and universal mail-in registration
late—the latter in 1996 when it was mandated under the 1993 National

Voter Registration Act. Notably, Minnesota is again the exception. It adopted universal mail-in registration in 1974 and motor voter registration in 1978. Additionally, most of these states used a nonvoting purge throughout the twentieth century, although the period of not voting before individuals were purged was slightly shorter in the high turnout states (about three years) than in the rest of the region (about three and a half years). Finally, none of the high turnout midwestern states adopted universal in-person early voting, and only North Dakota adopted universal absentee voting, in 1998. The polls were open on Election Day for a slightly shorter amount of time in these states throughout the period: about eleven hours on average, compared with twelve hours in the rest of the states in the region.

Generally, the electoral laws in the high turnout western states—Colorado, Idaho, Montana, Utah, and Wyoming—were somewhat expansive, though less consistently so than the institutions in the high turnout midwestern states. Although none of the western states imposed a property requirement, seven western states administered literacy tests. Interestingly, Wyoming, one of the high turnout states in the region, was one of these states; it used a literacy test until 1970. Further, each of the high turnout western states adopted fairly long residency requirements, ranging from 180 to 365 days from 1920 until the 1970s, when they became short or nonexistent. On average, the most restrictive residency requirement in the high turnout western states was 220 days, whereas the average length was 202 days in the other states in the region.

Although the western states do not appear very expansive with respect to their laws governing voter qualifications, they became more expansive with the rules regarding voter registration. Specifically, nearly all of the high turnout western states implemented permanent voter registration systems throughout the entire century. The exception was Wyoming, which adopted permanent registration in 1950. Registration closing dates in the western states also varied quite a bit throughout the century; yet on average voter registration closed much later in the high turnout states—about nineteen days before the general election, whereas on average they closed about thirty-two days before the election in the other western states. Additionally, these high turnout states vary in their tendency to adopt universal mail-in registration and motor voter registration—some adopted them in the 1970s, and others waited until the 1993 National Voter Registration Act (NVRA) required them to do so. Two of these states also instituted Election Day registration (EDR). Idaho and Wyoming both adopted EDR in 1994 to circumvent the 1993 NVRA's motor voter requirements. All these states had a nonvoting purge during the century, and the period of not voting before being purged was basically the same in the high turnout states and other western states (about three years on average). A few of the high turnout western states allowed citizens to vote early. Colorado adopted universal in-person early voting and absentee voting in 1992, with Idaho following in 1994 and Montana in 2000. Wyoming also adopted universal absentee voting in 1992. Finally, the polls were open for a comparable amount of time in the high turnout states and in the other states in the region—about twelve hours.

The high turnout states in the northeast—Connecticut and Rhode Island—share some expansive institutional features with the high turnout states in the other regions, but they seem to have the least consistently expansive electoral systems. Both of these states enacted some form of restrictive voting qualification for some period during the twentieth century. Rhode Island implemented a property requirement until 1948 and a poll tax until 1950, and Connecticut imposed a literacy test until the early 1970s. The high turnout northeastern states had residency requirements substantially longer than those of the other northeastern states and also the rest of the high turnout sample. On average, the most restrictive residency requirement in the high turnout northeastern states was 303 days, while it was 207 days in the other northeastern states.

These states, however, were somewhat more expansive in their voter registration requirements throughout the century. Connecticut had a permanent registration system from 1920 onward, and Rhode Island switched from a two-year periodic system to permanent registration in 1952; yet both were late adopters of universal mail-in registration and motor voter registration. Connecticut adopted universal mail-in in 1988 and motor voter in 1992, whereas Rhode Island waited to adopt mail-in and motor voter registration until the late 1990s in compliance with the NVRA. Neither state adopted Election Day registration. Although the average registration closing date in Connecticut from 1920 to 2000 was a mere twenty-three days, in Rhode Island it was a lengthy forty-nine days. This is especially long considering that the average closing date in the other northeastern states during the period was twenty-two days. Furthermore, each of these states adopted a nonvoting registration purge in the middle of the century; specifically, Connecticut enacted a nonvoting purge in 1946, and Rhode Island did so in 1952. Yet the purge periods tended to be longer in these states than in the rest of the region. On average, individuals were purged after five years of not voting in the high turnout states and after only four years in the rest of the region. Finally, both states kept their polls open for, on average, about thirteen hours on Election Day throughout the period;

and neither state implemented universal in-person early voting or absentee voting during the century.

Discussion

Even though the comparison of electoral institutions in the consistently high turnout nonsouthern states reveals that many of the "high turnout" states shared some of the same institutional mechanisms, there is no clear institutional standout. These states do not appear very homogeneous in their adoption of similar electoral institutions. No single institution, or pattern of institutional adoption, seems distinct between or within any of these routinely high turnout states. Trends do emerge, however. Generally, the high turnout states in the Midwest appear to be the most consistently expansive throughout the period, although their electoral laws were not completely cost-reducing, followed by the western states with fairly expansive institutions over time. The high turnout states in the Northeast appear to have the least consistently expansive institutions.

Overall, the routinely high turnout midwestern states share many institutional features and have enacted the most consistently expansive electoral laws throughout the century compared with the high turnout states in other regions; however, there is a lot of variation in the nature of the expansiveness and restrictiveness, even within the high turnout midwestern states. Furthermore, and perhaps less encouraging from an institutional reform standpoint, these high turnout nonsouthern states do not seem dramatically different from the other states in their regions. Although variation exists between the regions generally, though not strictly, there is not much institutional variation within the regions. Overall, the routinely high turnout states in the Midwest have adopted about the same expansive laws as the other midwestern states. Additionally, although the high turnout states in the West look institutionally alike and as a group are a bit less expansive than the high turnout midwestern states, there is not a lot of institutional variation between the high turnout western states and the rest of the western states. This suggests that some of the observed differences in turnout between the regions may be attributed to the nature of the electoral institutions; however, there may be more than an institutional story contributing to turnout differences between the states within regions.

This variation demonstrates both the strengths and the limitations of institutional reform with respect to boosting voter turnout, and it shows the error of a "one size fits all" reform perspective; instead, it underscores the importance of incrementalism in policy making. That is, since no single reform seems to matter much in shifting turnout patterns, though it appears that together they may be powerful, and since state-specific issues presumably also come into play, the findings of this study constitute an argument for policy variation. If one reform had seemed to make a real difference across all states, then that particular institution might be an appropriate candidate for a national reform; but this did not happen.

This book has shown that although expansive and restrictive electoral institutions have influenced twentieth-century state turnout in many important ways, these effects have not occurred in a vacuum, especially in the nonsouthern states. Electoral institutions structure voting, yet a state's political environment and political history also bear heavily on this relationship. It seems likely that although more expansive electoral institutions have positively affected voting in the nonsouthern states, the political profile of individual states outside the South is bolstered, or limited, by other demographic and political features. These additional state attributes might help explain why, when all else is institutionally equal within a region (for the most part), the climates of some states seem to encourage participation, so that they have higher voter turnout over time than their regional counterparts. These additional components may relate to some combination of ethnic and racial homogeneity, political culture, electoral competition, and partisanship and will be explored into the follow sections.[1]

Racial Homogeneity

A recurring, albeit somewhat implicit, theme throughout this book has been the impact of, and states' responses to, race and perceptions of race. In the United States, race and voting have been interwoven throughout this century and before. Indeed, a clear, largely racial, personification of the ideal electorate was embedded in the early roots of the republic. In his historical study on the origins of the American voting process during the 1800s, Richard Bensel characterized the popular notion of a representative participant in the American electoral process:

> The nation needed a core conception of an American citizen both as a model and as a constituting agent. As a model, the northern, rural, native-born, white, protestant male enshrined in suffrage law and social practice gave the other groups in American society something to emulate and, thus, reduced conflict that might have otherwise arisen had all contending values and identities had an equal claim on social legitimacy. (2004, 289)

This purebred characterization of the ideal American voter persisted beyond its early origins; it continued to shape debates over the changing structure of elections well into the twentieth century. Race clearly has influenced the nature of voting laws throughout the nation's history. It seems quite likely that in the states and regions where ethnic and racial homogeneity has persisted, there have also been more expansive electoral systems and greater confidence about participating in the electoral process. As I demonstrated in chapter 5, many restrictive electoral reforms had a real negative effect on voting in the states where they operated. These electoral institutions were typically instituted to limit voting among certain groups—those who did not fit the republican or societal norms of acceptability.

Historically, the states in and outside the South have maintained diverging perceptions of voting and elections. In the former, elections were marked by increasing volatility, whereas in the latter they were an effective manifestation of prescribed democracy. In effect,

[Elections] were peaceful and facilitating precisely where they were unnecessary to stability (e.g., much of the rural Northeast and Midwest, where the vast majority of the electorate was white, Protestant and native born) and were destabilizing precisely where conflict over the very basis of the American political system was at stake (e.g., along the border between North and South and in the larger cities). (Bensel 2004, 292)

Given the interconnectedness between issues of race and voting rules in the United States, it could be that electoral institutions have been consistently more expansive, and hence turnout rates are categorically higher, in regions and states that did not have to confront issues of "otherness" when structuring their electoral processes. In effect, the midwestern and western regions may have higher turnout, and have a longer history of electoral expansiveness, because they experienced less immigration and ethic migration than the states in the South and Northeast. Owing to their comparative homogeneity, the states in the Midwest and West did not face the need to discriminate and hence did not institute the widespread electoral restrictiveness and disenfranchisement predominating in lower turnout areas.[2]

The characterization of the Midwest as racially homogeneous compared with the rest of the country is fairly well founded when we explore the percentage of a midwestern state's average "nonwhite" population throughout the century.[3] This figure ranges from as low as 1.8% in Iowa to nearly 13% in Oklahoma; the average nonwhite population in the Midwest was almost

7%. Furthermore, five of the six midwestern states that had consistently high turnout from 1920 to 2000 tended to have the lowest average percentage of nonwhites compared with other states in the region. For example, on average throughout the period, less than 3% of both Minnesota's and North Dakota's populations were nonwhite. Similarly, the average nonwhite populations in both South Dakota and Indiana were about 5% during the period. There is one exception: Illinois had a relatively sizable nonwhite population—on average, 12% of its population.

Although it seems that many of the high turnout midwestern states were fairly homogeneous throughout the century, at least racially, the pattern in the West is even more striking. Among the western states, a state's nonwhite population ranged on average from nearly 3% in Idaho to a sizable 68% in Hawaii from 1920 to 2000, with an overall regional average of about 14%. In the West, it is quite clear that the five states with routinely high turnout were also those with the lowest percentage of nonwhites over time. In Idaho, Utah, and Wyoming, the average nonwhite population was about 3% during the period, whereas in Montana and Colorado it was between 5% and 6%.

The pattern of racial homogeneity and high turnout continues to some degree in the high turnout northeastern states. From 1920 to 2000, the average nonwhite population in the Northeast ranged from less than 1% in Vermont to 21% in Maryland. Although the average nonwhite populations in Rhode Island and Connecticut are not the lowest among states in the Northeast, they are below average for the region and comparable to the figures presented for the high turnout states in other regions. Specifically, in Rhode Island about 4% of the population, on average, was nonwhite throughout the period, although about 6% of Connecticut's population was nonwhite from 1920 to 2000. The average size of the nonwhite population in the Northeast was about 8%.

Overall, these statistics suggest that many of the high turnout states had small nonwhite populations throughout the century, and generally these states tended to be whiter than their regional counterparts. Of course this is not a rule, as demonstrated by the figures for Illinois, and the significance of the percentages is somewhat relative. Yet we can speculate that there is a real relationship between the size and history of a state's nonwhite population and its participation patterns. States that have not been forced to confront questions of "otherness" may have had less reason to constrict the electorate and have therefore fostered a more socialized and unlimited electorate.

It could also be that, in addition to tendencies toward racial homogeneity, comparatively low immigration rates and ethnic migration patterns have had a real effect on the expansiveness of state electoral laws and voting rates. Exploring this issue will require historical research beyond the scope of this book, but according to Clubb, Flanigan, and Zingale, effects attributed to immigration and migration seem likely:

> In the Northeast and Mid-Atlantic States, and several in upper Midwest (especially Illinois and Michigan), the proportion of foreign-born increased steadily until the mid-19th century, peaked around 1910, and declined thereafter. Many western and Midwestern states (i.e. Wisconsin, Minnesota, North Dakota, Nevada, California, and Washington) had a substantial number of foreign-born early settlers—30–45% of the population in early statehood; [this] proportion decreased until about 1910 when in these (and other) states, the decline became more precipitous. (1981, 107)

Consequently one may speculate that, similar to the effects of racial homogeneity, states witnessing comparably low instances of immigration and migration over time may experience higher turnout. Perhaps individuals who are native-born and have been in a region or state for a long time are more embedded in the community and therefore more likely to vote.

Political Culture and Social Capital

Several studies about American state politics have used the concept of political culture to explain variations in state political characteristics or policy outputs (see, e.g., Fitzpatrick and Hero 1988; Hutcheson and George 1973; Johnson 1976; Kincaid 1980, 1982; Luttbeg 1971; Patterson 1968; Peters and Welch 1978; Ritt 1974; Sharkansky 1969, 1970; Sharkansky and Hofferbert 1969). The notion of political culture might also help explain the persistence of high turnout in the nonsouthern states.[4] Daniel J. Elazar defined political culture as "the particular pattern of orientation to political action in which each political system is imbedded" (1972, 84). In Elazar's notable *American Federalism: A View from the States* (1972), he described three principal cultures found within the American states—moralist, individualist, and traditionalist—and identified the cultural type that prevailed in each of the forty-eight mainland states and 228 subareas of the states.[5] Further, in a systematic study of Elazar's (1972) "political culture," Sharkansky (1969) found that state political culture, measured as a one-dimensional scale ranging from moralism through individualism to traditionalism, is related to features of popular participation patterns, among other things. Within this framework, it could be that in some instances consistently high participation rates outside the South can be attributed, at least in part, to aspects of state political culture; furthermore, the high turnout states might share cultural characteristics.

Based on Elazar's description of moralism, individualism, and traditionalism, we can hypothesize about several political traits, including tendencies pertaining to political participation, that may be found in each type of culture. For example, Elazar contends that

> citizen participation in politics, as measured by voter turnout, clearly reflects the different predispositions in the fifty states based on their particular political cultures. It is reasonably clear that people who believe they can accomplish something positive through the political process are more likely to vote and otherwise become more active in politics than those having little faith in the efficacy of politics. Thus, it would be natural for moralistic types to be most active, traditionalistic types to be least, and individualistic types to fall somewhere in between, responding to specific elections differently. (1972, 129)

Elazar further observed that "during presidential elections, states of the moralistic political culture consistently lead in percentage of voters turned out, reflecting the internalization of those cultural norms by the citizenry at large" (1972, 130). Additionally, he posited that

> the moralistic and individualistic states generally make voting registration easier than traditionalistic states, though for slightly different reasons. The moralistic states wish to encourage broad political participation for all those who will put forth a minimum amount of effort to become participants, although in the individualistic states, there is a convergence between this view and the interest of the political organization to make voting as easy as possible for the segment of the population they influence most. (1972, 130)[6]

As such, Elazar's conceived "moralistic" political culture may be basically a stand-in for the high participation rates found in some of the nonsouthern states and the corresponding expansive electoral laws observed in this study.

In practice, many of the states Elazar characterized as "dominant moralistic" or of the "moralistic strain" have demonstrated consistently "high turnout" rates in this study. Specifically, four of the nine states that Elazar dubbed "dominant moralistic" were also classified as high turnout states from 1920 to 2000: Minnesota, North Dakota, Colorado, and Utah. Additionally, three of the eight states that Elazar classified as "moralistic dominant with a strong individualistic strain" were classified as high turnout in this study: Montana, South Dakota, and Idaho. Somewhat less associated with Elazar's expectations related to political culture and heightened participation, Connecticut, Rhode Island, Illinois, and Wyoming repeatedly exhibited high turnout and were classified by him as "individualistic dominant with a strong moralistic strain." Finally, Indiana was identified as a consistently high turnout state in this study but was considered "individualistic dominant" by Elazar. This comparison reveals that many of the states considered to have "moralistic" political cultures were, as Elazar posited, also characterized as consistently high turnout in this study. This connection suggests a relationship, perhaps somewhat loose, between high turnout and a component of political culture.

In addition to the seeming persistence of a prevalent "moralistic" political culture in the nonsouthern high turnout states, they might also have a disproportionate tendency to foster increased social capital (Putnam 2000). In effect, individuals in these states may have developed deeper communal bonds over time and, as a result, may participate more through these affiliations, networks, and relationships. More disaggregated studies have found that political participation appears to be geographically clustered (Cho and Rudolph 2008; Huckfeldt 1979, 1986; Huckfeldt and Sprague 1995; Oliver 2001). From this observation many scholars have posited that citizens' participatory behavior is heavily influenced by that of those who live near them. This is consistent with previous research that demonstrates a link between social context and political participation. Furthermore, by analyzing the spatial structure of participation, Cho and Rudolph found that "individuals are more likely to participate if those around them are likely to participate" (2008, 273). So it seems that perhaps the patterns generated by aspects of Elazar's "political culture," and social capital, may be perpetuated by reinforcing norms. This sort of behavioral and institutional path dependence could have led the handful of repeatedly high turnout nonsouthern states along a historical road of enhanced participation and voting tendencies; however, it will take a more in-depth individual-level study of these states to further probe this question.

Electoral Competition and Partisanship

Historically, elections in some states have a reputation for being more competitive than elections in other states; voter turnout thus could be consistently bolstered in the states where elections are frequently close. In fact, it could be that narrow vote margins (close races) during presidential and nonpresidential elections may help explain why voter turnout in some states is consistently high throughout the century. In the Midwest this seems true for at least two of the high turnout states, but it does not follow for the others. Specifically, among the high turnout states in the Midwest, on average Indiana and Illinois experienced the closest presidential and nonpresidential elections throughout the century, with vote margins (the difference between the winner and the loser) of about 13% during presidential election years and 9% and 13%, respectively, during nonpresidential election years; however, Minnesota and South Dakota routinely experienced average vote margins—about 16% separating the vote for the winner and the loser. Also, North Dakota consistently experienced the least competitive elections within the region during presidential and nonpresidential elections throughout the century.

In the West, Colorado and Montana appear to have had closer than average presidential elections during the period. Yet the other high turnout states in the region—Wyoming, Idaho, and Utah—appear to have had the least competition—or the largest vote margins—during presidential election years. These states do, however, have much closer vote margins during nonpresidential election years. Nonpresidential competition is closer than average in each these five high turnout states, and the vote margins were particularly narrow in Colorado and Wyoming. Also, in the Northeast, Connecticut had consistently close presidential and nonpresidential elections, on average, compared with the other northeastern states. Rhode Island's vote margins, however, were above average for the region, with slightly higher margins during nonpresidential election years.

Based on these comparisons, it appears that in some of the midwestern and western high turnout states the average closeness of elections may have bolstered participation rates; however, this does not seem to be so in all of the nonsouthern high turnout states. Of course, in addition to electoral competition, some states have had more entrenched political parties and witnessed more aggressive partisan vote mobilization efforts over time. This may have important effects on turnout. Achen (2006) posited that voting is an acquired competence, like other adult skills. By middle age, Achen claimed, most adults vote in consequential elections. He argued that they do so primarily because they see that they have a stake in the election at hand—that they have gained a grasp of politics. Yet Achen (2006) also posited that, to vote, one may need real political knowledge and perhaps a strong party identification, with the associated partisan preferences and political awareness. From this perspective, one might suppose that voters in these routinely high turnout nonsouthern states have developed and maintained a strength of political partisanship and political socialization that individuals in other states do not have. One might further contend that political party organizations may have been more effective mobilizing forces in these states than in others. Although this sort of analysis requires individual-level research beyond the scope of this book, a few aspects of nonsouthern partisanship may have led to disproportionately intense partisan ties and increased mobilization in the observed high turnout states and regions.

First, the Republican Party's strong hold over many states outside the South during the early years of the twentieth century could have dramatically affected the course of elections and voting behavior in this region. As Kleppner demonstrated, "The 1918 elections abruptly ended the Democratic resurgence, as the Republicans carried most of the non-Southern states and gained control of both the United States Senate and House. Two years later, the Republicans added to their legislative margins, won the presidency, and inaugurated a period of unified control of the national government that lasted for the rest of the decade (1987, 141). Further, this new Republican control during the first half of the century produced some degree of partisan solidarity in most of the affected regions. As Key stated, "[In the older states of the Northeast and the Middle West] the impact of sectionalism, in our peculiar historical and institutional setting, induced a fairly high degree of regional unity in national affairs which contributed to the entrenchment of Republicans in control of the state governments of the region" (1956, 24). These regional divides were potentially even further solidified and noticeable within regions at the state, county, and district levels. In particular, as Key suggested, "The cleavage between metropolitan residents and rural small-town dwellers has become a most significant foundation for dual systems of state politics" (1956, 230). Furthermore, with respect to partisanship and mobilization within states, there may have been noticeable differences between one-party and two-party systems, and even urban-rural divides.

Conclusion

The examination of the high turnout states outside the South presented in this chapter facilitates a discussion about their political attributes. It has illuminated some influential aspects of electoral politics, institutional and otherwise, that may have contributed to the consistently high turnout observed in many of the nonsouthern states throughout the century. One clear finding, especially for the states discussed in this chapter, is that there is no single institutional explanation for increased participation. Even though the expansiveness or restrictiveness of state electoral laws seems to have had a nontrivial effect on voting rates, one cannot look to the consistently high turnout states to identify an institutional solution. It seems that, on average, many of the nonsouthern states that experienced routinely high turnout throughout the twentieth century implemented more expansive laws than other states in their regions did and, in many cases, adopted them before many other states. But this is not a steadfast rule. In reality it seems that these high turnout states harbor an amalgam of qualities that, when combined with expansive electoral laws, may routinely bolster their turnout over time and lead to enduring institutional and behavioral patterns.

In many ways this analysis of high turnout in the nonsouthern states has raised more questions that it has resolved. Many aspects of these puzzles could, and should, be the basis of future research. For example, the state-level data in this book could be further disaggregated to determine whether the observed state-level turnout patterns and institutional effects are consistent at the county and district levels. Additionally, the historical role of political parties and variation in mobilization programs in these states and regions should be examined further, in addition to more single-state analyses on the underpinnings and effects of political capital and political culture. This could help illuminate various historical motivations that may have led state officials to expand or contract the electorate throughout the century.

SEVEN

Voting in the Southern States during and after Jim Crow

The dynamic struggle over voting rights in the southern states is fundamental to understanding twentieth-century political participation in the
United States. The prevalence of Jim Crow in this region dramatically influenced the nature of electoral politics and voting.[1] Despite many expansive,
equalizing electoral reforms instituted during the latter part of the century,
Jim Crow left an undeniable imprint on southern voting patterns. As I discussed in chapter 3, voting rates in the South were often significantly below
the national average throughout the twentieth century, and the individual
southern states have routinely garnered the lowest voter turnout in the nation. This situation is fueled by many conditions that dramatically affected
southern life during this century and before. Not only did the southern
states experience the systematic disenfranchisement of a large segment of
their eligible voting populations for several decades under Jim Crow, but
they also had the lowest income and education levels in the country, which
may have further depressed voting.

Although many scholars have addressed the widespread disenfranchisement of southern blacks—and in some cases poor whites—early in the
century, it is particularly relevant to this book because it illustrates the undeniable power of electoral institutions to shape, and in some instances
fundamentally limit, political participation. The effect of targeted disenfranchisement in the South was unprecedented. As Key stated, "The disenfranchisement movement gave the southern states the most impressive
system of obstacles between the voter and the ballot box known to the
democratic world" (1949, 555). No other region witnessed such richness
in experience, struggle, and history with respect to voting rights. The evolution of southern voting laws throughout the twentieth century provides a
vast mélange of electoral reform and associated outcomes and a fantasti-

cally varied framework for understanding the role of electoral institutions in shaping voting and elections in the United States. Even though some of these restrictive institutions existed outside the South, results suggest that they had a wider and more insidious effect on voting in the southern states than elsewhere. These laws tended to be implemented longer in this region and were often enforced more strictly than they were outside the South. Further, the consistent use of restrictive electoral institutions in the southern states dramatically shaped political socialization, which may have influenced voting rates even after these restrictions were eased.

The southern case study presented in this chapter seeks to isolate the impact of a variety of institutional factors and social forces on turnout in the South. While considering many relevant demographic and partisan variables, here I examine the peculiarities of voting in the southern states, paying particular attention to the historical and institutional mechanisms, party politics, and racism that contributed to the South's depressed participatory climate during, and to some extent even after, Jim Crow. By systematically evaluating the effect of changing laws pertaining to voter qualifications, voter registration, and voting procedures on southern turnout, we can draw conclusions about the past, and even the future, of voting in the South. With this in mind, I begin by tracing the tumultuous history of federal intervention aimed at ending southern Jim Crow and discuss the gains in voter participation generated by the 1964 National Civil Rights Act and the 1965 Voting Rights Act. Then I analyze the effects of restrictive and expansive electoral institutions on turnout during two distinct periods of institutional change: first, from 1920 to 1970, a time marked by the steady implementation of predominately restrictive institutions, and second, from 1972 to 2000, a time after the civil rights movement when there was a concerted effort to make southern voting laws more expansive. Finally, I consider the dampening effect of noncompetitive elections throughout the single-party South by examining the effects of electoral institutions during Democratic primary elections from 1920 to 1970.

Disenfranchisement in the South

The struggle over suffrage in the United States, particularly in the South, is rich with moments of expansion and contraction and with episodes of resistance and liberation. Though the rules governing voting and elections have generally been left to the states, in many instances southern Jim Crow voting practices were so egregious that the federal government had to supersede them with pivotal legislation. Indeed, the complicated history of voting in the South is fraught with instances where states exploited their power over elections under federalism and engaged in broad racist disenfranchisement so that the federal government, bound by democratic principle and rhetoric, was compelled to intervene. The federal government's decision to mediate voting practices in these states was colored by deeply political and partisan concerns (Black and Black 1987, 1992; Key 1949; Lawson 1976, 1985; Valelly 2004). Generally, the disenfranchisement of black citizens in the South reflected the region's overarching race and class issues, its struggle over political authority, and long-standing inequity. Moments of federal intervention in this history constitute breaking points—times when universal suffrage was demanded and was provided, to the extent possible, through federal legislation.

Unequal voting rights in the southern states began long before the twentieth century. Before the Civil War, the US Constitution did not provide any specific protections over voting or electoral practices. Early voting rules were entirely governed by the states; as such, the combination of slavery and restrictive state laws left the franchise to be exercised almost exclusively by white males. This changed in 1870 with the ratification of the Fifteenth Amendment. Section 1 of this pivotal constitutional amendment provided that the "right to vote shall not be denied or abridged on the basis of race, color, or previous condition of servitude" (US Constitution 1870). The amendment superseded all state laws that directly prohibited blacks from voting. To secure implementation, Congress also enacted the Force Act of 1871, which specified criminal penalties for interfering with the right to vote and provided federal election oversight (Davidson and Grofman 1994; Goldman 1990). As a result of this legislation, by the late nineteenth century countless recently freed slaves registered to vote in the former Confederate states—where in some cases black citizens constituted outright or near majorities of the eligible voting population (Key 1949; Lawson 1976). But this victory was short-lived.

The extension of the franchise to black citizens under the 1870s legislation was strongly resisted by the southern states. Using violence and intimidation, the Ku Klux Klan, the Knights of the White Camelia, and other extremist organizations tried to prevent enforcement of the Fifteenth Amendment. Many of the southern states also used implicitly racist institutional maneuvers to restrict participation. For example, several states adopted the white primary system, under which southern Democrats attempted to evade the Fifteenth Amendment by allowing political parties, touted as private organizations, to conduct elections and establish their own qualifications for members. Other disenfranchising laws became increasingly widespread; such laws included poll taxes, literacy tests, vouchers of "good character," and disqualification for "crimes of moral turpitude." Although these laws did not usually include overtly racist provisions, they were designed to disproportionately exclude black citizens by allowing white election officials to apply the procedures selectively. As a result, in the former Confederate states nearly all black citizens were effectively disenfranchised by 1910 (Black and Black 1987, 1992; Key 1949; Keyssar 2000, 2009; Lawson 1976; Valelly 2004).[2]

As I described in chapter 4, although variations of these restrictive laws existed in many nonsouthern states, the South was clearly home to Jim Crow. This region is unique not only in the sheer volume of disenfranchising laws enacted, but also in the racist way they were carried out. Of the 439 Jim Crow laws passed nationwide, 79% were implemented in southern states (Valelly 2004). Further, every southern state adopted one or more of the disenfranchising voting rules for some period during the twentieth century. For example, each southern state required the payment of a poll tax, typically six to twelve months before the election, and many required the payment of back taxes through 1901. Although the sums assessed may not seem significant by today's standards, in 1900 they were a lot of money. Valelly writes, "Consider the percentage of the annual income of a southern black farm laborer taken by a $1.00 poll tax and compare it to a contemporary equivalent payment. One dollar was about one-half of 1 percent of a black farm laborer's annual income circa 1900, assuming he worked every day of the year. That translates into about $135.00 in 2001 dollars" (2004, 125). Most people today would find it intolerable to pay this much to vote (or really, to pay anything at all). In addition to the direct cost of the poll tax, voting restrictions were intertwined with a socioeconomic system in which people on the lower rungs of the economic ladder were intimidated, ostracized, and disenfranchised in one way or another. As Lawson noted, "If they had acquired higher incomes and better education, southern blacks would have been more likely to sign up and cast their ballots. Victims of an enduring racial caste system, many blacks lacked the sense of political efficacy more commonly associated with individuals higher on the social and economic scale" (1985, 36).

The literacy test was also an impediment to black and, in many cases, white suffrage; however, since blacks suffered the most from a general lack of schooling and substandard segregated education in the South, they bore the heaviest burden when forced to prove they could read and write (Davidson and Grofman 1994; Key 1949; Lawson 1976). Therefore any literacy test, however impartially applied, would effectively curb voting among blacks—but we know that these tests were not administered impartially in the South. Even though literacy tests were somewhat common in many of the nonsouthern states, particularly those with substantial immigrant populations, the way they were carried out in the South was fueled by racism. As Lawson noted, "Registrars applied a double standard in administering tests that allowed most illiterate whites to enroll; in this way, the southern states differed from eleven of their northern neighbors that used literacy exams as a means of examining potential voters regardless of race" (1976, 87). It is clear that in addition to the mere existence of these laws, much of the hatred, dehumanization, and racism associated with these disenfranchising institutions were backed by the immense authority wielded by those enforcing them.

Although Jim Crow provisions were legal-institutional mechanisms found in the state law books, it was their enforcement, left wholly to the discretion of appointed election officials, that enabled racist predispositions to prevail. In the words of Richard Valelly, "Disenfranchisement was not *fully* legal. [To succeed] it required considerable trickery and intimidation on the part of its backers" (2004, 124). The county boards entrusted with oversight and implementation were essentially a law unto themselves. They applied the rules as they saw fit and functioned independently of each other, a system that ensured considerable diversity within and between states. Ultimately, by enforcing the laws so that they systematically disqualified blacks, southern registrars could preserve white supremacy (Black and Black 1987, 1992; Key 1949; Lawson 1976, 1985; Valelly 2004).

The intimidation within this oppressive political environment was flagrant, and its effectiveness in curbing registration and voting in the South was obvious. In the 1965 report titled *Voting in Mississippi*, the US Commission on Civil Rights found that "in many counties, the fear of economic or physical reprisal influenced the individual Negro in determining whether to attempt to register or vote" (1965, 21). According to one black citizen (Aaron Henry) testifying before the commission, "We are afraid of physical violence, economic reprisals, losing jobs, or not getting jobs" for making such attempts (1965, 21). The 1965 commission also found that

the low income and economic dependence of most Negroes in Mississippi has given rise to widespread fears that registration or voting will result in reprisals. These fears are intensified because Negroes in rural counties who attempt to register cannot hope to remain anonymous. Furthermore, fears of reprisals are not confined to Negroes with the lowest incomes. In some areas of Mississippi Negro teachers want to register and vote but fail to do so because they fear they will lose their jobs. When teachers themselves fail to participate, they set an example for those they teach. (1965, 39)

Restoring the rights impeded by these racist tactics took many decades.

Despite the victory concerning women's suffrage in 1920, black disenfranchisement in the South persisted. The 1940s, however, ushered in a few important gains in the struggle over equality and voting rights. In *Smith v. Allwright* (1944) the Supreme Court ruled that the Texas white primary violated the Fifteenth Amendment. This was an important victory for disenfranchised blacks since, as I will discuss later in this chapter, the white primary was vital to the institutional foundation of southern white supremacy. Observers surmised that if the Supreme Court "ever killed the white primary, the institutionally privileged position of white supremacist politicians would erode" (Valelly 2004, 158). The Court's decision produced immediate effects. Shortly after the white primary was eradicated, black voter registration drives in the South reemerged and experienced some success (Lawson 1976; Valelly 2004). Although several southern states experimented with additional restrictions to limit black participation after the white primary's demise, many were struck down by the federal courts over the next decade. It seemed that change was on the horizon, and the mediating hand of the federal government ensured that mechanisms for fostering equality and enfranchisement would soon come.

By the late 1950s, the momentum of the civil rights movement was impossible for elected representatives in Washington to ignore. In 1957 and 1960, Congress passed legislation that had important implications for voting in the states. The Civil Rights Act of 1957 created the Civil Rights Division within the Department of Justice and gave the Commission on Civil Rights and the attorney general authority to seek injunctions against violators of the Fifteenth Amendment (Davidson and Grofman 1994; Goldman 1990). Additionally, the Civil Rights Act of 1960 permitted federal courts to appoint voting referees to conduct voter registration after a judicial finding of discrimination. Although court decisions and these laws made it more difficult for the states to keep their black citizens disenfranchised, at least in theory, the strategy of case-by-case litigation had limited success. Literacy tests, poll taxes, and other formal and informal practices combined to keep black registration suppressed, particularly in Alabama, Louisiana, and Mississippi, and well below white registration rates in other southern states (Lawson 1985). The US Commission on Civil Rights, in its 1965 examination of voting practices in Mississippi, noted that "at the time of the Presidential election of 1964 it was estimated that more than 70% of the white voting age population of Mississippi, but less than 7% of its Negro voting age population, were registered to vote" (1965, 1). Furthermore, the report stated that

> Mississippi had by far the lowest rate of Negro registration and the greatest disparity between the rates of white and Negro registration of any other Southern state. The causes of this disparity are rooted in history; an examination of the development of voting laws in Mississippi indicates that the disenfranchisement of the Negro as a result of a deliberate State policy pursued over many years. (1965, 1)

Yet radical change was imminent. The 1964 National Civil Rights Act and the 1965 Voting Rights Act combated these infringements directly; however, as this book shows, their immediate effect on state voting rates varied.

Civil Rights Legislation and the Promise of Change

By 1965 a concerted effort to break the grip of state disenfranchisement had been under way for some time, but overall these efforts had achieved only modest success. Ultimately, state troopers' unprovoked attack on peaceful marchers crossing the Edmund Pettus Bridge in Selma, Alabama, on March 7, 1965, persuaded the president and Congress to overcome southern legislators' resistance to effective voting rights legislation and take action (Valelly 2004). Congress determined that the existing federal anti-discrimination laws were not sufficient to overcome state officials' resistance to enforcing the Fifteenth Amendment. Legislative hearings revealed that the Department of Justice's efforts to eliminate discriminatory election practices through piecemeal litigation had been unsuccessful in deracializing the registration process. As described in the *South Carolina v. Katzenbach* (1966) decision,

> Congress found that case-by-case litigation was inadequate to combat widespread and persistent discrimination in voting because of the inordinate amount of time and energy required to overcome the obstructionist tactics invariably encountered in these lawsuits. After enduring nearly a century of systematic resistance to the Fifteenth Amendment, Congress might well decide to shift the advantage of time and inertia from the perpetrators of the evil to its victims. (383 U.S. 301, 1966)

Accordingly, President Lyndon Johnson issued an urgent call for a strong voting rights law, and hearings began soon thereafter on the bill that would become the 1965 Voting Rights Act.

Arguably the Johnson administration's voting rights bill was greatly influenced by what had happened with the National Civil Rights Act of 1964. It had taken more than a year to push that act through Congress. It took only five months to enact the 1965 Voting Rights Act (Loevy 1997). The Voting Rights Act was extended in 1970, 1975, and 1982 and is generally considered the most successful piece of civil rights legislation ever adopted by Congress. The act codified and effected the Fifteenth Amendment's permanent guarantee that, throughout the nation, "no person shall be denied the right to vote on account of race or color." President Johnson signed the legislation into law on August 6, 1965.

Adopted at a time when African Americans were substantially disenfranchised in many southern states, the 1965 Voting Rights Act included measures to restore the right to vote, superseding disenfranchising laws in areas that had previously been left to individual states. As I discussed in chapter 4, section 4 of the act ended the use of literacy requirements for voting in Alabama, Georgia, Louisiana, Mississippi, South Carolina, and Virginia and in many counties of North Carolina. Section 5 stated that no voting changes were legally enforceable in these jurisdictions until approved either by a three-judge court in the District of Columbia or by the attorney general of the United States. Other sections authorized the attorney general to appoint federal voting examiners who could be sent into covered jurisdictions to ensure that legally qualified persons were free to register for federal, state, and local elections and to assign federal observers to oversee the conduct of elections (US Public Law 89–110). Ultimately this legislation eliminated the institutional underpinnings of Jim Crow and changed the face of voting in the South.

Touted by many as the greatest legislative achievements of the civil rights movement, the 1964 National Civil Rights Act and the 1965 Voting Rights Act had great success in curbing racial disenfranchisement in the South. Even though the effect of these acts is often portrayed as immediate and extensive, the legislation's effect on voting itself was not felt uniformly in all the southern states. There definitely were sweeping gains in voter registration; for example, in the Deep South, where Jim Crow politics had historically imposed the greatest repression, "voter registration jumped from about 33.8% of all black adults in 1964 to 56.6% in 1968, or a 67% increase, apparently due to compliance by state and local officials with the commands of the act and continued civil rights activism" (Valelly 2004,

4).[3] Yet despite dramatic increases in voter registration among southern blacks during this period, in many cases increases in actual turnout proved unsustainable, and in many of the southern states they were minimal. Though the significance of this legislation cannot be overstated, the postreform variation in southern voter turnout rates needs further analysis.[4]

Southern Turnout Rates after Federal Reform

The civil rights voting reforms undoubtedly changed the nature of participation in the southern states. By removing racist voting barriers, this legislation equalized the landscape for voting and elections throughout the region. We might expect that voter turnout increased unilaterally in the South after 1964, yet there is considerable variation in state-level voting rates. As displayed in figures 7.1 and 7.2, regional voting levels, aggregated across the southern states, remain consistently below average during presidential and nonpresidential election years from 1920 to 2000; however, the effect of the 1960s reforms on regional turnout is apparent. The size of the gap between voting levels in the southern states and the national figures decreased after Jim Crow was eliminated from the states where it was most entrenched. Overall, however, despite increases in the eligible voting population with the inclusion of women, blacks, and those eighteen and over throughout this period, southern turnout remained below the national average throughout the twentieth century.

Figure 7.1 shows that during presidential election years before the 1964 legislation, voter turnout in the southern states generally ranged from a staggering 15% to 45% below the national average. This corresponds to actual state voting rates (as shown in online appendix A) of only 10% to 30% during presidential election years, when voter turnout is typically at its peak. As shown in figure 7.2, there is more variation in southern turnout during nonpresidential election years. Once again, however, turnout in nonpresidential election years was significantly below the national average, ranging from 10% to 40% below the national average, with a tendency toward rates of 30% to 40% below. Despite portraying a dismal picture of southern voting rates, these figures offer evidence that turnout improved to some extent after many of the restrictive voting laws were removed during the mid-1960s.

In particular, although the regional trends presented in the aggregate figures smooth the interstate variation, the state-by-state trends presented in appendix A illustrate the immediate positive effects the 1964 National Civil Rights Act and 1965 Voting Rights Act generated in many of the

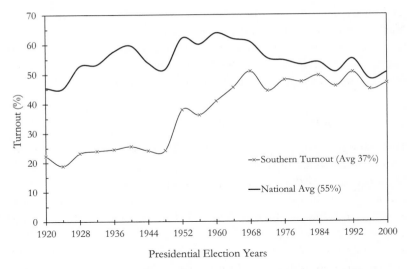

7.1. Southern presidential election year voter turnout trends, 1920–2000

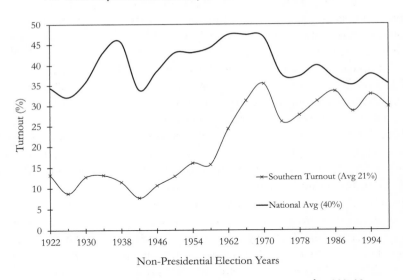

7.2. Southern nonpresidential election year voter turnout trends, 1922–98

southern states. Specifically, voter turnout improved in all eleven southern states during the 1964 presidential election, shortly after the National Civil Rights Act was passed. Additionally, during the following 1966 nonpresidential elections, voting rates increased in all the southern states except Louisiana and Texas. Yet the boost in voting rates, coinciding with and seemingly promoted by these reforms, was unsustainable in many of the states. Although voter turnout increased again in all the southern states during the 1968 presidential election, it then decreased in all the southern states during the 1972 election. Additionally, during the 1970 nonpresidential elections, turnout increased in all the southern states except Louisiana, Mississippi, and North Carolina, yet turnout declined in Alabama, Arkansas, Tennessee, and Texas during the 1974 election. These figures suggest that although southern blacks may have been registering in record numbers soon after the passage of the 1964 National Civil Rights Act and 1965 Voting Rights Act, the legislation did not necessarily lead to sweeping and sustainable increases in actual voter turnout throughout the South.[5] Indeed, even though the gap between southern and national voting rates decreased after the legislation was passed, a significant difference remained between voting trends in the southern states and the rest of the nation.

The variation in turnout gains and losses before and after the 1960s legislation raises important questions about the overarching voting culture in this region. Perhaps the legacy of Jim Crow made it unlikely that there would be massive and sustained increases in voting rates despite the federal intervention. After decades when political activity was discouraged or denied and people lived with rampant racism, humiliation, and violence, it may have taken something grander than the sheer ability to vote to mobilize the southern masses (Rosenstone and Hansen 1993). Despite this liberating legislation, a suffrage problem lingered in the southern states. In addition to the practice and reality of Jim Crow, many southerners, especially blacks, suffered immense economic and educational hardship. As Lawson wrote,

> Many of those [blacks] who remained disenfranchised suffered from the same socioeconomic handicaps that curtailed political participation by the poor and ill educated throughout the nation. In addition, fear and intimidation continued to hamper prospective black registrants in the South. Breaking down the habit of non-voting nurtured throughout the years by white supremacy, required not only increased federal intervention but also the resumption of grass roots civil rights activities like those conducted in the early 1960s. (1985, 298)

This sort of mobilization did not materialize in the South beyond the civil rights movement (Rosenstone and Hansen 1993), and after decades of limitation it seems it may take more than reduced voting costs to stimulate participation in this region.

Over the past two centuries, political socialization in the South has been permeated with racist, violent, targeted nonvoting norms. For an effective policy solution to emerge, we must first understand and appreciate the gravity of these institutional effects throughout the region's history. Understanding the magnitude of Jim Crow's influence on southern voting history could help inform policy solutions for the future. With this in mind, in the following sections I further examine the effect that limiting political institutions had on southern voting throughout the twentieth century. First, I use empirical analyses to evaluate the effects of electoral institutions during two distinct periods of institutional change—one decidedly restrictive and the other intentionally expansive. Then I assess the importance of electoral competition compared with electoral institutions during competitive primary elections in the single-party South from 1920 to 1970.

Restrictive and Expansive Periods of Institutional Change in the South, 1920–2000

Given the evolution of state policies and federal intervention in the southern states throughout the twentieth century, two distinct institutional periods have emerged. Institutional restrictiveness dominated the electoral landscape in the southern states before the civil rights movement, and a concerted effort to make electoral institutions more inclusive began in the early 1970s. Accordingly, here I aim to evaluate the effect of electoral institutions during these two distinct periods, since once the disproportionately restrictive institutions were removed, effects associated with expansive reforms might emerge. Table 7.1 presents the results from the empirical analysis on the effects that southern electoral institutions had on voting rates during presidential and nonpresidential election years during these two periods of change: 1920–70 and 1972–2000. As I discussed in chapter 4, the first period encapsulates the years when restrictive laws flourished, and the second period, after the limiting laws were eradicated or significantly eased, marks the period of concerted expansiveness. The data and statistical method used in these analyses are comparable to the models employed in chapter 5.[6]

As expected, findings in the period-specific models support the notion that many of the restrictive voting qualifications depressed voter turnout in the South during the first part of the century. As shown in table 7.1, during presidential election years from 1920 to 1968 (model 1), property requirements decreased turnout by 4.2 percentage points and poll taxes depressed it by an impressive 8.2 percentage points. Long residency requirements also had a statistically significant negative effect on presidential election year turnout; as the length of the state's most restrictive residency requirement increased by 100 days, southern voter turnout decreased by nearly 1 percentage point. Additionally, during nonpresidential election years from 1922 to 1970 (model 2), poll taxes depressed southern turnout by over 6 percentage points. The magnitude of each of these effects is very comparable to the estimates presented in the aggregate models from chapter 5 (tables 5.1 and 5.3) that spanned the entire century.

Voter registration rules also appear to have had some effect on voting rates from 1920 to 1970—a time when voting and registration were comparably limited. Indeed, in the early period, periodic voter registration systems were very common and were often criticized as unnecessarily cumbersome. Results suggest that with the move from an inefficient periodic registration system to a more efficient permanent registration system, southern turnout in presidential election years increased by 2.5 percentage points (model 1). Additionally, registration closing dates had a statistically significant effect on turnout during the early period in presidential and nonpresidential election years; that is, as a state's closing date moved ten days further from Election Day—so registration had to be completed earlier—voter turnout declined by about half a percentage point in both the presidential (model 1) and nonpresidential specifications (model 2). This is consistent with the presidential model presented in chapter 5.

Unlike the results in chapter 5, however, it seems that increasing poll hours were associated with a statistically significant decrease in southern turnout during presidential election years (model 1). As shown by the significant, positive squared term, this relationship is curvilinear. When the marginal effects of the poll hours and poll hours squared terms are calculated, it appears that longer poll hours predict decreased southern presidential turnout during the early period. Yet a difference exists between states with short polling windows and those that keep their polls open for eleven hours or more. It seems that after eleven hours, keeping the polls open longer is associated with a slight increasing effect on voting rates. Consistent with chapter 5, however, polls hours did not have a statistically significant effect on turnout during nonpresidential election years (model 2).

During the later period from 1972 to 2000 when none of the restrictive voting qualifications were implemented by the states, there appear to be few effective expansive institutions in the southern states. Similar to the findings during the early period, early registration closing dates continued to depress turnout later in the century. For every ten days that the closing date was moved away from Election Day, turnout declined by

Table 7.1 Southern Voter Turnout by Reform Period, 1920–2000

Variable	Model 1: Presidential, 1920–68	Model 2: Nonpresidential, 1922–70	Model 3: Presidential, 1972–2000	Model 4: Nonpresidential, 1974–98
Voting qualifications:				
Property requirement	−4.222** (1.228)	−1.242 (1.633)	... ...	... ...
Literacy test	1.697 (1.897)	2.979 (1.878)	... ...	... ...
Poll tax	−8.168** (1.174)	−6.069** (1.284)	... ...	... ...
Residency requirement	−0.007 (0.003)	−0.006 (0.004)	... ...	... ...
Voter registration:				
Frequency of periodic registration	0.025** (0.010)	0.010 (0.015)	0.018 (0.013)	−0.016 (0.016)
Nonvoting purge period	0.001 (0.015)	0.017 (0.019)	0.751 (0.866)	−4.490** (1.840)
Universal mail-in registration	... ...	... ...	−1.132 (1.138)	−0.930 (2.455)
Motor voter registration	... ...	... ...	... ...	... ...
Registration closing date	−0.044** (0.011)	−0.038** (0.011)	−0.171** (0.049)	−0.157** (0.058)
Election Day registration	... ...	... ...	... ...	... ...
Voting procedures:				
Hours polls are open	−7.575** (2.102)	1.266 (2.794)	−7.315** (2.290)	−12.208** (4.384)
Hours polls are open squared	0.359** (0.107)	−0.045 (0.143)	0.382** (0.104)	0.547** (0.207)
In-person early voting	... ...	... ...	−0.429 (1.210)	−0.394 (2.877)
Universal absentee voting	... ...	... ...	2.127 (2.097)	... ...

	(1)	(2)	(3)	(4)
Electoral calendar:				
Gubernatorial race	4.886** (1.112)	3.070* (1.511)	−2.039* (0.937)	2.948* (1.408)
Senate race	0.658 (0.657)	0.959 (0.655)	0.385 (0.487)	4.302** (0.946)
Contested House seats	0.016 (0.018)	0.034 (0.019)	−0.037** (0.012)	0.008 (0.035)
Initiatives on ballot	−0.342 (0.380)	0.022 (0.525)	−0.171 (0.412)	1.410 (1.252)
Vote margin	−0.077** (0.029)	−0.065** (0.018)	0.022 (0.032)	−0.174** (0.026)
Demographics:				
Education	0.395 (0.228)	−0.233 (0.266)	0.146 (0.148)	0.193 (0.236)
Per capita income	−1.060 (0.733)	−1.820* (0.849)	−0.500 (0.293)	−1.384** (0.288)
Black population	−0.044 (0.094)	−0.161 (0.101)	−0.058 (0.090)	−0.198 (0.144)
Age 45 or above	0.106 (0.265)	1.023** (0.283)	0.478** (0.144)	0.276 (0.208)
Constant	68.491** (9.558)	4.369 (12.034)	70.870** (15.059)	110.356** (24.562)
State fixed effects	No	No	No	No
Year fixed effects	Yes	Yes	Yes	Yes
N	143	143	88	73
R^2	0.910	0.845	0.891	0.729

Note: Panel-corrected standard errors are in parentheses.

*$p < .05$

**$p < .01$

nearly 2 percentage points during presidential election years (model 3) and by about 1.5 percentage points during nonpresidential election years (model 4). The magnitude of this effect was quite a bit larger during the later period (1972–2000) than during the early period (1920–70). This suggests that once the explicit limitations to voting were removed, early closing dates presented a more formidable barrier to participation. Additionally, universal mail-in registration was associated with an unexpected 4.5 percentage point decrease (model 4) in turnout during nonpresidential election years. Additionally, during this period, long poll hours were associated with decreased southern turnout rates during both presidential and nonpresidential election years (models 3 and 4); however, again the relationship is curvilinear, and marginal effects suggest that there are some increasing properties associated with poll hours that extend beyond the eleven-hour mark.

Overall, the findings from the period-specific models presented in table 7.1 are very similar to those in the aggregated models on southern turnout presented in chapter 5. This is especially true for the results from the early period (1920–70), and the findings are mostly the same during the later period (1972–2000). In particular, the results during the early period (models 1 and 2) pertaining to poll taxes in both presidential and nonpresidential election years and property requirements during presidential years are comparable to the findings in chapter 5. If anything, the magnitudes of the results in table 7.1 are slightly larger during presidential election years than they were in chapter 5. The findings about early closing dates are also nearly identical during presidential election years. There is a bit more variation, however, in the findings for the later period (models 3 and 4) compared with the results in chapter 5. For example, the analysis of turnout during nonpresidential election years in the later period reveals that mail-in registration is statistically significant (though not in expected direction), but it was not statistically significant at all in the aggregate analyses (table 5.3). The results for early closing dates are also more substantial in the later period. Finally, long poll hours had a notable effect on southern turnout in both the early and late periods, but they did not have a statistically significant effect on aggregate southern turnout in chapter 5.

Overall, comparing the two periods of institutional change shows that the results in chapter 5 are robust across both of the period-specific specifications. Despite the differences in the nature of southern electoral rules during these two periods, the effects of the restrictive rules during the early period do not swamp the effects of the expansive institutions in the later period. Indeed, the results presented here underscore the finding that expansive electoral institutions have done little to alter participation in the southern states. This is significant, since the goal of expansive reform efforts since midcentury has been to increase voter registration and turnout. Instead, the results continue to suggest that expansive institutional reforms (beyond the removal of restrictive voting provisions) have not increased turnout in the place where there is the most to gain—the routinely low turnout southern states. The consistency of these findings across institutional periods further highlights the importance of considering a state's political history and norms when pursuing electoral reform. Indeed, even when the period of restrictive electoral laws is isolated, there are still no gains from the expansive provisions. The South's history of Jim Crow voting laws and limited electoral competitiveness (and its poor socioeconomic conditions) may affect the ability of expansive reforms to generate gains in participation. To examine whether this finding is sensitive to the level of electoral competition in the voting environment, in the following section I will evaluate the role of electoral institutions in shaping voting rates in southern primary elections.

Examining Institutional Effects during Primary Elections

Although the findings of this study suggest that restrictive electoral institutions played a major role in suppressing voter turnout in the southern states, we should not forget that throughout the first half of the century general elections in most of the region were not competitive. During the years of Democratic dominance in the South, the real electoral contest was the primary election. In effect, "because Democratic nominees ordinarily faced no serious competition in general elections, the Democratic primaries actually functioned as the sole arenas of meaningful choice in state politics" (Black and Black 1987, 84). Further, the lack of competition in general elections was instrumental in maintaining the one-party South. As Key stated, "It [was] fundamental to Democratic supremacy in the South that the party's nominees shall go without effective challenge in the general election" (1949, 424).

Many have argued that a lack of partisan competition discouraged voting in the South and that this absence of real electoral competition largely explains the region's consistently low turnout, setting aside the influence of restrictive laws in limiting turnout or portraying them as secondary at best. Key notably argued that "the one-party system (or perhaps the absence of a two-party system) contributes in large degree to the low electoral interest in the South; its development paralleled the evolution of suffrage limitations, whose adoption, in a sense, marked the demise of tendencies toward the re-establishment of a two-party system" (1949, 551). Even though the lack of partisan competition presumably had a real part in dampening voting rates in the South, the analyses presented here have consistently demonstrated that electoral institutions also had an effect (albeit sometimes modest) on voter turnout in the southern states, even after controlling for the competitiveness of the race (vote margin and concurrent elections). Yet we can further explore the relationship between electoral competition and electoral institutions in the South by examining voter turnout during primary elections early in the century, a time when the Democratic Party's monopoly over southern politics was steadfast.

In addition to the limited competitiveness of general elections, southern Democrats restricted voting in these "real" contests by employing a white primary system. During the years following Reconstruction, the white primary system was one of the most pronounced barriers used to restrict black participation while building coalitions among southern whites. White primaries existed exclusively in the eleven southern states in the early part of the twentieth century and before.[7] White primaries were first used informally by various Democratic organizations throughout the South at the end of the Civil War, and they were used more systematically once the federal troops were withdrawn. In the early years, Democrats used white primaries to keep their factions from forming coalitions with blacks and to reduce the favors blacks could extort from them. It is no coincidence that white primaries began while Republicans and third-party Populists had a lot of support among poor whites and blacks in the South and consequently posed a viable threat to Democratic power. In this early period, black and white voter registration rates were nearly equal, so the white primary was seen more as a mechanism for building white coalitions than as a means to disenfranchise blacks. This changed somewhat in the twentieth century, however, when disenfranchising blacks became a primary objective throughout much of the South (Hine 2003; Keyssar 2000).

The overt racial restrictiveness of white primary elections is hard to conceive by modern standards. At the time, however, in *Newberry v. United States* (1921), a case not related to white primaries, the US Supreme Court effectively signaled its willingness to treat primary elections as private party functions, thereby opening the door to the proliferation of the white primary in the single-party Democratic South. After the *Newberry* ruling, many southern state legislators, frustrated after several years of Reconstruction, surmised that the courts would not provide constitutional protection to

African Americans who wanted to vote in primaries and seized the opportunity to institutionally disenfranchise them.

There is no denying the racist motivations for the use of the white primary in the southern states. This was particularly true in Texas, where it flourished most proudly. The introduction to the 1952 Texas Electoral Code plainly stated, "The influence of the Klan was responsible for the enactment of a statute in 1923 by the thirty-eight state legislatures disqualifying Negroes from voting in Democratic primary elections" (Texas Code 1952, XXVI). As the racist sentiments associated with the white primary became clearer, the US Supreme Court could not remain complacent. When the Texas legislature passed a white primary law in 1923, it thrust Texans (and the Texas white primary) into the center of a struggle that ultimately led the Supreme Court to declare all white primaries unconstitutional.

On March 7, 1927, in *Nixon v. Herndon*, the Supreme Court unanimously declared the white primary statute unconstitutional for violating the "equal protection" clause of the Fourteenth Amendment. The decision, however, left open the possibility that the party could do privately what the state could not do officially. White Democrats in Texas, and in other states throughout the South, took only a few months to respond to this opportunity and ultimately restored the white primary. Many state legislatures enacted new statutes giving the executive committee of each state party the power to decide who could vote in its primary. Accordingly, the Democratic executive committees in most southern states adopted resolutions allowing only whites to vote in the Democratic primary (the *white* primary).

Southern Democrats were successful in barring African Americans from Democratic primary elections under the pretext that the political party was a private club and thus not subject to federal laws prohibiting discrimination. Even though the white primary restricted the qualification of voters at the primary election and not during the general election, as I noted before, in the single-party South primary elections were the "real" elections (Key 1949). Since the Democratic Party was the majority party, the candidates it nominated in its primary always won the general election, so the difference between the primary and the general election was mostly figurative. By denying African Americans the vote in the primary, states implicitly disenfranchised them from the general election, not by explicitly barring them but by creating an environment where nonwhite voters had no stake in the outcome, no authentic candidates to support, and no real contest to turn out for. Interestingly, there is some sense that white primaries were also used to unite southern whites in majority coalitions. They allowed white elites to form coalitions with poor whites and essentially kept poor whites from forming coalitions with other groups, again rendering the general election effectively meaningless.

Finally in 1944, after much legal strife over the issue in Texas and elsewhere, the Supreme Court ruled in *Smith v. Allwright* that the Texas white primary violated the Fifteenth Amendment. The Court found that various state laws made the Texas primary an integral part of the general electoral process, so blacks could not constitutionally be prohibited from voting in the Democratic primary, even by party officials. Of course the Smith decision did not end all attempts to limit political participation among African Americans, given the widespread implementation of other restrictive electoral institutions at the time, but it ended the white primary in Texas and throughout the South.

Together, the limited electoral competitiveness fostered within the single-party South and the white primary system widely used by the southern states make southern primary elections an interesting setting for exploring the effects of electoral institutions. First, southern primaries were more competitive than general elections during the pre–civil rights era, so by looking at them we can better discern the role that increased competition (even within-party competition) had on voting rates as compared with electoral institutions. Further, one would expect the white primary to have a sizable effect on turnout during primaries, not general elections. Shifting the focus to the primary contest will illuminate the effect of a variety of electoral institutions, especially the white primary, on southern turnout during comparably competitive primary elections.

Table 7.2 presents the results from the empirical analysis conducted on voter turnout in the southern states during primary elections from 1920 to 1970.[8] During this subset of years the Democratic Party had a strong hold over politics in the region; in all, this period lasted from the end of Reconstruction to the end of the civil rights era. This time frame also includes variation in election years with and without the white primary system, which, as I noted earlier, was eradicated by 1948 under *Smith v. Allwright*. Data on vote totals from the primary elections were taken from Heard and Strong's *Southern Primaries and Elections, 1920–1949* (1950) and Bartley and Graham's *Southern Elections: County and Precinct Data, 1950–1972* (1978). As shown in figure 7.3, voting rates during the period were often higher for gubernatorial primaries (17% on average) than for US Senate primaries (13% on average). Accordingly, model 1 in table 7.2 presents the results on southern primary turnout when a gubernatorial election is considered the highest race on the ballot, and model 2 presents the results

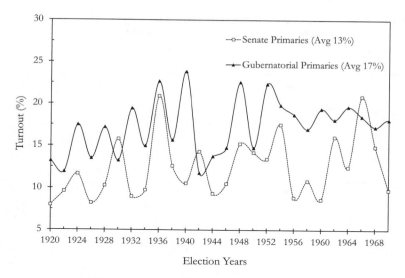

7.3. Southern voter turnout trends during primary elections, 1920–70

when a US Senate race is considered the highest race. The analysis was run both ways to examine whether the selection of which race is considered the highest race on the ballot affects the results in a systematic way. Any differences that exist between the specifications are pointed out in the discussion of results.

First, table 7.2 demonstrates the sizable, and perhaps surprising, positive effect that the white primary had on southern voter turnout during primary elections from 1920 to 1970.[9] The results suggest that the white primary increased voter turnout by just over 6 percentage points during gubernatorial elections (model 1) and by over 8 percentage points during senatorial elections (model 2). This is interesting, since the white primary's turnout-increasing effect is often masked by simpler descriptive approaches to depicting turnout variation and is typically thought to be overwhelmed by the massively restrictive combination of electoral institutions that flourished in the southern states. Further, at first one might expect this limiting law to decrease, not increase, participation, since in practice the provision mandated a white electorate in states that had sizable black populations. Although the aggregate data used in the analysis constrain the conclusions one can reach about the particular groups for which voting rates increased, it seems reasonable to expect that the white primary may have boosted the number of white voters in the primary in relation to the size of the state's black population.

Table 7.2 Southern Voter Turnout during Primary Elections, 1920–70

Variable	Model 1: Governor Highest Race		Model 2: Senate Highest Race	
Voting qualifications:				
White primary	6.233*	(2.974)	8.387**	(2.983)
Property requirement	−2.698	(5.608)	3.324	(5.558)
Literacy test	−8.097	(4.990)	−12.172*	(5.689)
Poll tax	−2.848	(2.395)	−3.433	(2.492)
Residency requirement	−0.005	(0.005)	−0.004	(0.006)
Voter registration:				
Frequency of periodic registration	0.107**	(0.041)	0.092*	(0.044)
Nonvoting purge period	0.047	(0.028)	0.024	(0.030)
Registration closing date	−0.041	(0.038)	−0.053	(0.041)
Voting procedures:				
Hours polls are open	2.152	(7.010)	1.905	(7.952)
Hours polls are open squared	−0.096	(0.350)	−0.085	(0.393)
Electoral calendar:				
Vote margin	0.028	(0.021)	0.033	(0.019)
Demographics:				
Education	0.686	(0.688)	0.537	(0.699)
Per capita income	−2.764*	(1.179)	−2.535*	(1.195)
Black population	0.429	(0.390)	0.589	(0.394)
Other population	21.201	(14.913)	19.154	(14.360)
Age 45 or above	2.679**	(0.666)	2.943**	(0.703)
Constant	−66.167	(42.744)	−74.304	(44.200)
State fixed effects	Yes		Yes	
Year fixed effects	Yes		Yes	
N	286		286	
R^2	0.535		0.486	

Note: Panel-corrected standard errors are in parentheses.
*$p < .05$
**$p < .01$

Further work will have to be done to evaluate the nuances of this relationship, since interaction terms in the models presented here were not statistically significant. Yet there is reason to suspect that the effects of the white primary were exacerbated by race relations, as informed by Key's (1949) racial threat hypothesis, which argued that efforts to maintain political control were more aggressive and pronounced in areas with higher concentrations of African Americans (see also Blalock 1967; Blumer 1958; Bobo 1983; Kousser 1974; Quillian 1995; Tajfel, Billig, and Bundy 1971). A number of other scholars have also demonstrated that political environments grow more hostile to minority groups as their respective numbers increase (see, e.g., Avery and Fine 2012; Giles and Hertz 1994; Glaser 1994; Hill and Leighley 1999; Krueger and Mueller 2001; Matthews and Prothro 1963). By stacking the deck in favor of white political preferences, the white primary offered whites a way to control political outcomes despite the sizable black populations in the southern states. Thus it seems reasonable to suspect that in the single-party states where the white primary flourished—the same states where black populations were large—whites had an increasing incentive to participate in selecting Democratic representatives, and they seized this opportunity at the expense of southern blacks.

In addition to examining the effects of the white primary, table 7.2 aimed to evaluate the effects of other electoral institutions in a more competitive electoral environment. This was motivated in response to scholars, particularly Key (1949), who suggested that lack of competition, not restrictive electoral laws per se, fostered low voting rates in the southern states; although many have challenged Key's theory (Kousser 1974; Redding 2003; Rusk 1970; Rusk and Stucker 1978), these claims are rarely examined with respect to primary elections or general elections preceded by a white primary. In theory, examining institutional effects during competitive primary elections shows the impact of institutions in a more even-handed framework. Yet as shown in table 7.2, few electoral institutions—restrictive or expansive—affected voter turnout during primary elections from 1920 to 1970. Beyond the effects of the white primary, it seems that literacy tests were the only voting qualification that affected turnout during primary elections. As shown in model 2, the literacy test decreased southern turnout in Senate primaries by about 12 percentage points. This result was not statistically significant at the conventional threshold of $p < .05$ in gubernatorial elections (model 1), but the effect is in the same direction and also sizable. Note that, unlike the models of general elections presented in chapter 5, the literacy test, not the poll tax, is shown to affect participation during primary elections. Table 7.2 also demonstrates that at least one expansive provision positively influenced primary voting rates. Specifically, as a state moved from a periodic to a permanent voter registration system during this period, overall turnout increased by almost 11 percentage points in gubernatorial primaries (model 1) and by over 9 percentage points in senatorial primaries (model 2).

Overall, these findings suggest that even within the comparably more competitive primary elections from 1920 to 1970, at least three electoral institutions—the white primary, literacy tests, and permanent voter registration—had an effect on primary voting rates. The history of restrictiveness and nonvoting norms created by these institutions has shaped the character of voting and elections for southern blacks, and perhaps whites in the region as well. In his important *Southern Politics in State and Nation,* V. O. Key suggested that southern suffrage laws merely formalized a situation that had already become a fact of southern political life. He asserted that "the absence of a presidential contest, the nature of suffrage rights, and Negro disenfranchisement result in a low turnout of voters. The habit of nonvoting grows and the electorate by custom becomes limited" (1949, 508); yet Key was not convinced that electoral institutions depressed turnout as much as civil rights reformers of a later era thought. This study, however–like others–has repeatedly demonstrated that electoral institutions did indeed have a real effect on southern voting rates throughout the century (see Kousser 1974, 1999). Specifically, this chapter has illuminated the dominance of restrictive voting rules and their consistently depressing effect on voting throughout the South.

Conclusion

This chapter has further explored the origins and impact of the oppressive voting norms that impeded southern voting throughout the first half of the twentieth century. It has focused on two important aspects of institutions and voting in the South: the pre- and post–civil rights periods with their different approaches to structuring voting rights and the effect that electoral institutions, especially the white primary, had on voting during more competitive primary elections from 1920 to 1970. Although some might argue that we already know a sufficient amount about the effects of Jim Crow in the South and that, in this sense, a historical framework is unnecessary, this book contends that there is a relationship between the restrictive voting culture of the South's past and its continuing low turnout today. It could be that these voting patterns are at least partly rooted in the legacy of Jim Crow and the depressed voting culture that system promoted. If so, this dreary reality may trump purely institutional attempts at improvement. Even though the southern voting culture was noticeably altered by the passage and implementation of the 1964 National Civil Rights Act and 1965 Voting Rights Act, the South continues to garner the lowest voting rates in the nation. Over the past century, many expansive reforms have been enacted to make voting less costly for the individual and ultimately increase turnout; yet, as I have shown throughout this book, the effect of recent institutional reforms on voting rates in the South has been minimal.

That result suggests that this low turnout may be attributable to a long history of not voting, coupled with a depressed socioeconomic climate. As Lawson stated, although the civil rights legislation made democratic equality possible in a literal sense, "modern-day reformers [have] failed to provide southern blacks with the economic means to accompany guarantees of political freedom" (1985, 273). Further, as suggested by Matthews and Prothro, "How much more can the size of the Negro vote in the South be increased without first revolutionizing the social and economic structure of the region, without first altering the pattern of subordination within which southern Negroes live?" (1966, 20). When historically repressive voting norms are coupled with a poor socioeconomic climate, it may be that the types of electoral reform that could effectively improve voting rates reside in categories of race, class, and education and that overtly electoral mechanisms are only secondary issues. Given the South's dramatic history of limiting voting, it seems there is no one institutional answer to its depressed turnout rates.

If the ultimate goal of modern cost-reducing electoral reforms is to increase national participation, then we must pay particular attention to how the states and their voting histories differ. The southern states have a long history of enacting restrictive voting laws, which may continue to suppress voting today. Because of these states' history of restrictive voting socialization, racism, and poverty, engaging the latent voting culture and participatory spirit might require a multifaceted solution. Although it is necessary to continue enacting reforms that make voting less costly in a direct sense, work also must be done to improve the region's depressed economic and educational situation and stimulate political attentiveness and mobilization.

EIGHT

Conclusion: The Future of Electoral Reform

Voting is fundamental to the American political system. Through the ballot box, the governed are able to express their consent with the political process (or their disapproval of it), alter or maintain the status quo, and foster democratic representation. Electoral institutions provide the framework for this critical mechanism, setting the boundaries of participation throughout the twentieth century and before. It has been widely noted, however, that the structure of the American electoral system, especially early in the century, has disproportionately placed the burden of participating on the individual. Politicians and voters alike have realized that the costs of voting are vast and the rewards minimal. It has been argued that without substantial reform to ease the costs of participation, the institution itself creates a disincentive to vote so that turnout suffers. Indeed, if institutions systematically affect political behavior, it seems reasonable to expect electoral institutions—and the ever-present possibility of institutional change—to hold great promise for reshaping participation norms in American elections.

Understanding this dynamic relationship is complicated, however. This book has dealt with one piece of the process—the effects of a variety of electoral institutions on participation rates throughout the twentieth century. Central to the story is the American federal system, which grants individual states the power to determine who may vote and how costly the process will be. As I have shown throughout, the states have taken very different approaches to structuring participation. Electoral reform has been used over the years to constrain participation among certain groups and, more recently, as a solution for improving national voting rates. However, by examining expansive and restrictive laws together, this book has shown that there has been an asymmetry in the effects of institutional change. On the one hand, restrictive electoral institutions have systematically contributed to low voter turnout in many southern and nonsouthern states throughout the twentieth century; yet the effects associated with expansive reforms have arguably been modest and varied; the absence of positive effects in the southern states is especially noteworthy. Taken together, these findings suggest that despite recent calls for national election reform, a single institutional fix may not be universally successful.

Instead, I argue that variation in state voting rates might be due to some blending of institutions and political context. Accordingly, I highlight the importance of political, geographical, and historical context as necessary conditions for understanding and generating change from electoral reform. This is similar to the larger literature on American exceptionalism that posits a cultural basis for political behavior, with some role for institutions, but differs from most canonical turnout models, which often ignore institutions or treat them as deterministic. The differences in historical or geographical context that I stress pertain to state voting habits and patterns that are due to social circumstances (e.g., racial and social disposition, political history, and previous approaches to rule making), and they further show how important political environment is in shaping institutional effects. For example, the empirical results I present reveal that expansive institutions are not a panacea when favorable historical and cultural conditions do not exist. Although exploring specific individual-level and state-by-state relationships awaits future work, this book has demonstrated important differences between the southern and nonsouthern states.

Ultimately, my goal has been to examine a process that is both historical and dynamic and to sketch a bigger picture about incentives and disincentives in American elections. The root of these relationships is in the exceptionalism of both electoral environments and outcomes that is afforded (and perpetuated) by the American federal system. Indeed, each of the American states has a unique institutional profile (and institutional history) that defines past and maybe even future institutions. This variation affects state participation rates and subsequent rule changes. It is poised as the beginning of a larger research agenda on how specific institutions interact with political context at the aggregate and individual levels and on how these laws originated in the first place. It also offers perspective on the bounds of electoral reform as we move through the twenty-first century.

At least three research paths could be pursued in light of the findings I have presented. First, exploring the origins of the electoral institutions I have discussed would be a substantial contribution to those works (like this one) that examine institutional effects. Obviously electoral rules are the product of political processes. Indeed, electoral institutions are incredibly important to political actors in the states and at the national level, so institutional changes to the governance of elections are often contentious and very partisan. By exploring the origin of these laws, one could reveal the *politics* behind the creation and evolution of state electoral institutions. In particular, one could evaluate the view that economists commonly hold about federalism—that institutions match preferences and demographic heterogeneity or homogeneity that have been sorted into jurisdictions— and determine where and when this framework holds. One could also explore the intense partisan, racial, and class struggles that have shaped reform discussions throughout American history, particularly those aiming to remedy injustices (see, e.g., Redding's impressive work on disenfranchisement laws in North Carolina [2003]).

Future work could also build on existing research to further examine how changing election laws can alter the motivations of interest groups, political parties, and elected officials as well as voters. For example, in 2008, Barack Obama strategically mobilized voters using newly available early voting laws. From research on the use of direct democracy in the American states we know that individuals are more likely to vote when salient initiatives appear on state ballots, but also that party strategies change as well (Smith and Tolbert 2007; Tolbert and Smith 2005). Political parties place initiatives on state ballots to mobilize their partisan base or divide the electorate using wedge issues (Donovan, Tolbert, and Smith 2008; Nicholson 2005; Smith 2001). Restrictive voter registration laws in the South were paired with weak political parties and weak party mobilizing institutions, which all contributed to decreased voter turnout (Hill and Leighley 1992; Key 1949; Rosenstone and Hansen 1993). By exploring the political underpinnings of electoral reform from a number of vantage points, we might be able to determine how and when varying electoral laws may be used strategically to benefit many political players.

Finally, it is important to examine the varying effects of electoral laws on the composition of the electorate. Over time it has become clear that the rules governing elections in the American states have stacked the deck in favor of certain groups and implicitly, or sometimes even explicitly, disenfranchised others (Leighley 1995; Patterson 2002; Piven and Cloward 1988, 2000; Wolfinger and Rosenstone 1980). Alleviating socioeconomic vote bias has been one of the motivations for electoral reform. Indeed, many studies have pointed out the differential effects associated with electoral reform that may exist across groups, but they fail to reach consensus on the direction of these effects. Future work could more explicitly examine whether institutional effects are big enough to shift the balance of participation between income groups. For example, some have identified greater increases in turnout among disadvantaged citizens (Avery and Peffley 2005; Highton 2004; Mitchell and Wlezien 1995; Wolfinger and Rosenstone 1980) or infrequent voters (Stein and Vonnahme 2008), while others have found little or no significant difference across income groups after reform (Knack and White 2000; Stein 1998). Some studies even warn of the potential for "perverse consequences" following electoral reform in which turnout among advantaged groups rises the most, leading to a presumed net increase in political inequality (Berinsky 2005; Berinsky, Burns, and Traugott 2001; Karp and Banducci 2000; Rigby and Springer 2011), which should be studied further, especially in relation to recent convenience reform initiatives.

The Future of Electoral Reform in the United States

The common thread guiding the evolution of elections and voting behavior throughout the twentieth century (and since) has been the role of American federalism in shaping the electoral landscape. As this book has shown, despite the enactment over time of federal electoral laws that have typically aimed to limit state autonomy to some degree, variation in electoral institutions still abounds both between states and within states over time. Yet reformers and politicians frequently tout blanket national electoral reforms that invariably stifle the diversity and utility of voting practices in the individual states.

For example, throughout the year preceding the 2004 presidential election, the *New York Times* ran an editorial series on improving the quality of American elections and increasing interest and participation in politics. To conclude, on the morning before the election, the *Times* issued a twelve-point plan proposing a variety of institutional methods that would effectively reform the American electoral system. The list was largely motivated by the assertion that "first and foremost, it is patently obvious that presidential elections, at least, should be conducted under uniform rules" (November 7, 2004). Although this remark was probably intended to resonate with those still unsettled by the unmistakable failure of various state electoral systems on election night in 2000, it is reminiscent of the rhetoric used by scholars and activists pleading for federal electoral reform more broadly: for the federal government to supersede American federalism and construct uniform, far-reaching electoral policy. In urging this, they suggest that we actually know which institutional designs would increase fairness and participation throughout the nation and, more important, that there is some systematic evidence and consensus about what these uniform rules should be. Of course this is generally not the case, and the results presented in this book make the success of such blanket reforms seem questionable at best.

Ignoring variation in state political climates and electoral history, those touting national reforms have often assumed that a single expansive electoral reform would produce an equivalent effect wherever it was implemented, regardless of geography or political history. It is thus not surprising that reformers have been disappointed over the past few years by the small impact many federal reform initiatives seem to have had on participation (such as the National Voter Registration Act in 1993 and the Help America Vote Act in 2002). To date, most of what we know about political participation in the United States is limited by a monolithic picture of national elections. This affects reform discussions, and those touting national-level reforms often lose sight of the possibility that state-specific and regional-specific issues might undermine the success of national measures.

But this book describes federalism as a constitutive feature of American voting and elections; we cannot make truly useful policy prescriptions for improving political participation until we appreciate the unique manifestations of state electoral institutions and how much they effectively, or ineffectively, govern voting in individual states. We must also consider historical context and the overall institutional profile of the state when making our policy recommendations. Further, we must modify our expectations about national electoral reform and strive to identify where and when institutional changes might be most necessary and successful.

Even though expansive institutional changes over the past few decades seem to have stopped the decline in national turnout, voting rates in many of the American states have not increased. This has led reformers and scholars to wonder whether there is an institutional solution that can actually foster substantial increases in voting. I suggest that lowering voting costs through institutional reforms perhaps only allows those already interested in voting to take advantage of the new procedure and does not generate new voters. Additionally, something outside the institutional framework may be contributing to patterns of nonvoting. Over eighty years of institutional change reveals that there is no universal cure-all for improving low turnout rates wherever they exist. In particular, there are important differences between the observable effects associated with institutional changes in the southern and nonsouthern states. So it may be that to truly improve voting rates we need to implement targeted reforms in conjunction with a long-term strategy for civic reengagement.

There is also the question of implementation. Do states and their election boards have enough money to effectively carry out national or state-initiated reform policies? Without adequate funding and proper implementation, the potential of cost-reducing electoral reforms will not be realized. To date, fiscal commitment to recent national programs has been inconsistent. For example, to help pay for the electoral reforms mandated by the Help America Vote Act (2002), the law authorized a total of nearly $3.9 billion over three fiscal years. Yet Congress severely underfunded the law by appropriating only $1.5 billion in 2003 and $500 million more in pending appropriations for 2004, leaving $1.86 billion that had not been fully appropriated. Given tightening budgets, particularly in the states, where and how are electoral reforms prioritized—or even possible? Further, do states have the manpower to physically carry out the changes associated with dramatically cost-reducing electoral reforms? And will electoral reform continue to be a partisan hot potato?

It is also clear that electoral reform is a high-stakes political game. Although this study ended with the historic 2000 presidential election—where problems in Florida highlighted the decentralized electoral system, a product of American federalism—the story did not stop there. What followed was a great irony. The decade began with this notable election, whose results informed millions of Americans that because of state-level variation in voting procedures their votes might not be counted correctly, or counted at all. It was an election that set the stage for another century's worth of electoral reforms. In its wake there was a storm of initiatives aimed at easing the vote and scrutinizing voting technology to make sure future votes are counted correctly. But more quietly, the Bush era also ended with a wave of restrictions—the first major systemic restriction on the right to vote in many years—in the form of voter identification laws. This culminated in the *Crawford v. Marion County Election Board* (2008) ruling in which, with another divided Supreme Court decision, Indiana's voter photo identification law was upheld as a valid state regulation. This decision, and the increasing adoption of photo identification laws (sixteen states, many of them southern, required voters to present a photo ID in order to vote in November 2012), is for many observers reminiscent of a bygone era of race-based restrictions. Given the notable implications of restrictive laws on participation demonstrated in this book, one might wonder what the course of electoral reform, and the priorities it reflects, will look like through the twenty-first century. Will the political parties keep using reform to stack the electoral deck in their favor? Has a new era of different, but nonetheless restrictive, electoral laws begun? Will the progression of voting rights and electoral reform in the United States forever be plagued by progress followed by backsliding?

Because widespread electoral participation is vital to the health of American democracy, electoral reform is essential in those places where voting rates wane. But the approach we take to reform in the twenty-first century must be more nuanced and informed than previous national attempts. States' independent needs must be identified, and steps must be taken to reform the voting and institutional culture in areas that have been consistently depressed. I suggest that targeted state and local reforms may be more prudent than nationalized attempts. Yet the policy recommendations conveyed here imply an interesting paradox. Although we might believe that reforms targeted to state conditions make sense (and this book has made a powerful case for them) and could be effective, it is unlikely that federal authorities would impose varying rules on individual states, particularly in the interest of fairness and funding. In the absence of new strategies, however, the future of electoral reform looks bleak. We cannot continue to revisit previous initiatives and expect different results. We need to look to the varying experiences in the individual states to determine whether electoral reform is necessary and how local publics may respond to change. By embracing the variation afforded by American federalism, we will have a better understanding of how the states have shaped the nation throughout the twentieth century and into the twenty-first.

APPENDIX A

State-by-State Voter Turnout Rates Compared with the Average National Voter Turnout Rate during Election Years, 1920–2000
   Available online only at www.press.uchicago.edu/sites/springer/

Mississippi Voter Registration Application Form

SWORN WRITTEN APPLICATION FOR REGISTRATION

(By reason of the provisions of Sections 241, 241-A and 244 of the Constitution of Mississippi and relevant statutes of the State of Mississippi, the applicant for registration, if not physically disabled is required to fill in this form in his own handwriting in the presence of the registrar and without assistance or suggestion of any person or memorandum.)

1. Write the date of this application. . . . .

2. What it your full name? . . . .

3. State your age and date of birth . . . .

4. What is your occupation? . . . .

5. Where is your business carried on? (Give city, town or village, and street address, if any, but if none, post office address.) If not engaged in business, so state. . . . .

6. By whom are you employed? (Give name and street address, if any, but if none, post office address.) If not employed, so state. . . . .

7. Where is your place of residence in the county and district where you propose to register? (Give city, town or village, and street address, if any, but if none, post office address.) . . . .

8. Are you a citizen of the United States and an inhabitant of Mississippi? . . . .

9. How long have you resided in Mississippi?. . . . .

10. How long have you resided in the election district or precinct in which you propose to register? . . . .

11. State your last previous places of residence. (Give street address, if any, but if none, post office address.) . . . .

12. Are you a minister of the gospel in charge of an organized church, or the wife of such a minister? If so, what church? (Give address its each instance,) . . . .

13. Check which oath you desire to take: (1) General . . . . (2) Minister's: . . . . (3) Minister's wife: . . . . (4) If under 21 years at present, but will be 21 years old by date of general election. . . . .

14. If there is more than one person of your same name in the precinct, by what name do you wish to be called?. . . . .

15. Have you ever been convicted of any of the following crimes: bribery, theft, arson, obtaining money or goods under false pretenses, perjury, forgery, embezzlement, or bigamy? . . . .

16. Have you ever been convicted of any other crime (excepting misdemeanors for traffic violations)? . . . .

17. If your answer to question 15 or 16 is "Yes", name the crime or crimes of which you have been convicted, and the year, court, and place of such conviction or convictions: . . . .

18. Write and copy in the space below, Section . . . . of the Constitution of Mississippi: (Instructions to Registrar: You will designate the Section of the Constitution and point out same to applicant). . . . .

19. Write in the space below a reasonable interpretation (the meaning) of the Section of the Constitution of Mississippi which you have just copied: . . . .

20. Write in the space below a statement setting forth your understanding of the duties and obligations of citizenship under a constitutional form of government. . . . .

21. Sign the oath or affirmation referred to in question 13, and which is:

> NOTE: Registrar give applicant oath selected under question 13, Mark out that portion of oath that is not applicable.

> NOTE: Registrar. In registering voters in Cities and Towns not all in one election district, the name of such city or town may be substituted in the Oath for the Election District.

(a) GENERAL and/or SPECIAL OATH:

I, ... , do solemnly swear (or affirm) that I am twenty-one years old (or I will be before the next election in this County) and that I will have resided in this State two years, and . . . . Election District of . . . . County one year next preceding the ensuing election, and am now in good faith a resident of the same, and that I am not disqualified from voting by reason of having been convicted of any crime named in the Constitution of this State as a disqualification to be an elector; that I will truly answer all questions propounded to me concerning my antecedents so far as they relate to my right to vote, and also as to my residence before my citizenship in this District; that I will faithfully support the Constitution of the United States and of the State of Mississippi, and will bear true faith and allegiance to the same, So Help Me God.

. . . .
Applicant's Signature to Oath

(b) OATH OF MINISTER and/or MINISTER'S WIFE:

I, ... , do solemnly swear (or affirm) that I am twenty-one years old (or I will be before the next election in this County) and that I am a Minister, or the wife of a Minister, of the Gospel in charge of an organized church, and that I will have resided two years in this State and in . . . . Election District of . . . . County six months next preceding the ensuing election, and am now in good faith a resident of the same, and that I am not disqualified from voting by reason of having been convicted of any crime named in the Constitution of this State as a disqualification to be an elector; that I will truly answer all questions propounded to me concerning my antecedents so far as they relate to my right to vote, and also as to my residence before my citizenship in this District; that I will faithfully support the Constitution of the United States and of the State of Mississippi, and will bear true faith and allegiance to the same. So Help Me God.

. . . .
Applicant's Signature to Oath

. . . .
Applicant's Signature to Application
(The Applicant will also sign his name here)

STATE OF MISSISSIPPI
County of . . . .
Sworn to and subscribed before me by the within named . . . . .on
this the . . . . day of. . . . . , 19. . . . . .

. . . .
County Registrar

(SHAL)
Is applicant of good moral character?. . . . .
If not, why?. . . . .
Does applicant qualify?. . . . .
Passed . . . . Failed . . . .

. . . .
County Registrar

Source: United States Commission on Civil Rights, *Voting in Mississippi: A Report of the US Commission on Civil Rights* (Washington, DC: US Government Printing Office, 1965).

Descriptive Statistics, Presidential Election Years, 1920–2000

Variable	Measurement	Mean	SD	Min	Max
Dependent variable:					
Voter turnout	Total number of presidential votes divided by the state's voting age population (%)				
All states		55.72	14.57	6.64	82.97
Non-South		61.26	9.01	37.03	82.97
South		36.56	13.88	6.64	58.80
Independent variables:					
Voting qualifications:					
Property requirement	State has a property requirement: 1 = Yes, 0 = No				
All states		0.05	0.23	0	1
Non-South		0.01	0.10	0	1
South		0.21	0.41	0	1
Literacy test	State has a literacy test: 1 = Yes, 0 = No				
All states		0.23	0.42	0	1
Non-South		0.18	0.39	0	1
South		0.37	0.48	0	1
Poll tax	State has a poll tax: 1 = Yes, 0 = No				
All states		0.13	0.34	0	1
Non-South		0.05	0.22	0	1
South		0.40	0.49	0	1
Residency requirement	Length (in days) of a state's most restrictive residency requirement				
All states		227.27	191.43	0	730
Non-South		204.55	161.51	0	730
South		305.87	255.82	0	730

Variable	Measurement	Mean	SD	Min	Max
Voter registration:					
Frequency of periodic registration	Number of years before one has to reregister; states with permanent registration are assigned 100				
All states		84.65	35.31	1	100
Non-South		85.46	34.61	1	100
South		81.84	37.56	1	100
Nonvoting purge period	Number of years of not voting before one is purged; states without a nonvoting purge are assigned 100				
All states		49.16	48.28	2	100
Non-South		44.67	47.91	2	100
South		64.68	46.39	2	100
Universal mail-in registration	State has universal mail-in voter registration: 1 = Yes, 0 = No				
All states		0.21	0.41	0	1
Non-South		0.22	0.42	0	1
South		0.16	0.37	0	1
Motor voter registration	State has motor voter registration: 1 = Yes, 0 = No				
All states		0.12	0.33	0	1
Non-South		0.12	0.33	0	1
South		0.12	0.32	0	1
Registration closing date	Number of days between the close of registration and Election Day.				
All states		27.93	27.03	0	180
Non-South		25.30	21.33	0	180
South		37.05	39.76	10	180
Election Day registration	State has EDR: 1 = Yes, 0 = No				
All states		0.03	0.17	0	1
Non-South		0.04	0.20	0	1
South		. . .	. . .	. . .	. . .
Voting procedures:					
Hours polls are open	Number of hours the polls are open on Election Day				
All states		11.51	1.91	4	15
Non-South		11.68	1.87	4	15
South		10.92	1.94	7	14
Hours polls are open squared	Number of hours the polls are open on Election Day (squared)				
All states		136.14	39.34	16	225
Non-South		139.94	38.34	16	225
South		122.99	40.03	49	196

Variable	Measurement	Mean	SD	Min	Max
In-person early voting	State has in-person early voting: 1 = Yes, 0 = No				
All states		0.03	0.18	0	1
Non-South		0.03	0.17	0	1
South		0.04	0.19	0	1
Universal absentee voting	State has universal absentee voting: 1 = Yes, 0 = No				
All states		0.05	0.22	0	1
Non-South		0.06	0.24	0	1
South		0.01	0.07	0	1
Electoral calendar:					
Gubernatorial race	Gubernatorial race on the ballot: 1 = Yes, 0 = No				
All states		0.50	0.50	0	1
Non-South		0.53	0.50	0	1
South		0.40	0.49	0	1
Senate race	Senate race on the ballot: 1 = Yes, 0 = No				
All states		0.67	0.47	0	1
Non-South		0.67	0.47	0	1
South		0.67	0.47	0	1
Contested House seats	% of congressional seats contested by the two major parties				
All states		86.50	25.27	0	100
Non-South		95.81	11.53	0	100
South		54.29	32.44	0	100
Initiatives on the ballot	Number of initiatives on the ballot				
All states		0.86	2.05	0	18
Non-South		1.02	2.22	0	18
South		0.30	1.14	0	8
Vote margin	Difference between votes for winner and loser divided by total votes cast (%)				
All states		19.05	17.17	0.01	97.15
Non-South		16.59	12.79	0.06	88.08
South		27.59	25.64	0.01	97.15
State demographics:					
Education	% of state population age 25 years and older who graduated from high school				
All states		46.72	23.62	8.48	91.80
Non-South		49.01	23.34	8.96	91.80
South		38.82	22.90	8.48	86.60

Variable	Measurement	Mean	SD	Min	Max
Per capita income	State's per capita income in 2000 dollars ($1,000 increments)				
All states		14.11	8.53	0.65	41.45
Non-South		14.80	8.57	0.99	41.45
South		11.73	7.96	0.65	31.21
Black population	% of a state's total population black				
All states		9.29	11.15	0.03	52.23
Non-South		4.31	4.74	0.03	27.89
South		26.52	9.69	11.53	52.23
Other population	% of a state's total population "other" (neither white nor black)				
All states		3.42	7.90	0.01	73.93
Non-South		4.06	8.76	0.00	73.93
South		1.22	2.49	0.01	17.49
Age 45 or above	% of a state's total population 45 years of age and older				
All states		28.04	5.10	14	40
Non-South		28.66	4.63	15	40
South		25.89	6.03	14	40

Note: During presidential election years from 1920 to 2000, *N* is 1,030 for all states, 799 for the nonsouthern states, and 231 for the southern states.

Source: Validated presidential vote totals from 1920 to 2000 are available by state from the clerk of the US House of Representatives. The population data I used to calculate the voting age population (VAP) were taken from the *Statistical Abstracts of the United States* (US Census Bureau, 1900–2002). I compiled data on state electoral institutions using official state codebooks and state session laws. Where there was ambiguity, I contacted state electoral officials. Electoral calendar and state demographic data are available from a variety of sources, including *The Book of the States* (Council of State Governments, 1935–2004), *America Votes* (Congressional Quarterly Election Research Center, 1954–2002), and the *Statistical Abstract of the United States* (US Census Bureau, 1900–2002).

Descriptive Statistics, Nonpresidential Election Years, 1922–98

Variable	Measurement	Mean	SD	Min	Max
Dependent variable:					
Voter turnout	Total number of votes for the highest race on the ballot divided by the state's voting age population (%)				
All states		41.58	14.88	1.86	75.42
Non-South		47.31	9.68	19.31	75.42
South		21.42	12.19	1.86	52.16
Independent variables:					
Voting qualifications:					
Property requirement	State has a property requirement: 1 = Yes, 0 = No				
All states		0.05	0.22	0	1
Non-South		0.01	0.10	0	1
South		0.20	0.40	0	1
Literacy test	State has a literacy test: 1 = Yes, 0 = No				
All states		0.22	0.42	0	1
Non-South		0.18	0.39	0	1
South		0.37	0.48	0	1
Poll tax	State has a poll tax: 1 = Yes, 0 = No				
All states		0.13	0.34	0	1
Non-South		0.05	0.23	0	1
South		0.41	0.49	0	1
Residency requirement	Length (in days) of a state's most restrictive residency requirement				
All states		228.87	191.87	0	730
Non-South		204.77	161.59	0	730
South		313.68	255.91	0	730

Variable	Measurement	Mean	SD	Min	Max
Voter registration:					
Frequency of periodic registration	Number of years before one has to reregister; states with permanent registration are assigned 100				
All states		84.99	34.98	1	100
Non-South		86.12	33.96	1	100
South		81.02	38.19	1	100
Nonvoting purge period	Number of years of not voting before one is purged; states without a nonvoting purge are assigned 100				
All states		46.35	48.05	2	100
Non-South		41.20	47.27	2	100
South		64.45	46.46	2	100
Universal mail-in registration	State has universal mail-in voter registration: 1 = Yes, 0 = No				
All states		0.19	0.39	0	1
Non-South		0.20	0.40	0	1
South		0.14	0.35	0	1
Motor voter registration	State has motor voter registration: 1 = Yes, 0 = No				
All states		0.09	0.29	0	1
Non-South		0.10	0.30	0	1
South		0.07	0.25	0	1
Registration closing date	Number of days between the close of registration and Election Day				
All states		28.26	27.67	0	180
Non-South		25.55	21.77	0	180
South		37.78	40.99	10	180
Election Day registration	State has EDR: 1 = Yes, 0 = No				
All states		0.03	0.17	0	1
Non-South		0.04	0.19	0	1
South		. . .	. . .	. . .	. . .
Voting procedures:					
Hours polls are open	Number of hours the polls are open on Election Day				
All states		11.50	1.90	4	15
Non-South		11.67	1.86	4	15
South		10.90	1.91	7	14
Hours polls are open squared	Number of hours the polls are open on Election Day (squared)				
All states		135.86	39.05	16	225
Non-South		139.69	38.18	16	225
South		122.41	39.16	49	196

Variable	Measurement	Mean	SD	Min	Max
In-person early voting	State has in-person early voting: 1 = Yes, 0 = No				
All states		0.02	0.15	0	1
Non-South		0.02	0.14	0	1
South		0.03	0.16	0	1
Universal absentee voting	State has universal absentee voting: 1 = Yes, 0 = No				
All states		0.04	0.19	0	1
Non-South		0.05	0.22	0	1
South		. . .	. . .	. . .	. . .
Electoral calendar:					
Gubernatorial race	Gubernatorial race on the ballot: 1 = Yes, 0 = No				
All states		0.70	0.46	0	1
Non-South		0.73	0.44	0	1
South		0.59	0.49	0	1
Senate race	Senate race on the ballot: 1 = Yes, 0 = No				
All states		0.67	0.47	0	1
Non-South		0.68	0.47	0	1
South		0.65	0.48	0	1
Contested House seats	% of congressional seats contested by the two major parties				
All states		83.34	28.53	0	100
Non-South		94.37	13.86	0	100
South		44.52	32.69	0	100
Initiatives on the ballot	Number of initiatives on the ballot				
All states		0.72	1.75	0	18
Non-South		0.86	1.91	0	18
South		0.21	0.88	0	7
Vote margin	Difference between votes for winner and loser divided by total votes cast (%)				
All states		23.87	25.19	0	100
Non-South		16.38	14.15	0	89.42
South		50.20	35.72	0.39	100
State demographics:					
Education	% of state population age 25 years and older who graduated from high school				
All states		46.41	22.83	9.02	92
Non-South		48.83	22.53	9.48	92
South		37.92	21.87	9.02	82.60
Per capita income	State's per capita income in 2000 dollars ($1,000 increments)				

Variable	Measurement	Mean	SD	Min	Max
All states		14.11	8.12	0.90	39.20
Non-South		14.84	8.11	1.35	39.20
South		11.52	7.61	0.90	29.55
Black population	% of a state's total population black				
All states		9.18	11.01	0.03	51.79
Non-South		4.31	4.70	0.03	27.34
South		26.31	9.65	11.60	51.79
Other population	% of a state's total population "other" (neither white nor black)				
All states		3.24	7.62	0.01	72.11
Non-South		3.84	8.44	0.01	72.11
South		1.11	2.34	0.01	16.71
Age 45 or above	% of a state's total population 45 years of age and older				
All states		28.05	4.87	15	40
Non-South		28.68	4.37	15	40
South		25.86	5.82	15	40

Note: During nonpresidential election years from 1922 to 1998, N is 976 for all states, 760 for the nonsouthern states, and 216 for the southern states.

Source: Validated vote totals for US Senate and House races from 1922 to 1998 are available by state from the clerk of the US House of Representatives. Vote totals for gubernatorial races during this period are available from the Congressional Quarterly Election Research Center's *Guide to US Elections* (2001). The population data I used to calculate the voting age population (VAP) were taken from the *Statistical Abstracts of the United States* (US Census Bureau, 1900–2002). I compiled data on state electoral institutions using official state codebooks and state session laws. Where there was ambiguity, I contacted state electoral officials. Electoral calendar and state demographic data are available from a variety of sources, including *The Book of the States* (Council of State Governments, 1935–2004), *America Votes* (Congressional Quarterly Election Research Center, 1954–2002), and the *Statistical Abstract of the United States* (US Census Bureau, 1900–2002).

NOTES

CHAPTER ONE

1. The Progressive electoral reforms occurred, ironically, in the name of democratic control of government, and were not necessarily implemented to encourage increases in voting.

2. Of course the literature on voter turnout is much more comprehensive than this statement suggests. One could fill a library with observational and experimental analyses exploring various dimensions of the topic. This book illustrates three research paths that are particularly relevant to this study, but the discussion is not meant to be comprehensive.

CHAPTER TWO

1. It is worth noting that some scholars have also shown the gap between the preferences of voters and nonvoters to be generally small (Bennett and Resnick 1990; Erikson 1995; Highton 2004; Norrander 1989; Wolfinger and Rosenstone 1980).

2. Although the level of participation in US national elections is very low from a comparative perspective, comparative data have also shown that Americans are very active in groups and in campaign work. They also typically face a greater variety of national, state, and local elections and referenda than citizens in many other nations (Powell 1982; Verba, Schlozman, and Brady 1995).

3. Individual-level research has been vastly important to our understanding of American elections and the American voter. The relationship between socioeconomic status and participation developed most fully by Verba and Nie (1972; see also Almond and Verba 1963; Barnes and Kaase 1979; Campbell et al. 1960; Milbrath 1965; Nie, Verba, and Petrocik 1999; Rosenstone and Hansen 1993) is widely considered to be the major finding about political participation within behavioral research, and one of the most robust results within the study of American politics more generally. From this extensive literature, we have learned that people with high levels of education and income are more likely to participate in politics than those with low levels (Acock and Scott 1980; Barnes and Kaase 1979; Conway 1991; Dalton 1988; Leighley 1990; Salisbury 1980; Verba, Nie, and Kim 1978; Verba et al. 1993a). This line of research has also explored, among other things, generational effects (Jennings 1979; Jennings and Markus 1988; Jennings and Niemi 1981) and the effect

of race on one's propensity to vote (Bobo and Gilliam 1990; Ellison and Gay 1989; Uhlaner, Cain, and Kiewiet 1989; Verba et al. 1993b).

4. Several studies have shown that turnout is high among those who are registered (Erikson 1981; Glass, Squire, and Wolfinger 1984; Piven and Cloward 1988; Squire, Wolfinger, and Glass 1987). More recently, however, some have questioned this result, particularly in an increasingly relaxed registration environment (Brown and Wedeking 2006; Hanmer 2009; Highton 1997). It may be that voters factor the costs of voting into the initial costs of registration; that is, a costly voting process may lead to lower registration overall but to higher turnout among those who do register.

5. This is not to say that scholars have ignored the effects of restrictive laws on voting; this is of course false (see, e.g., Key 1949; Kousser 1999; Lawson 1976). Rather, there are gains to be made from studying the effects of expansive *and* restrictive laws together over time.

6. Others have argued that state context is important by focusing on the effects of social capital or state racial and ethnic context (see, for example, Campbell 2000; Ewald 2009; Hero 2007; Hill and Leighley 1992; Putnam 2000).

CHAPTER THREE

1. Since voter turnout is one step removed from voter registration, there is more potential for noise to be introduced by analyzing the effects of registration laws when turnout, rather than voter registration, is used as the dependent variable. However, because states run their own registration programs, some states have more inflated registration rolls than others. In fact, Piven and Cloward (2000) estimated that "deadwood registrants"—those who are deceased or have moved and may be registered elsewhere but whose names nevertheless remain on the registration rosters—compose on average 10% to 15% of the names on the official state registration rolls, and this percentage varies widely across the states. In fact, there are numerous examples of state-reported registration figures exceeding 100% of the voting age population (VAP), particularly before the National Voting Rights Act. Since it is not entirely clear that finding sizable effects on registration rates would imply much about turnout effects (for example, there will presumably be some registrants who register via motor voter but do not vote on Election Day), it would be ideal to estimate two models: one for voter registration and another for voter turnout. Unfortunately, the quality of voter registration data is categorically poor and varies greatly by state and over time. Thus, comparing registration levels is perhaps more problematic than comparing turnout levels. Owing to the poor quality of twentieth-century state-level registration data and this book's overarching focus on the participatory outcome of various electoral institutions, I concentrate exclusively on state-level voter turnout rates.

2. After much consideration, I used the "highest race on the ballot" rather than the "race with the highest turnout overall" when calculating state turnout rates. First, using the highest race on the ballot employs a systematic comparable turnout measure across states and time and does not introduce selection bias into the analysis. Additionally, constructing the turnout measure using the race with the highest turnout overall does not produce a significant difference in the statistical or substantive evaluation of voting rates (or the rankings presented here). In most cases the race with the highest turnout overall *was* the highest race on the ballot. Further, the Pearson correlation between the two measures during the election years evaluated in

this study is .99, which suggests that there is not a statistically significant difference between the alternative measures.

3. Validated vote totals for presidential, senatorial, and congressional races from 1920 to 2000 were provided by the clerk of the US House of Representatives. Vote totals for gubernatorial races during this period were found in the Congressional Quarterly's *Guide to the U.S. Elections* (2001).

4. Population data were taken from the US Census Bureau's *Statistical Abstracts of the United States*. Linear interpolation was used to generate between-census population estimates. Before the ratification of the Twenty-Sixth Amendment in 1971, the VAP was calculated for those twenty-one years of age and over. Before 1971, four states allowed individuals under twenty-one to vote. In 1943 Georgia allowed those eighteen and over to vote. In 1955 Kentucky let those eighteen and over vote. And beginning in 1960, Alaska allowed those nineteen and over to vote, and Hawaii let those twenty and over vote. The VAP for these states was calculated accordingly.

5. Alaska and Hawaii did not gain statehood until 1959, so they enter the time series at the 1960 presidential election (see figures 3.5 and 3.6). Also, as shown in figure 3.10, nonpresidential turnout rates do not exist for Louisiana in 1978, 1982, 1990, and 1994. This reflects a unique election rule in Louisiana stipulating that a candidate who receives 50% or more of the vote in the primary election automatically wins, and no general election is held. If no candidate secures 50% or more of the vote in the primary election, then the general election is a runoff between the top two candidates. The former scenario occurred during the four omitted nonpresidential years.

6. The most widely given reason for the bad prediction was that the pollsters had stopped questioning individuals too early. Roper's September 9 poll showed Dewey with a lead of 52.2 to 37.1 percent, so he confidently announced that he would not do any more polling during the campaign.

7. The 1972 decline in turnout should be viewed with some skepticism. Although the decline occurred in principle, it can be attributed at least in part to the reduction in the national voting age from twenty-one to eighteen after the ratification of the Twenty-Sixth Amendment. This change artificially swelled the denominator in the turnout equation and created an observable decline similar to what happened after the national enfranchisement of women in 1920. Of course, this election was also held during a time of great unrest about the Vietnam War, which may have had a real and unique depressing effect on 1972 turnout rates.

8. Of course, quantitative analysis is required to systematically test this relationship. This is provided in chapter 5.

CHAPTER FOUR

1. Given the eighty-year span of this study, there are no data on the actual implementation of state electoral institutions (e.g., whether they were strictly enforced). I therefore concentrate on state adoption and elimination years, assuming that the laws are enforced in accord with the statutory provisions. The possibility that these laws may be carried out unevenly is a certain but unavoidable limitation of this approach (for more on implementation, see Bassi, Morton, and Trounstine 2013; Burden and Neiheisel 2013; Hanmer 2009; Piven and Cloward 1988).

2. Age is also an important qualification for voting. Although I take changes in state voting age into account when calculating voter turnout, lowering the voting age is not expected to affect state turnout in the same way as the other institutional

changes I examine. Further, in addition to limited variation over time, it is not clear how a change in the voting age would have altered voting rates from a theoretical standpoint. On the one hand, reducing the voting age enfranchised a large group of people (those eighteen to twenty years of age) all at once, which may be expected to raise turnout. But this increase in the qualified population occurred among those least likely to vote. So one might expect a decline in turnout after the change. For these reasons, voting age itself is not treated as an electoral institution in this study.

3. After much consideration, I decided not to include felon disenfranchisement among voting qualifications. All but two states (Maine and Vermont) disenfranchised felons for some period between 1920 and 2000, and very few changes were made to these laws over the century. Although there is some variation in the permanency of state felon disenfranchisement laws—for example, whether the ability to vote is reinstated after some period—classifying this distinction is very subjective given the way state laws were written (Manza and Uggen 2006). There is also some variation in which populations are disenfranchised (e.g., prisoners, parolees, probationers, ex-felons). Unfortunately, data are available only on the number of prisoners in the states before 1972. This measure grossly underestimates the total disenfranchised population, especially during the latter part of the century (see Keyssar 2000; Manza and Uggen 2006; Miles 2004); thus it seems inappropriate to include this measure in the study's empirical analyses. As a test, the main empirical models I present throughout the book were estimated including the state prisoner population variable as a rough proxy for felon disenfranchisement. The variable was not statistically significant in any of the models, and the other findings were robust. Given the consistent presence of felon disenfranchisement in the states throughout the twentieth century and the inability to reliably measure the disenfranchised population over the period of this study, I conclude that there is little reason to suspect the law would dramatically affect state turnout beyond the effects of the institutions discussed and in addition to the state fixed effects that were estimated.

4. Although the 1965 Voting Rights Act eliminated property requirements for federal elections, many states continued to implement them for voting on bond issues or special assessments.

5. Appendix B presents an example of the literacy test used in Mississippi during the 1950s.

6. Alabama adopted the Boswell Amendment in 1946, just after the white primary was declared unconstitutional by the Supreme Court, making the timing of these additional restrictions somewhat unsurprising.

7. The 1965 Voting Rights Act eliminated the literacy test for voting in forty counties in North Carolina rather than in all counties.

8. From 1964 into the early 1970s, Alabama, Mississippi, Texas, and Virginia continued to require the payment of a poll tax to qualify for voting in nonfederal elections.

9. As shown in table 4.1, Alabama, Nevada, Texas, and Virginia continued to assess a poll tax after 1964, seemingly in opposition to the Twenty-Fourth Amendment. In each of these states, resistance and litigation slowed the removal of the tax, which was abolished by the Supreme Court two years later in *Harper v. Virginia State Board of Elections* (1966).

10. Voter registration currently exists in every state except North Dakota, which eliminated it in 1951.

11. In addition to the motor voter provision, the 1993 National Voter Registration Act required states to allow voter registration at government agencies such as welfare

offices. By allowing widespread access to registration materials, agency registration programs were expected to have a positive impact on voter registration and turnout; however, under the NVRA (1993), most states adopted agency-based registration at the exact time they implemented motor voter programs. Therefore agency registration is almost perfectly correlated with the enactment of motor voter programs. Since both reforms made registration more convenient and accessible (e.g., lowered the costs) and were enacted at generally the same time, I include only motor voter. See Piven and Cloward (1988, 2000) for more on agency registration.

12. In addition to the voting procedures evaluated here, there is some evidence that state-level variation in ballot design may affect participation. Exploring the evolution of the physical ballot in the fifty states over time is beyond the scope of this book, but see Carson and Roberts (2013) about ballot effects during congressional elections.

CHAPTER FIVE

1. The District of Columbia was not included in this study. Although Washington, DC, is often treated as a state, it lacks many of the important institutional qualities relevant to this study. Most important, its citizens were not allowed to vote in presidential elections until 1961, after the ratification of the Twenty-Third Amendment.

2. Alaska and Hawaii were not US states and did not have national elections from 1920 to 1958, so these twenty observations were omitted for both states. As I noted in chapter 3, Louisiana had no general election in 1978, 1982, 1990, or 1994. In the estimations focusing on all states, this yields an N of 1,030 [$(50 \times 21) - 10 - 10 = 1,030$] during presidential election years and an N of 976 [$(50 \times 20) - 10 - 10 - 4 = 976$] during nonpresidential election years. In the estimations focusing on the thirty-nine nonsouthern states, this yields an N of 799 [$(39 \times 21) - 10 - 10 = 799$] during presidential election years and an N of 760 [$(39 \times 20) - 10 - 10 = 760$] during nonpresidential election years. Similarly, in the estimations of the eleven southern states, this yields an N of 231 [$(11 \times 21) = 231$] during presidential election years and an N of 216 [$(11 \times 20) - 4 = 216$] during nonpresidential election years.

3. Practically speaking, 1920 is also the first year for which reliable validated vote totals are available from the clerk of the US House of Representatives. Before 1920 vote totals are questionable because of the role partisan political machines played in the voting process and the wide variation in reporting standards in state and local elections. Beginning this study in 1920 affords a consistent and systematic measure of the dependent variable from a reliable source and encompasses a period when women are included in the denominator term (and never again excluded).

4. Fixed-effects models are appropriate if one wants to make inferences about the observed units, whereas the random-effects model (which assumes that the effects are drawn from some random distribution) is appropriate if one thinks of the observed units as a sample from a larger population and wants to make inferences about the larger population. In the time-series cross-sectional (TSCS) data used in this study, the units (the fifty states) are fixed, and my aim is not to extend inferences to a larger, hypothetical population of similar states.

5. Panel-corrected standard errors (PCSEs) are similar to White's heteroskedasticity-consistent standard errors for cross-sectional estimators, but they are better because they take advantage of the information provided by the panel structure of the data. Simulations indicate that PCSEs are very accurate for $T > 15$. This is true even when

the errors meet the Gauss-Markov assumptions. Thus there is no cost, and some potential gain, to using PCSEs in place of the usual OLS standard errors (Beck and Katz 1995, 1996).

6.   As I noted earlier, North Dakota eliminated voter registration in 1951. Since it had many of the electoral institutions of interest here before and after 1951, I did not drop it from the analysis. After 1951, it is coded as not having any of the voter registration laws; but since it is the only state without a registration requirement, the effect of "no registration" on turnout rates could not be reliably evaluated. Alternatively, some scholars assume that having no registration is equivalent to having Election Day registration (EDR) and code North Dakota's registration laws in that fashion. Although the results are robust across alternative specifications, in the analyses presented here I chose not to conflate the EDR results by classifying a state that does not strictly have EDR as if it did.

7.   Some studies examining the effects of motor voter programs on registration and turnout have characterized their implementation in a given state (Knack 1995; Piven and Cloward 1988, 2000; Rhine 1995). In such work, motor voter implementation is often coded as either "active" or "passive." Active implementation requires motor vehicle employees to formally ask patrons whether they would like to register to vote. Presumably an active dialogue would take place, and the person would be given an explicit opportunity to register. States that implemented motor voter passively merely made the registration forms available on a desk or table within the agency but did not explicitly call attention to the option. In some cases government agents were rewarded for registering individuals. For example, Oklahoma law stipulated in 2000 that "motor license agents shall received 50 cents per valid voter registration application, or application for changes in voter registration, taken by themselves and employees of the motor license agent's office taken at the agent's office, payable by the State Election board" (Oklahoma State Code 2004, sec. 4–109.3). Incentives like this were offered to entice agency employees to enthusiastically comply; however, the way the process was carried out within individual states was left to the discretion of state officials and was almost never systematically verified or enforced. Although there is reason to suspect that states with active motor voter systems may have experienced larger increases in participation than states with passive systems, classifying the states in this way is rather subjective. Given the unreliability of such accounts, a simple dummy coding is superior, or at least is less potentially biased than studies that assess the quality of implementation.

8.   Despite the way the variables are coded, the correlation between Election Day registration and registration closing date is minimal. The correlation ranges from −0.22 to −0.29 in the various specifications, and it is not statistically significant at the $p \leq .05$ significance level.

9.   Oregon adopted a statewide vote-by-mail system (VBM) for all elections in 1998. Estimation problems arise with respect to VBM's effect on voter turnout, since Oregon is the only state that has VBM and had it only for two years during the span of the study. Therefore I have not included it in this analysis (for more on VBM, see Berinsky, Burns, and Traugott 2001; Mutch 1992; Southwell and Burchett 1997, 2000a, and 2000b).

10. Using aggregate data to study patterns of participation identified in research on individual-level behavior may raise concerns about the ecological fallacy. Of course the use of aggregate data in this study is appropriate and desirable, since the vari-

ables of interest pertain to state electoral institutions and state effects. However, the statistical models would be underspecified and potentially biased if demographic controls were not included. For this purpose I have included five key demographic controls. These are variables that have been shown to consistently affect individual-level behavior, yet their effects are not theorized about, or tested, at the individual level in this study. Instead, I observe general state trends. This is a limitation of using aggregate data exclusively, but it is not inherently a problem given my focus and goals.

11. Per capita income statistics from 1920 to 2000 are from the Bureau of Economic Analysis in the US Department of Commerce. They were adjusted for inflation and calculated in 2000 dollars using the Consumer Price Index published by the US Bureau of Labor Statistics, 1920–2000.

12. After serious consideration, I omitted an urban-rural state classification and a measure of partisan mobilization from this work. Although many subnational studies focus on the importance of urban-rural influences throughout the country, it does not seem that this distinction is important at the state level. Entire states are hard to classify in this way, and most of the variation in an urban-rural classification is lost when applied to an aggregated state analysis. Additionally, the historical role of political parties in the states, and partisan mobilization efforts in particular, has undoubtedly been important in shaping participation rates throughout the century; however, no suitable historical measure of state-level mobilization exists for the duration of this study. Some have employed David Mayhew's (1986) "traditional party organization" (TPO) scores in an attempt to capture this sort of classification; however, the TPO scores do not vary over time and are therefore inappropriate for this analysis.

13. Owing to my focus on aggregate, state-level data, we must be mindful of ecological inference issues. Namely, the statistical models presented throughout this book cannot account for how the electoral institutions being studied would have differentially affected individuals within a given state (drawing conclusions about individual-level behavior rather than aggregate behavior). Consequently, we should keep in mind that the effect the regressions presented here are estimating is the average institutional effect on turnout, which, for example, may not correspond to the average effect of law changes for blacks in the Jim Crow South (which we would expect to be large) or the average effect on whites during the same period (which we would expect to be comparatively small). Given the aggregate-level data used in this book, one must be cautious about the ecological fallacy, which assumes that individual members of a group have the average characteristics of the group at large. In other words, statistics that accurately describe the group characteristics do not necessarily apply to individuals within that group, and the results presented here are mindful of such limitations.

14. Chow tests confirm the need to run separate regression analyses for presidential and nonpresidential election years. The null hypothesis of no structural difference was rejected at the $p \leq .01$ confidence level.

15. Portions of the empirical work presented in this chapter are also found in Springer (2006) and Springer (2012).

16. The model is run on the separate regions to control for the unique institutional and political trends observed in the South that might erroneously influence the estimates of institutional effects outside the South when the regions are combined. A

Chow test indicates that structural differences exist between the southern and non-southern states during election years from 1920 to 2000. In regional specifications for both presidential election years and nonpresidential election years, the null hypothesis of no structural difference was rejected at the $p \leq .01$ confidence level.

17. For each model, two null hypotheses were tested: that the year dummies and the state dummies were not jointly significant. Using a general Wald test (F test), both null hypotheses were rejected at the $p \leq .01$ significance level.

18. Note that the fit of the models is inflated by the addition of several statistically significant state and year dummy variables. As a crude reference, one can compare the R^2 term for the models estimated with and without the state and year fixed effects to determine how much variance is being explained by the fixed effects versus the electoral institutions, state demographics, and electoral calendar indicators. For example, as shown in table 5.1, the R^2 term for the model estimated on the non-southern states is .77 when the fixed effects are included and only .44 when they are removed. Similarly, the R^2 term for the model estimated on the southern states is .92 when the fixed effects are included and .82 when they are removed. While this hints at the modest effect institutions have had on turnout over time, running the analysis without the fixed effects risks exaggerating the effects of the institutions and misspecifying the model in the ways I outlined earlier in the chapter. Although including fixed effects is a conservative modeling strategy, it seems the most appropriate for this type of study.

19. To determine whether these results were a function of Rhode Island's sole use of the law, the model was also estimated dropping the property requirement from the analysis (since it existed in only one state). The results were comparable across the models, underscoring the robustness of the finding for Rhode Island.

20. The variables are correlated at .38 ($p < .05$).

21. Interactions between race and each of the restrictive voting laws were tested. Most of them were not statistically significant, so they were not included in the final specification.

22. The models were also estimated using a classification of "active" or "passive" motor voter implementation (Knack 1995; Piven and Cloward 1988; Rhine 1995). The result (that motor voter registration did not have a statistically significant effect on turnout) was robust across all specifications.

23. I ran additional models to test the possibility that an interactive relationship may exist between the electoral institution and vote margin variables—that electoral reforms may have a more pronounced effect in competitive than in noncompetitive electoral settings (Patterson and Caldeira 1983; Leighley 2001). No statistically significant interactive effects were detected in the southern models. There were statistically significant interactive effects with both the literacy test and EDR and electoral competition in the nonsouthern states; however, because the magnitudes of the effects were minuscule and the substantive effect was nonexistent, these results were not included.

24. The EDR count variable ranged from one to eight years in the nonsouthern sample, reflecting a range in marginal effects of 1.35 to 10.82 depending on the number of years the state implemented EDR.

25. The literacy test count variable ranged from one to thirteen years in the nonsouthern sample. This corresponds to a range in marginal effects of −1.19 to 1.64 depending on the number of years the state had the restriction.

CHAPTER SIX

1. State-level political ideology would also be an interesting aspect of political context to examine here. Unfortunately no over-time measure of state ideology exists for the time span of this study (see Berry et al. [1998, 2007] for data on the modern period). This would be an interesting avenue for future work, especially for research pertaining to the underpinnings of the adoption of, and changes to, various state electoral laws rather than an examination of their effects.

2. This hypothesis does not rest on the presumption that nonwhites do not vote, or vote less frequently than whites. Instead, it suggests that an indirect relationship may exist between the size of a state's nonwhite population, the nature of the state's electoral laws, and the propensity for high voter turnout. It could be that the size of a state's nonwhite population affects the state's tendencies toward the adoption of expansive or restrictive electoral laws, which in turn affects participation rates. That is, racial homogeneity may play a role in a state's adoption of particular types of electoral rules, which may alter its voting culture and political history.

3. A state's nonwhite population is measured as the sum of the state's black population and any other nonwhite groups.

4. In this book, political culture is considered to be "like all culture, rooted in the cumulative historical experiences of particular groups of people" (Elazar 1972, 89).

5. Generally, Elazar's (1972) conception of "political culture" has an amorphous quality, but perhaps there is something useful about the spirit of the framework for this study. Although his research techniques in devising the state political culture designations admittedly are imprecise (they are largely based on his judgment, informed by years of observation and assumptions about the migration patterns of particular religious groups) and do not really lend themselves to direct measurement, Elazar's conception of political culture may tap into some of the cultural predispositions that could affect the voting behavior of state citizens. Even though some researchers have moved beyond his political culture typology, the three types do clearly imply fundamentally different collective attitudes toward political participation and imposition of institutional barriers.

6. Interestingly, testing Elazar's claims, Sharkansky found that "the states that place high on the Traditional end of the scale (and therefore low on Moralism) tend to show low voter turnout and illiberal suffrage regulations, underdeveloped government bureaucracy, and low scores on several measures of tax effort, government spending, and public services" (1969, 78).

CHAPTER SEVEN

1. The term Jim Crow refers to a racial caste system that existed primarily in the eleven southern states and additional border states (those slave states that did not secede) during the period from Reconstruction through the mid-1960s. Jim Crow connotes a series of discriminatory antiblack and antiminority laws and practices that permeated this region and greatly affected the quality of life for those under its sway. Many racist practices are associated with Jim Crow, but the focus of this chapter is its effect on voting rights. In this realm especially the weight of Jim Crow was immense. As noted by historian Steven F. Lawson, "The nearly total loss of the franchise during the 1890s coincided with the rigid imposition of Jim Crow laws. Both forms of discrimination marked the termination of any flexibility in race relations that previously existed, and completed the degradation of the Negro into a separate and unequal position within Southern life" (1976, 11).

2. There is also evidence that whites—especially poor whites—were adversely affected by restrictive voting laws in the South (although not necessarily to the same extent) even if they were not the direct targets of the laws (Key 1949; Kousser 1999; Rusk and Stucker 1978).

3. The Deep South is defined as the first seven states that seceded from the Union: Alabama, Florida, Georgia, Louisiana, Mississippi, South Carolina, and Texas.

4. This is an important place to remind readers that the voter turnout statistics I present in this study are aggregated at the state level. As a result, this book can make no claims about individual-level voting or about who the voters (or nonvoters) were during these election years. Although significant gains may have occurred with respect to voting among blacks after the 1960 reforms (see Reichley 1987; Rosenstone and Hansen 1993), the data I used cannot differentiate the race of the voters from the aggregate statistics. They can only indicate that overall voter turnout did not increase uniformly across all the southern states, as we might expect after the restrictive voting laws associated with Jim Crow were eradicated. It may be that voting increased among blacks at the expense of voting among whites in this region, but with the state-level data I used I cannot decipher that trend, and trying would only introduce ecological inference problems.

5. Of course the increases observed in the southern states after the implementation of the 1964 National Civil Rights Act and 1965 Voting Rights Act are especially impressive when compared with the counterfactual of the legislation having not being implemented at all. My point is that the civil rights legislation did not provide a one-stop fix for southern turnout, as one might expect. In fact, voting rates in the South continued to be low even after the restrictive voting laws were removed, although they were generally higher than they had been before the reforms.

6. State fixed effects were not included in the models presented in table 7.1. Not only are the southern states very similar on several dimensions during these subsets of years, but the samples are very small, making the inclusion of state fixed effects too restrictive for statistical estimation.

7. Alabama, Arkansas, Florida, Georgia, Louisiana, Mississippi, North Carolina, Tennessee, and Texas held white primaries through the 1944 election; South Carolina held a white primary though the 1946 election; and Virginia stopped using the white primary after the election in 1928.

8. The model specifications presented in table 7.2 are similar to those presented in other sections of the study; however, I omitted several institutional variables that were not implemented during the subset of years being considered. These include universal mail-in voter registration, motor voter registration, Election Day registration, in-person early voting, and universal absentee voting. Additionally, many of the electoral calendar variables were not appropriate for the analysis of primary elections.

9. The white primary variable is coded dichotomously by state (e.g., 1 = a year the state had the white primary; 0 = no white primary in the state). There were 286 observations during this period. The mean value was 0.476, with a standard deviation of 0.500.

WORKS CITED

Abramson, Paul, and John Aldrich. 1982. "The Decline of Electoral Participation in America." *American Political Science Review* 76:502–21.

Achen, Christopher. 1986. *The Statistical Analysis of Quasi-Experiments*. Berkeley: University of California Press.

————. 2006. "Expressive Bayesian Voters and Their Turnout Decisions: Empirical Implications of a Theoretical Model." Paper presented at the annual conference, Society for Political Methodology.

Acock, Alan C., and Wilbur J. Scott. 1980. "A Model for Predicting Behavior: The Effect of Attitude and Social Class on High and Low Visibility Political Participation." *Social Psychology Quarterly* 43:59–72.

Aldrich, John. 1993. "Rational Choice and Turnout." *American Journal of Political Science* 37:246–78.

Almond, Gabriel, and Sidney Verba. 1963. *The Civic Culture*. Princeton, NJ: Princeton University Press.

Althaus, Scott, and Todd Trautman. 2008. "The Impact of Television Market Size on Voter Turnout in American Elections." *American Politics Research* 36:824–56.

Ansolabehere, Stephen, and David M. Konisky. 2006. "The Introduction of Voter Registration and Its Effect on Turnout." *Political Analysis* 14:83–100.

Avery, James M., and Jeffrey A. Fine. 2012. "Racial Composition, White Racial Attitudes, and Black Representation: Testing the Racial Threat Hypothesis in the United States Senate." *Political Behavior* 34 (3): 391–410.

Avery, James M., and Mark Peffley. 2005. "Voter Registration Requirements, Voter Turnout, and Welfare Eligibility Policy: Class Bias Matters. *State Politics and Policy Quarterly* 5 (1): 47–67.

Avey, Michael J. 1989. *The Demobilization of American Voters: A Comprehensive Theory of Voter Turnout*. New York: Greenwood Press.

Bachrach, Peter. 1967. *The Theory of Democratic Elitism*. Boston: Little, Brown.

Barnes, Samuel, and Max Kaase. 1979. *Political Action: Mass Participation in Five Western Democracies*. Beverly Hills, CA: Sage.

Bartels, Larry. 2008. *Unequal Democracy: The Political Economy of the New Gilded Age*. Princeton, NJ: Princeton University Press.

Bartley, Numan V., and Hugh D. Graham. 1978. *Southern Elections: County and Precinct Data, 1950–1972*. Baton Rouge: Louisiana State University Press.

Bassi, Anna, Rebecca Morton, and Jessica Trounstine. 2013. "Reaping Political Benefits: Local Implementation of State and Federal Election Law." Working paper, available from the authors.

Beck, Nathaniel. 2000. "Time-Series Cross-Section Data: What Have We Learned in the Past Few Years?" *Annual Review of Political Science* 4:271–93.

Beck, Nathaniel, and Jonathan Katz. 1995. "What to Do (and Not to Do) with Time-Series-Cross-Section Data in Comparative Politics." *American Political Science Review* 89:634–47.

———. 1996. "Nuisance vs. Substance: Specifying and Estimating Time-Series-Cross-Section Models." *Political Analysis* 6:1–36.

Bennett, Stephen, and David Resnick. 1990. "The Implications of Non-voting for Democracy in the United States." *American Journal of Political Science* 34:771–802.

Bensel, Richard. 2004. *The American Ballot Box in the Mid-Nineteenth Century.* New York: Cambridge University Press.

Berinsky, Adam. 2005. "The Perverse Consequences of Electoral Reform in the United States." *American Politics Research* 33:471–91.

Berinsky, Adam, Nancy Burns, and Michael Traugott. 2001. "Who Votes by Mail? A Dynamic Model of Individual-Level Consequences of Voting-by-Mail Systems." *Public Opinion Quarterly* 65:178–97.

Berry, William D., Evan J. Ringquist, Richard C. Fording, and Russell L. Hanson. 1998. "Measuring Citizen and Government Ideology in the American States, 1960–93." *American Journal of Political Science* 42 (1): 327–48.

———. 2007. "The Measurement and Stability of State Citizen Ideology." *State Politics and Policy Quarterly* 7 (2): 111–32.

Black, Earl, and Merle Black. 1987. *Politics and Society in the South.* Cambridge, MA: Harvard University Press.

———. 1992. *The Vital South: How Presidents Are Elected.* Cambridge, MA: Harvard University Press.

Blalock, Hubert M. 1967. *Toward a Theory of Minority-Group Relations.* New York: John Wiley.

Blumer, Herbert. 1958. "Race Prejudice as a Sense of Group Position." *Pacific Sociological Review* 1 (1): 3–7.

Bobo, Lawrence. 1983. "Whites' Opposition to Busing: Symbolic Racism or Realistic Group Conflict?" *Journal of Personality and Social Psychology* 45 (6): 1196–1210.

Bobo, Lawrence, and Frank D. Gilliam Jr. 1990. "Race, Sociopolitical Participation and Black Empowerment." *American Political Science Review* 84:377–93.

Bolinger, Bruce C., and Edward H. Gaylord. 1977. *California: Special Articles on California Electoral Laws.* St. Paul: West.

Boyd, Richard W. 1981. "Decline of US Voter Turnout: Structural Explanations." *American Politics Quarterly* 9:133–59.

———. 1986. "Election Calendars and Voter Turnout." *American Politics Quarterly* 14:89–104.

———. 1989. "The Effects of Primaries and Statewide Races on Voter Turnout." *Journal of Politics* 51:730–39.

Brians, Craig, and Bernard Grofman. 1999. "When Registration Barriers Fall, Who Votes? An Empirical Test of a Rational Choice Model." *Public Choice* 99:161–76.

———. 2001. "Election Day Registration's Effect on U.S. Voter Turnout." *Social Science Quarterly* 82:170–83.

Brody, Richard A. 1978. "The Puzzle of Political Participation in America." In *The New*

American Political System, edited by Samuel Hutchison Beer and Anthony King, 287–324. Washington, DC: American Enterprise Institute.

Brown, Robert, and Justin Wedeking. 2006. "People Who Have Their Tickets but Do Not Use Them: 'Motor Voter,' Registration, Turnout Revisited." *American Politics Research* 34:479–504.

Burden, Barry, and Jacob Neiheisel. 2013. "Election Administration and the Pure Effect of Voter Registration on Turnout." *Political Research Quarterly* 66:77–90.

Burnham, Walter Dean. 1965. "The Changing Shape of the American Political Universe." *American Political Science Review* 59:7–28.

———. 1970. *Critical Elections and the Mainsprings of American Politics*. New York: Norton.

———. 1982. *The Current Crisis in American Politics*. New York: Oxford University Press.

———. 1986. "Those High Nineteenth-Century American Voting Turnouts: Fact or Fiction?" *Journal of Interdisciplinary History* 16 (Spring): 613–44.

———. 1987. "The Turnout Problem." In *Elections American Style*, edited by A. James Reichley, 97–133. Washington, DC: Brookings Institution Press.

Cain, Bruce E., Todd Donovan, and Caroline J. Tolbert, eds. 2008. *Democracy in the States: Experiments in Election Reform*. Washington, DC: Brookings Institution Press.

Campbell, Andrea. 2003. How Policies Make Citizens: Senior Political Activism and the American Welfare State. Princeton, NJ: Princeton University Press.

Campbell, Angus, Philip Converse, Warren Miller, and Donald Stokes. 1960. *The American Voter*. Chicago: University of Chicago Press.

Campbell, David E. 2000. "Social Capital and Service Learning." *PS: Political Science and Politics* 33:641–45.

Carson, Jamie L., and Jason M. Roberts. 2013. *Ambition, Competition, and Electoral Reform: The Politics of Congressional Elections across Time*. Ann Arbor: University of Michigan Press.

Cassel, Carol. 1979. "Change in Electoral Participation in the South." *Journal of Politics* 41:907–17.

Cho, Wendy Tam, and Thomas J. Rudolph. 2008. "Emanating Political Participation: Untangling the Spatial Structure behind Participation." *British Journal of Political Science* 38:273–89.

Citrin, Jack, Eric Schickler, and John Sides. 2003. "More Democracy or More Democrats? The Impact of Increased Turnout on Senate Elections." *American Journal of Political Science* 47:75–90.

Civil Rights Act of 1957. US Public Law 85–315, Eighty-Fifth Congress of the United States of America (HR 6127). Approved September 9, 1957.

Civil Rights Act of 1960. US Public Law 86–449. Eighty-Sixth Congress of the United States of America (HR 8601). Approved May 6, 1960.

Civil Rights Act of 1964. US Public Law 88–352. Eighty-Eighth Congress of the United States of America (HR 7152). Passed July 2, 1964.

Clerk of the US House of Representatives. 1920–2000 (biennial editions). *Statistics of Congressional and Presidential Elections*. Washington, DC: US House of Representatives Historical Documents.

Clubb, Jerome M., William H. Flanigan, and Nancy H. Zingale. 1981. *Analyzing Electoral History: A Guide to the Study of American Voter Behavior*. Beverly Hills, CA: Sage.

Congressional Quarterly Election Research Center. 1954–2002. *America Votes*. Vols. 1–25. Washington, DC: Congressional Quarterly Press.

———. 2001. *Guide to the U.S. Elections*. 4th ed. Washington, DC: Congressional Quarterly Press.

Constitution of the United States of America, Fifteenth Amendment, Sections 1–2. Ratified February 3, 1870.

Constitution of the United States of America, Twenty-Fourth Amendment, Sections 1–2. Ratified January 23, 1964.

Conway, M. Margaret. 1991. *Political Participation in the United States*. Washington, DC: Congressional Quarterly Press.

Council of State Governments. 1935–2004. *The Book of the States*. Vols. 1–36. Chicago: Council of State Governments.

Crawford v. Marion County Election Board (2008). 553 U.S. 181. Decided April 28, 2008.

Crewe, Ivor. 1981. "Electoral Participation." In *Democracy at the Polls: A Comparative Study of Competitive National Elections*, edited by David Butler, Howard R. Penniman, and Austin Ranney, 216–63. Washington, DC: American Enterprise Institute for Public Policy Research.

Crocker, Royce. 1996. *Voter Registration and Turnout: 1948–1998*. Washington, DC: Library of Congress, Congressional Research Service.

Dalton, Russell J. 1988. *Citizen Politics in Western Democracies*. Chatham, NJ: Chatham House.

Davidson, Chandler, and Bernard Grofman. 1994. *Quiet Revolution in the South*. Princeton, NJ: Princeton University Press.

Donovan, Todd, Caroline Tolbert, and Daniel Smith. 2008. "Priming Presidential Votes by Direct Democracy." *Journal of Politics* 70:1217–31.

Downs, Anthony. 1957. *An Economic Theory of Democracy*. New York: Harper and Row.

Dubin, Jeffrey, and Gretchen Kaslow. 1996. "Comparing Absentee and Precinct Voters: A View over Time." *Political Behavior* 18:369–92.

Dunn v. Blumstein (1972). 405 U.S. 330. Decided March 21, 1972.

Dye, Thomas R. 1984. "Party and Policy in the States." *Journal of Politics* 46:1097–1116.

Eckstein, Harry. 1975. "Case Study and Theory in Political Science." In *Handbook of Political Science*, vol. 7, *Strategies of Inquiry*, edited by Fred I. Greenstein and Nelson W. Polsby, 79–137. Reading, MA: Addison-Wesley.

Elazar, Daniel Judah. 1972. *American Federalism: A View from the States*. New York: Crowell.

Ellison, Christopher G., and David A. Gay. 1989. "Black Political Participation Revisited: A Test of Compensatory, Ethnic Community and Public Arena Models." *Social Science Quarterly* 70:101–19.

Erikson, Robert. 1981. "Why Do People Vote? Because They Are Registered." *American Politics Quarterly* 9:259–76.

———. 1995. "State Turnout and Presidential Voting—A Closer Look." *American Politics Quarterly* 23:387–96.

Ewald, Alec C. 2009. *The Way We Vote*. Nashville, TN: Vanderbilt University Press.

Fellowes, Matthew, and Gretchen Rowe. 2004. "Politics and the New American Welfare States." *American Journal of Political Science* 48:362–73.

Fenster, Mark J. 1994. "The Impact of Allowing Day of Registration Voting on Turnout in US Elections from 1960 to 1992." *American Politics Quarterly* 22:74–87.

Filer, John, Lawrence Kenny, and Rebecca Morton. 1993. "Redistribution, Income, and Voting." *American Journal of Political Science* 37:63–87.

Fitzgerald, Mary. 2005. "Greater Convenience but Not Greater Turnout: The Impact of Alternative Voting Methods on Electoral Participation in the United States." *American Politics Research* 33:842–67.

Fitzpatrick, Jody, and Rodney Hero. 1988. "Political Culture and Political Characteristics of the American States: A Consideration of Some Old and New Questions." *Western Political Quarterly* 41:145–53.

Force Act of 1871 (also called the Civil Rights Act of 1871 or the Ku Klux Klan Act of 1871). United States Public Law 42–22. Forty-Second Congress of the United States of America (H.R. 1293). Approved April 20, 1871.

Franklin, Daniel, and Eric Grier. 1997. "Effects of Motor Voter Legislation: Voter Turnout, Registration, and Partisan Advantage in the 1992 Presidential Election." *American Politics Quarterly* 25:104–17.

Gans, Curtis B. 1978. "The Empty Ballot Box: Reflections on Non-voters in America." *Public Opinion*, September/October, 54–57.

———. 1987. *Creating the Opportunity: How Voting Laws Affect Voter Turnout.* Washington, DC: Committee for the Study of the American Electorate.

Geering, John. 2004. "What Is a Case Study and What Is It Good For?" *American Political Science Review* 98:341–54.

———. 2007. "The Case Study: What It Is and What It Does." In *Oxford Handbook of Comparative Politics*, edited by Carles Boix and Susan Stokes, 90–122. London: Oxford University Press.

George, Alexander, and Andrew Bennett. 2004. *Case Studies and Theory Development in the Social Sciences.* Cambridge, MA: MIT Press.

Giles, Micheal, and Kaenan Hertz. 1994. "Racial Threat and Partisan Identification." *American Political Science Review* 88 (2): 317–26.

Glaser, James M. 1994. "Back to the Black Belt: Racial Environment and White Racial Attitudes in the South." *Journal of Politics* 56 (1): 21–41.

Glass, David P., Peverill Squire, and Raymond Wolfinger. 1984. "Voter Turnout: An International Comparison." *Public Opinion*, December/January, 49–55.

Goldman, Robert M. 1990. *A Free Ballot and a Fair Count: The Department of Justice and the Enforcement of Voting Rights in the South, 1877–1893.* New York: Garland.

Gomez, Brad, Thomas Hansford, and George Krause. 2007. "The Republicans Should Pray for Rain: Weather, Turnout, and Voting in U.S. Presidential Elections." *Journal of Politics* 69:649–63.

Gosnell, Harold F. 1930. *Why Europe Votes.* Chicago: University of Chicago Press.

Griffin, John, and Brian Newman. 2005. "Are Voters Better Represented?" *Journal of Politics* 67:1206–27.

———. 2008. *Minority Report: Evaluating Political Equality in America.* Chicago: University of Chicago Press.

Gronke, Paul, Eva Galanes-Rosenbaum, and Peter Miller. 2007. "Early Voting and Turnout." *PS: Political Science and Politics* 40 (4): 639–45.

———. 2008. "Early Voting and Voter Turnout." In *Democracy in the States: Experiments in Election Reform*, edited by Bruce Cain, Todd Donovan, and Caroline Tolbert, 68–82. Washington, DC: Brookings Institution Press.

Gronke, Paul, Eva Galanes-Rosenbaum, Peter A. Miller, and Daniel Toffey. 2008. "Convenience Voting." *Annual Review of Political Science* 11:437–55.

Guinier, Lani. 1994. *Tyranny of the Majority: Fundamental Fairness in Representative Democracy.* New York: Free Press.

Hajnal, Zoltan L. 2010. *America's Unequal Democracy: Race, Turnout, and Representation in City Politics.* New York: Cambridge University Press.

Hamilton, Alexander, James Madison, and John Jay. 1961. *The Federalist Papers: A Collection of Essays Written in Support of the Constitution of the United States.* Edited by R. P. Fairfield. New York: Anchor Books.

Hanmer, Michael. 2009. *Discount Voting: Voter Registration Reforms and Their Effects*. New York: Cambridge University Press.

Hansen, John Mark. 2001. "Early Voting, Unrestricted Absentee Voting, and Voting by Mail." Unpublished Report of the Task Force on the Federal Election System.

Harper v. Virginia Board of Elections (1966). 383 U.S. 663. Decided March 24, 1966.

Heard, Alexander, and Donald S. Strong. 1950. *Southern Primaries and Elections, 1920–1949*. Montgomery: University of Alabama Press.

Help America Vote Act of 2002. United States Public Law 107–252. One Hundred and Seventh Congress of the United States of America (H.R. 3295; S 565). Approved October 29, 2002.

Hero, Rodney. 2007. *Racial Diversity and Social Capital: Equality and Community in America*. New York: Cambridge University Press.

Highton, Benjamin. 1997. "Easy Registration and Voter Turnout." *Journal of Politics* 59:565–75.

———. 2004. "Registration and Voting in the United States." *Perspectives on Politics* 2: 507–15.

Highton, Benjamin, and Raymond Wolfinger 1998. "Estimating the Effects of the National Voter Registration Act of 1993." *Political Behavior* 20:79–104.

Hill, Kim Quaile, and Jan Leighley. 1992. "The Policy Consequences of Class Bias in State Electorates." *American Journal of Political Science* 36 (2): 351–65.

———. 1999. "Racial Diversity, Voter Turnout, and Mobilizing Institutions in the United States." *American Politics Research* 27 (3): 275–95.

Hine, Darlene Clark. 2003. *Black Victory: The Rise and Fall of the White Primary in Texas*. Columbia: University of Missouri Press.

Hofstetter, Richard. 1973. "Inter-party Competition and Electoral Turnout: The Case of Indiana." *American Journal of Political Science* 17:351–66.

Huang, Chi, and Todd Shields. 2000. "Interpretation of Interaction Effects in Logit and Probit Analyses: Reconsidering the Relationship between Registration Laws, Education, and Voter Turnout." *American Politics Quarterly* 28:80–95.

Huckfeldt, Robert. 1979. "Political Participation and the Neighborhood Social Context." *American Journal of Political Science* 23:579–92.

———. 1986. *Politics in Context: Assimilation and Conflict in Urban Neighborhoods*. New York: Agathon.

Huckfeldt, Robert, and John Sprague. 1995. *Citizens, Politics, and Social Communication: Information and Influence in an Election Campaign*. New York: Cambridge University Press.

Hutcheson, John D., and Taylor George. 1973. "Religious Variables, Political System Characteristics, and Policy Outputs in the American States." *American Journal of Political Science* 17:414–21.

Jackman, Robert W. 1987. "Political Institution and Voter Turnout in the Industrial Democracies." *American Political Science Review* 81:405–23.

Jackson, Robert A. 1997. "The Mobilization of the U.S. State Electorate in the 1998 and 1990 Elections." *Journal of Politics* 59:520–37.

Jacobson, Gary C. 1978. "The Effects of Campaign Spending in Congressional Elections." *American Political Science Review* 72 (2): 469–91.

———. 1990. "The Effects of Campaign Spending in House Elections: New Evidence for Old Arguments." *American Journal of Political Science* 34 (May): 334–62.

Jennings, M. Kent. 1979. "Another Look at the Life Cycle and Political Participation." *American Journal of Political Science* 73:755–71.

Jennings, M. Kent, and Gregory B. Markus. 1988. "Political Involvement in the Later Years: A Longitudinal Study." *American Journal of Political Science* 32:302–16.

Jennings M. Kent, and Richard G. Niemi 1981. *Generations and Politics: A Panel Study of Young Adults and Their Parents.* Princeton, NJ: Princeton University Press.

Johnson, Charles A. 1976. "Political Culture in American States." *American Journal of Political Science* 20:491–509.

Juenke, Eric Gonzalez, and Julie Marie Shepard. 2008. "Vote Centers and Voter Turnout." In *Democracy in the States: Experiments in Election Reform,* edited by Bruce Cain, Todd Donovan, and Caroline Tolbert, 55–67. Washington, DC: Brookings Institution Press.

Karp, Jeffery, and Susan Banducci. 2000. "Going Postal: How All-Mail Elections Influence Turnout." *Political Behavior* 22:223–39.

———. 2001. "Absentee Voting, Mobilization, and Participation." *American Politics Research* 29:183–95.

Kelley, Stanley, Richard Ayers, and William Bowen. 1967. "Registration and Voting: Putting First Things First." *American Political Science Review* 61:359–79.

Key, V. O. 1949. *Southern Politics in State and Nation.* New York: Vintage Books.

———. 1956. *American State Politics: An Introduction.* New York: Knopf.

———. 1966. *Politics, Parties, and Pressure Groups.* New York: Crowell.

Keyssar, Alexander. 2000. *The Right to Vote: The Contested History of Democracy in the United States.* New York: Basic Books.

———. 2009. *The Right to Vote: The Contested History of Democracy in the United States.* Rev. ed. New York: Basic Books.

Kim, J. O., J. R. Petrocik, and S. N. Enokson. 1975. "Voter Turnout among the American States: Systemic and Individual Components. *American Political Science Review* 69:107–23.

Kincaid, John. 1980. "Political Cultures of the American Compound Republic." *Publius* 10:1–15.

———. 1982. "Dimensions and Effects of America's Political Cultures." *Journal of American Culture* 5:84–92.

King, Gary, Robert O. Keohane, and Sidney Verba. 1994. *Designing Social Inquiry: Scientific Inference in Qualitative Research.* Princeton, NJ: Princeton University Press.

———. 1995. "The Importance of Research Design in Political Science." *American Political Science Review* 89:475–81.

Kirkpatrick, Charles. 1967. "Statement by Commissioner Kirkpatrick on Literacy Tests." New York: President's Commission on Registration and Voting Participation.

Kleppner, Paul. 1982. *Who Voted? The Dynamics of Electoral Turnout, 1870–1980.* New York: Praeger.

———. 1987. *Continuity and Change in Electoral Politics, 1893–1928.* Westport, CT: Greenwood Press.

Knack, Stephen. 1995. "Does Motor Voter Work? Evidence from State-Level Data." *Journal of Politics* 57:796–811.

———. 2001. "Election-Day Registration—The Second Wave." *American Politics Research* 29:65–78.

Knack, Stephen, and Martha Kropf. 2003. "Voided Ballots in the 1996 Presidential Election: A County-Level Analysis." *Journal of Politics* 65:881–97.

Knack, Stephen, and James White. 2000. "Election-Day Registration and Turnout Inequality." *Political Behavior* 22:29–44.

Kousser, Morgan J. 1974. *The Shaping of Southern Politics: Suffrage Restriction and the Establishment of the One-Party South, 1880–1910.* New Haven, CT: Yale University Press.

———. 1999. *Colorblind Injustice: Minority Voting Rights and the Undoing of the Second Reconstruction.* Chapel Hill: University of North Carolina Press.

Kousser, Thad, and Megan Mullin. 2007. "Does Voting by Mail Increase Participation? Using Matching to Analyze a Natural Experiment." *Political Analysis* 15:428–45.

Kristensen, Ida, and Greg Wawro. 2003. "Lagging the Dog? The Robustness of Panel Corrected Standard Errors in the Presence of Serial Correlation and Observation Specific Effects." Paper presented at the annual conference, Society for Political Methodology.

Krueger, Brian S., and Paul D. Mueller. 2001. "Moderating Backlash: Racial Mobilization, Partisan Coalitions, and Public Policy in the American States." *State Politics and Policy Quarterly* 1 (2): 165–79.

Lawson, Steven F. 1976. *Black Ballots: Voting Rights in the South, 1944–1969.* New York: Columbia University Press.

———. 1985. *In Pursuit of Power: Southern Blacks and Electoral Politics, 1965–1982.* New York: Columbia University Press.

Lazarsfeld, Paul, and Allen Barton. 1951. "Qualitative Measurement in the Social Sciences: Classification, Typologies, and Indices." In *The Policy Sciences,* edited by Daniel Lerner and Harold D. Lasswell, 155–92. Stanford, CA: Stanford University Press.

Leighley, Jan E. 1990. "Social Interaction and Contextual Influences on Political Participation." *American Politics Quarterly* 18:459–75.

———. 1995. "Attitudes, Opportunities, and Incentives: A Field Essay on Political Participation." *Political Research Quarterly* 48 (March): 181–209.

———. 2001. *Strength in Numbers? The Political Mobilization of Racial and Ethnic Minorities.* Princeton, NJ: Princeton University Press.

Lewis-Beck, Michael, Helmut Norpoth, William G. Jacoby, and Hebert Weisberg. 2008. *The American Voter Revisited.* Ann Arbor: University of Michigan Press.

Lijphart, Arend. 1994. *Electoral Systems and Party Systems: A Study of Twenty-Seven Democracies, 1945–1990.* New York: Oxford University Press.

———. 1997. "Unequal Participation: Democracy's Unresolved Dilemma." *American Political Science Review* 91:1–14.

Lipset, Seymour Martin. 1996. *American Exceptionalism: A Double-Edged Sword.* New York: Norton.

Loevy, Robert D. 1997. *The Civil Rights Act of 1964: The Passage of the Law That Ended Racial Segregation.* New York: State University of New York Press.

Luttbeg, Norman. 1971. "Classifying the American States: An Empirical Attempt to Identify Internal Variations." *Midwest Journal of Political Science* 15:703–21.

Mahoney, James, and Gary Goertz. 2006. "A Tale of Two Cultures: Contrasting Quantitative and Qualitative Research." *Political Analysis* 14:227–49.

Manza, Jeff, and Christopher Uggen. 2006. *Locked Out: Felon Disenfranchisement and American Democracy.* New York: Oxford University Press.

Martin, Paul. 2003. "Voting's Rewards: Voter Turnout, Attentive Publics, and Congressional Allocation of Federal Money." *American Journal of Political Science* 47:110–27.

Martinez, Michael, and D. Hill. 1999. "Did Motor Voter Work?" *American Politics Quarterly* 27:296–315.

Matthews, Donald R., and James W. Prothro. 1963. "Social and Economic Factors and Negro Voter Registration in the South." *American Political Science Review* 57 (1): 24–44.

———. 1966. *Negroes and the New Southern Politics.* New York: Harcourt, Brace and World.

Mayhew, David R. 1986. *Placing Parties in American Politics: Organization, Electoral Settings, and Government Activity in the Twentieth Century.* Princeton, NJ: Princeton University Press.

McDonald, Michael. 2002. "The Turnout Rate among Eligible Voters in the States, 1980–2000." *State Politics and Policy Quarterly* 2:199–212.

McDonald, Michael, and Samuel Popkin. 2001. "The Myth of the Vanishing Voter." *American Political Science Review* 95:963–74.

McGerr, Michael E. 1986. *The Decline of Popular Politics: The American North, 1865–1928.* New York: Oxford University Press.

———. 2003. *A Fierce Discontent: The Rise and Fall of the Progressive Movement in America, 1870–1920.* New York: Free Press.

Milbrath, Lester W. 1965. *Political Participation.* Chicago: Rand McNally.

Miles, Thomas. 2004. "Felon Disenfranchisement and Voter Turnout." *Journal of Legal Studies* 33:85–129.

Mill, John Stuart. 1962. *Considerations on Representative Government.* 1861. Chicago: University of Chicago Press.

Miller, Warren E., and J. Merrill Shanks. 1996. *The New American Voter.* Cambridge, MA: Harvard University Press.

Mills, C. Wright. 1956. *The Power Elite.* New York: Oxford University Press.

Mitchell, Glenn E., and Christopher Wlezien. 1995. "The Impact of Legal Constraints on Voter Registration, Turnout, and the Composition of the American Electorate." *Political Behavior* 17:179–202.

Munck, Gerardo Luis. 1998. "Canons of Research Design in Qualitative Analysis." *Studies in Comparative International Development* 33:18–45.

Mutch, Robert E. 1992. "Voting by Mail." *State Legislatures* 18:29–31.

National Voter Registration Act of 1993. United States Public Law 103–31. One Hundred and Third Congress of the United States of America. Approved May 20, 1993.

Neeley, Grant, and Lilliard Richardson. 2001. "Who Is Early Voting? An Individual Level Examination." *Social Science Journal* 38:381–92.

Newberry v. United States (1921). 256 U.S. 232. Decided May 2, 1921.

New York Times, Editorial Section, November 7, 2004.

Nicholson, Stephen P. 2005. *Voting the Agenda: Candidates, Elections, and Ballot Propositions.* Princeton, NJ: Princeton University Press.

Nie, Norman H., Jane Junn, and Kenneth Stehlik-Barry. 1996. *Education and Democratic Citizenship in America.* Chicago: University of Chicago Press.

Nie, Norman H., Sidney Verba, and John R. Petrocik. 1999. *The Changing American Voter.* Cambridge, MA: Harvard University Press.

Nixon v. Herndon (1927). 273 U.S. 536. Decided March 7, 1927.

Norrander, Barbara. 1989. "Ideological Representativeness of Presidential Primary Voters." *American Journal of Political Science* 33:570–87.

Oklahoma State Code. 2004. 2004 Cumulative Supplement to the Oklahoma Statutes Annotated. West Publishing.

Oliver, Eric. 1996. "The Effects of Eligibility Restrictions and Party Activity on Absentee Voting and Overall Turnout." *American Journal of Political Science* 40:498–513.

———. 2001. *Democracy in Suburbia.* Princeton, NJ: Princeton University Press.

Onuf, Peter. 1996. "Federalism, Republicanism, and the Origins of American Sectionalism." In *All Over the Map: Rethinking American Regions,* edited by Edward Ayers, Patricia Limerick, Stephen Nissenbaum, and Peter Onuf, 11–37. Baltimore: Johns Hopkins University Press.

Oregon v. Mitchell (1970). 400 U.S. 112. Decided December 21, 1970.

Pape, William J. 1939. *Report of Election Laws Commission*. Hartford: Connecticut Election Laws Commission.

Patterson, Samuel C. 1968. "The Political Cultures of the American States." *Journal of Politics* 30:187–209.

Patterson, Samuel, and Gregory Caldeira. 1983. "Getting Out the Vote: Participation in Gubernatorial Elections." *American Political Science Review* 77:675–89.

———. 1985. "Mailing In the Vote: Correlates and Consequences of Absentee Voting." *American Journal of Political Science* 29:766–88.

Patterson, Thomas E. 2002. *The Vanishing Voter: Public Involvement in an Age of Uncertainty*. New York: Knopf.

Peters, John, and Susan Welch. 1978. "Politics, Corruption, and Political Culture: A View from the State Legislature." *American Politics Quarterly* 6:345–56.

Pierson, Paul. 2004. *Politics in Time: History, Institutions, and Social Analysis*. Princeton, NJ: Princeton University Press.

Pitkin, Hanna F. 1967. *The Concept of Representation*. Berkeley: University of California Press.

Piven, Frances Fox, and Richard A. Cloward. 1988. *Why Americans Don't Vote*. New York: Pantheon Books.

———. 2000. *Why Americans Still Don't Vote and Why Politicians Want It That Way*. Boston: Beacon Press.

Powell, Bingham G. 1982. *Contemporary Democracies: Participation, Stability, and Violence*. Cambridge, MA: Harvard University Press.

———. 1986. "American Voter Turnout in Comparative Perspective." *American Political Science Review* 80:17–43.

Putnam, Robert D. 2000. *Bowling Alone: The Collapse and Revival of American Community*. New York: Simon and Schuster.

Quillian, Lincoln. 1995. "Prejudice as a Response to Perceived Group Threat: Population Composition and Anti-immigrant and Racial Prejudice in Europe." *American Sociological Review* 60 (4): 586–611.

Redding, Kent. 2003. *Making Race, Making Power: North Carolina's Road to Disenfranchisement*. Urbana: University of Illinois Press.

Reichley, A. James. 1987. "The Electoral System." In *Elections American* Style, edited by A. James Reichley, 1–28. Washington, DC: Brookings Institution Press.

Research Staff of the Legislative Research Commission. 1957. *Election Laws in Kentucky*. Research Publication 52. Frankfort, KY: Legislative Research Commission.

Rhine, Staci L. 1995. "Registration Reform and Turnout Change in the American States." *American Politics Quarterly* 23:409–26.

———. 1996. "An Analysis of the Impact of Registration Factors on Turnout in 1992." *Political Behavior* 18:171–85.

Richardson, Lilliard E., and Grant W. Neeley. 1996. "The Impact of Early Voting on Turnout: The 1994 Elections in Tennessee." *State and Local Government Review* 28:173–79.

Rigby, Elizabeth, and Melanie J. Springer. 2011. "Does Electoral Reform Increase (or Decrease) Political Equality?" *Political Research Quarterly* 64:420–34.

Riker, William, and Peter Ordeshook. 1968. "A Theory of the Calculus of Voting." *American Political Science Review* 62:25–42.

Ritt, Leonard. 1974. "Political Cultures and Political Reform: A Research Note." *Publius* 4:127–33.

Rosenstone, Steven J., and John Mark Hansen. 1993. *Mobilization, Participation, and Democracy in America*. New York: Macmillan.

Rosenstone, Steven J., and Raymond E. Wolfinger. 1978. "The Effect of Registration Laws on Voter Turnout." *American Political Science Review* 72:22–46.

Rusk, Jerrold. 1970. "The Effect of the Australian Ballot Reform on Split-Ticket Voting: 1876–1908." *American Political Science Review* 64:1220–38.

———. 1974. "Comment: The American Electoral Universe: Speculation and Evidence." *American Political Science Review* 68:1028–49.

Rusk, Jerrold, and John J. Stucker. 1978. "The Effect of the Southern System of Election Laws on Voting Participation: A Reply to V. O. Key." In *The History of American Electoral Behavior*, edited by Joel H. Silbey, Allan G. Bogue, and William H. Flanigan, 198–250. Princeton, NJ: Princeton University Press.

Salisbury, Robert H. 1980. *Citizen Participation in the Public Schools*. Lexington, KY: Lexington Books.

Schattschneider, E. E. 1960. *The Semisovereign People: A Realist's View of Democracy in America*. New York: Holt, Rinehart and Winston.

Shachar, R., and B. Nalebuff. 1999. "Follow the Leader: Theory and Evidence on Political Participation." *American Economic Review* 89:525–47.

Sharkansky, Ira. 1969. "The Utility of Elazar's Political Culture: A Research Note." *Polity* 2:67–83.

———. 1970. *Regionalism in American Politics*. Indianapolis, IN: Bobbs-Merrill.

Sharkansky, Ira, and Richard Hofferbert. 1969. "Dimensions of State Politics, Economics, and Public Policy." *American Political Science Review* 63 (3): 867–79.

Smith, Daniel, and Caroline Tolbert. 2007. "The Instrumental and Educative Effects of Ballot Measures: Research on Direct Democracy in the American States." *State Politics and Policy Quarterly* 7 (4): 416–45.

Smith, Mark A. 2001. "The Contingent Effects of Ballot Initiatives and Candidate Races on Turnout." *American Journal of Political Science* 45:700–706.

Smith v. Allwright (1944). 321 U.S. 649. Decided April 3, 1944.

Smolka, Richard G. 1977. *Election Day Registration: The Minnesota and Wisconsin Experience in 1976*. Washington, DC: American Enterprise Institute for Public Policy Research.

Smolka, Richard G., and Jack E. Rossotti. 1975. *Registering Voters by Mail: The Maryland and New Jersey Experience*. Washington, DC: American Enterprise Institute for Public Policy Research.

South Carolina v. Katzenbach (1966). 383 U.S. 301. Decided March 7, 1966.

Southwell, Priscilla, and Justin Burchett. 1997. "Survey of Vote-by-Mail Senate Election in the State of Oregon." *PS: Political Science and Politics* 91:53–57.

———. 2000a. "The Effect of All-Mail Elections on Voter Turnout." *American Politics Quarterly* 28:72–79.

———. 2000b. "Does Changing the Rules Change the Players? The Effect of All-Mail Elections on the Composition of the Electorate." *Social Science Quarterly* 81:837–45.

Springer, Melanie J. 2006. "Electoral Institutions, Voter Turnout, and American Democracy: The States, 1920–2000." PhD diss., Columbia University.

———. 2012. "State Electoral Institutions and Voter Turnout in Presidential Elections, 1920–2000." *State Politics and Policy Quarterly* 12 (3): 252–83.

Squire, Peverill, Raymond Wolfinger, and D. P. Glass. 1987. "Residential Mobility and Voter Turnout. *American Political Science Review* 81:45–65.

Stein, Robert. 1998. "Introduction: Early Voting." *Public Opinion Quarterly* 62:57–69.

Stein, Robert, and Patricia A. Garcia-Monet. 1997. "Voting Early, but Not Often." *Social Science Quarterly* 78:657–71.

Stein, Robert, Jan Leighley, and Christopher Owens. 2005. "Alternative Modes of Balloting: Early Voting, Absentee Voting and Late Voter Registration." Report to the Federal Commission on Electoral Reform.

Stein, Robert, and Greg Vonnahme. 2006. "Election Day Vote Centers and Voter Turnout." Paper presented at the annual conference, Midwest Political Science Association.

———. 2007. "Turning Out Newly Registered Voters: The Effects of Election Day Vote Centers." Paper presented at the annual conference, Midwest Political Science Association.

Stimson, James A. 1985. "Regression in Space and Time: A Statistical Essay." *American Journal of Political Science* 9:914–47.

Tajfel, Henri, M. G. Billig, and R. P. Bundy. 1971. "Social Categorization and Intergroup Behavior." *European Journal of Social Psychology* 1 (2): 149–78.

Teixeira, Ruy A. 1992. *The Disappearing American Voter*. Washington, DC: Brookings Institution Press.

Thompson, Dennis F. 2002. *Just Elections: Creating a Fair Electoral Process in the United States*. Chicago: University of Chicago Press.

Timpone, Richard J. 1998. "Structure, Behavior, and Voter Turnout in the United States." *American Political Science Review* 92:145–58.

———. 2002. "Estimating Aggregate Policy Reform Effects: New Baselines for Registration, Participation, and Representation." *Political Analysis* 10:154–77.

Tocqueville, Alexis de. 1948. *Democracy in America*. Vols. 1 and 2. New York: Knopf.

Tolbert, Caroline, Todd Donovan, Bridgett King, and Shaun Bowler. 2008. "Election Day Registration, Competition, and Voter Turnout." In *Democracy in the States: Experiments in Election Reform*, edited by Bruce Cain, Todd Donovan, and Caroline Tolbert, 83–98. Washington, DC: Brookings Institution Press.

Tolbert, Caroline, and Daniel Smith. 2005. "The Educative Effects of Ballot Initiatives on Voter Turnout." *American Political Research* 33:283–309.

Traugott, Michael W. 2004. "Why Electoral Reform Has Failed: If You Build It, Will They Come?" In *Rethinking the Vote: The Politics and Prospects of American Electoral Reform*, edited by Ann N. Crigler, Marion R. Just, and Edward J. McCaffery, 167–84. New York: Oxford University Press.

Uhlaner, Carole J., Bruce E. Cain, and D. Roderick Kiewiet 1989. "Political Participation of Ethnic Minorities in the 1980s." *Political Behavior* 11:199–225.

US Census Bureau. 1900–2002. *Statistical Abstract of the United States*. Washington, DC: Government Printing Office.

US Commission on Civil Rights. 1965. *Voting in Mississippi: A Report of the US Commission on Civil Rights*. Washington, DC: Government Printing Office.

US Department of Commerce. *Per Capita Income, 1920–2000*. Washington, DC: Government Printing Office, Bureau of Economic Analysis.

Valelly, Richard M. 2004. *The Two Reconstructions*. Chicago: University of Chicago Press.

Verba, Sidney, and Norman H. Nie. 1972. *Participation in America: Political Democracy and Social Equality*. New York: Harper and Row.

Verba, Sidney, Norman H. Nie, and Jae-on Kim. 1978. *Participation and Political Equality*. Cambridge, MA: Cambridge University Press.

Verba, Sidney, Kay Schlozman, and Henry Brady. 1995. *Voice and Equality: Civic Voluntarism in America*. Cambridge, MA: Harvard University Press.

Verba, Sidney, Kay Schlozman, Henry Brady, and Norman Nie. 1993a. "Who Participates? What Do They Say?" *American Political Science Review* 87:303–18.

———. 1993b. "Race, Ethnicity, and Political Resources: Participation in the United States." *British Journal of Political Science* 23:453–97.

Voting Rights Act of 1965. United States Public Law 89–110. Eighty-Ninth Congress of the United States of America (S1564). Passed August 6, 1965.

Wattenberg, Martin P. 1998. "Turnout Decline in the U.S. and Other Advanced Industrialized Democracies." Irvine, CA: Center for the Study of Democracy.

———. 2002. *Where Have All the Voters Gone?* Cambridge, MA: Harvard University Press.

Whitby, Kenny J. 2007. "The Effect of Black Descriptive Representation on Black Electoral Turnout in the 2004 Elections." *Social Science Quarterly* 88:4.

Wolfinger, Raymond E., Benjamin Highton, and Megan Mullin. 2005. "How Postregistration Laws Affect the Turnout of Citizens Registered to Vote." *State Politics and Policy Quarterly* 5:1–23.

Wolfinger, Raymond E., and Steven J. Rosenstone. 1980. *Who Votes?* New Haven, CT: Yale University Press.

INDEX

southern states (*continued*)
149; effect of voter registration rules
on voting rates, 149, 152; little effect of
expansive electoral institutions on voter
participation, 152–53; voter turnout
by reform period, *150–51*; voting rate
improvements after federal reform unsustainable in many states, 146–47
Squire, Peverill, 16
state-by-state voter turnout rates compared
with the average national voter turnout
rate during election years, 1920–2000,
171
state demographic indicators, 105; and
voter turnout, 94–95, 113
state electoral institutions: allow states to
structure political environment through
institutional design, 19–20, 23; defined
as laws and procedures governing registration and voting, 2; effects are dependent on a state's political history and
social context, 1, 2, 3, 24–25; implications of, 79–81; regional differences in,
79; total number of states with various
laws over time, *80. See also* literacy tests;
poll taxes; property requirements; voter
qualifications
state electoral institutions, effects on
twentieth-century voter turnout in
the states, 7, 20–23, 86–114; differences in effects in southern and
nonsouthern states, 109; direct effects
on voter turnout, 2, 19, 20–23; effects
in nonpresidential election years,
1922–1998, 109–12, *110*; effects
over time, 105–7; and importance of
political environment, 164; measurement of, 89; potential mechanisms for
change in political participation, 112;
and southern voter turnout during
presidential election years, *100*; and
state demographics, 94–95; substantial
negative effect of restrictive voting qualifications, 96–104; voter qualifications,
90; voter registration, 90–93; voting
procedures, 93
states, regional classification of, *30*
states' rights and voting laws, debates
over, 1

state turnout, high and low throughout
century, 41–44; domination of highest
ten category for most years by nonsouthern states, 41; domination of high
turnout category in both presidential
and nonpresidential elections by western states, 41; domination of high turnout category in presidential elections
by midwestern states, 41; domination
of lowest turnout category by southern
states, 41, 44; high turnout nonsouthern
states, 115–36; ranking of states with
consistently high turnout throughout
century, nonpresidential election years,
42–43; ranking of states with consistently high turnout throughout century,
presidential election years, *42*; ranking
of states with consistently low turnout
throughout century, nonpresidential
election years, *44–45*; ranking of states
with consistently low turnout throughout century, presidential election
years, *43*
state turnout, noninstitutional effects,
104–5; ballot initiatives, 104; electoral calendar measures, 93–94, 104;
gubernatorial races, 104; political
competition, 104–5; state demographic
indicators, 105
state turnout, nonpresidential election
years, 1922–1998, 40–41
state turnout, presidential election years,
1920–2000: decreased turnout in
most states in 1980, 1988, and 1996,
39–40; increased turnout in southern
states in 1964 and 1968, 39; 1952
race, increase in turnout in all fifty
states, 38; 1960 race, highest participation rates since 1900, 39; 1964 race,
decline in state voting rates in all
midwestern and northeastern states,
39; 1968 race, decline in state voting
rates in all but three midwestern and
northeastern states, 39; 1972 race,
decreased turnout in all states, 39; 1976
race, decreased turnout in most states
except those in the South, 39; steady
increase in voter turnout from 1928 to
1940, 38

adopted later closing dates that other Western states, 125; all had a nonvoting purge during the century, 125–26; experienced closest nonpresidential elections throughout the century, 134; identification of high turnout states, 1920–2000, *120*; more racially homogeneous than other states in region, 130; nearly all adopted permanent voter registration systems throughout twentieth century, 125; region dominated high turnout category in both presidential and nonpresidential elections, 41

West Virginia, turnout rates higher than average at beginning of century and below average at end of century, 51

white primary, 139, 154–60, 194n7; based on pretext that Democratic Party was a private club and not subject to federal laws, 154–55; began while Republicans and Populists enjoyed support among poor whites and blacks in the South, 154; institutional effects on voter turnout during primary elections, 1920–1970, *158*–60; positive effect on southern voter turnout during primary elections from 1920 to 1970, *157*–60; used to unite southern whites in majority coalitions, 155–56; vital to southern white supremacy, 142

White's heteroskedasticity-consistent standard errors for cross-sectional estimators, 189n5

Wolfinger, Raymond, 16, 21

women's suffrage, 3, 38, 86, 142

Wyoming: adoption of Election Day registration in 1994, 125; adoption of permanent voter registration in 1950, 125; adoption of universal absentee voting in 1992, 126; turnout above national average in all presidential and nonpresidential election years from 1920 to 2000, 46, 49, 120

CHICAGO STUDIES IN AMERICAN POLITICS

A series edited by Benjamin I. Page, Susan Herbst, Lawrence R. Jacobs, and Adam J. Berinsky